The Handbook of Global Outsourcing and Offshoring

The Handbook of Global Outsourcing and Offshoring

The Definitive Guide to Strategy and Operations

3rd edition

Ilan Oshri
Professor of Technology and Globalisation, Loughborough University, UK

Julia Kotlarsky
Professor of Technology and Global Sourcing, Aston University, UK

Leslie P. Willcocks
Professor of Management, London School of Economics, London, UK

palgrave
macmillan

First published 2015 by
PALGRAVE MACMILLAN

Palgrave Macmillan in the UK is an imprint of Macmillan Publishers Limited, registered in England, company number 785998, of Houndmills, Basingstoke, Hampshire RG21 6XS.

Palgrave Macmillan in the US is a division of St Martin's Press LLC, 175 Fifth Avenue, New York, NY 10010.

Palgrave Macmillan is the global academic imprint of the above companies and has companies and representatives throughout the world.

Palgrave® and Macmillan® are registered trademarks in the United States, the United Kingdom, Europe and other countries.

ISBN 978–1–137–43742–6

This book is printed on paper suitable for recycling and made from fully managed and sustained forest sources. Logging, pulping and manufacturing processes are expected to conform to the environmental regulations of the country of origin.

A catalogue record for this book is available from the British Library.

Library of Congress Cataloging-in-Publication Data
Oshri, Ilan.
   The handbook of global outsourcing and offshoring : the definitive guide to strategy and operations / Ilan Oshri, Professor of Technology and Globalisation, Loughborough University, Julia Kotlarsky, Professor of Technology and Global Sourcing, Aston University, UK, Leslie P. Willcocks, Professor of Information Systems, London School of Economics, London, UK. — Third edition.
       pages   cm
   ISBN 978–1–137–43742–6 (hardback)
   1. Offshore outsourcing.   2. Contracting out.   I. Kotlarsky, Julia.
   II. Willcocks, Leslie.   III. Title.
   HD2365.O82 2015
   658.4′058—dc23   2014038183

Contents

List of Tables and Figures

Tables

Figures

Acknowledgements

The first edition of this book, published in 2009, was inspired by the insights and learning we gained from being a part of a group of passionate individuals – practitioners and academics – whom we met in industry events, academic conferences and while working together on joint research and consultancy projects.

One event that in particular inspired us to update this book is our annual Global Sourcing Workshop (www.globalsourcing.org.uk). This annual gathering of researchers and practitioners is now in its ninth year and has created a community that discusses strategic, operational, technical and social aspects of global sourcing. We have learned a lot from each participant and will ever be grateful to them for sharing with us their experience and research.

We are also thankful to colleagues who adopted this book in their teaching and corporate training.

Case Study Contributors

Erran Carmel is the Dean and Professor of Information Technology Department, Kogod School of Business at American University. Erran studies the globalisation of technology work. He has visited hundreds of firms in over 20 countries. He has published over 100 articles and 10 case studies. He recently completed his third book, which deals with how time zone separation impacts global coordination of work. His previous books are *Global Software Teams* and *Offshoring Information Technology*.

Rudy Hirschheim is the Ourso Family Distinguished Professor of Information Systems at Louisiana State University. He was previously a faculty member at the University of Houston, the London School of Economics (University of London) and Templeton College (University of Oxford). He has a PhD in Information Systems from the University of London. He was the Founding Editor of the John Wiley Series in Information Systems in 1985. He is Senior Editor for the journal *Information & Organization* and on the editorial boards of the journals *Information Systems Journal, Journal of Strategic Information Systems, Journal of Management Information Systems, Journal of Information Technology, Wirtschaftsinformatik/Business & Information Systems Engineering* and *Strategic Outsourcing*.

Evgeny Kaganer is an Assistant Professor at IESE Business School where he teaches MBA and executive courses in IT strategy and virtual enterprise. His research focuses on social and mobile technologies and their impact on individuals, organisations and business models. He has published in *MIT Sloan Management Review, Communications of the ACM, Journal of the AIS* and *European Journal of Information Systems*. His work on the use of social and mobile technologies in business and education has also been cited in major media outlets, such as the *Financial Times, Business Week* and *San Francisco Chronicle*, among others.

Rajiv Kishore is an Associate Professor in the School of Management at the State University of New York at Buffalo. His interests are in improving organisational and IT performance through the effective management of global outsourcing projects, new forms of IT outsourcing including crowdsourcing, technology and innovation management, and strategic IT management. His papers have been published in *MIS Quarterly, Journal of Management Information Systems, IEEE Transactions on Engineering Management, Communications of the ACM, Decision Support Systems* and *Information & Management*, among others. Rajiv has consulted with a number of large companies, some of which include BellSouth, Blue Cross Blue Shield of Minnesota, IBM and Pioneer Standard Electronics.

Onook Oh is a Visiting Assistant Professor in the University of Colorado Denver Business School. He was a research associate at the Center for Collaboration Science in the University of Nebraska Omaha and an Assistant Professor of the Warwick Business School. He is interested in theorising the information systems infrastructure, its techno-social impacts on our everyday lives and technology-mediated collective sense-making under crisis situations. He is a recipient of multiple NSF-funded projects with these research topics. He published his researches in *MIS Quarterly, Communications of the AIS, AIS Transactions on Human–Computer Interaction* and *Information Systems Management*, among others.

Ken Schulz is Vice President of Corporate Marketing, Pactera Technology International Ltd. Ken has 20 years of experience in the IT industry, including 12 years in outsourcing services. Before joining Pactera in 2006, Ken worked at HP for ten years where as Engineering Manager he was tasked with increasing IT capabilities and capacity by establishing offshore software engineering resources in India. Prior to joining HP, Ken was Management Consultant on IT strategy and applications for Fortune 500 clients at PriceWaterhouseCoopers. Ken holds an MBA from the University of California at Berkeley and a Bachelor's Degree in Information Systems from Cal Poly at San Luis Obispo.

Sandra Sieber is a Professor and Chair of the Department of Information Systems at IESE Business School. She is also the Academic Director of the IESE Global Executive MBA. She has worked extensively on the impact of information and communication technologies on organisational and individual work practices, being especially interested in the most recent developments due to the impact of social media on organisations. Sieber has published scholarly and general articles in national and international journals, magazines and newspapers and has contributed to several books.

Mark Skilton has over 30 years of experience in a wide variety of customer-facing and provider solutions strategies, consulting to board level in operating model transformations and value creation, including big data, social media and digital infrastructure transformation. Mark has held International Standards Body Chair positions with the Open Group and is currently a member of the ISO JC38 distributed computing standards for cloud computing. He has graduated from Sheffield and Cambridge Universities and Warwick Business School. Currently, he is holding part-time position as Professor of Practice in Information Systems Management at Warwick Business School.

Introduction

The global IT outsourcing (ITO) market has increased each year since 1989, when global ITO was only a US$10 billion market. On conservative estimates, by the end of 2014 it exceeded US$700 billion. On some estimates, the market will see a 4.8% compound annual growth through to the end of 2018 as more is outsourced and new service lines and delivery locations are added. Looking at the global business process outsourcing (BPO) and IT services market by region, in 2013 North America was 42% of the market, Europe, Middle East and Africa (EMEA) 34%, Japan 10%, the rest of Asia Pacific 9% and Latin America 5%. However, for the first time, in 2014 growth in outsourcing services in Europe exceeded growth in the USA. Offshoring and offshore outsourcing are certainly expanding. By 2015, over 125 offshore locations have been providing ITO and BPO services for more than five years and are seeking to mature their service capabilities. Furthermore, today clients are facing a large variety of alternatives to choose from when making sourcing decisions, which means that they need to take into account a number of considerations to be able to make the right decision. Therefore, it has become increasingly important to understand the phenomenon, not least as a basis for suggesting what directions it will take, its impacts, how it has been conducted and how its management can be better facilitated.

These points are particularly pertinent because recent evidence has suggested that a number of offshore outsourcing relationships and offshoring projects have failed to live up to some of their promises. The reasons for this are many, ranging from poor quality delivered by suppliers to rising management costs that result in frustration and disappointment. Collaboration between remote sites and the ability to share and transfer knowledge between dispersed teams have also been mentioned as imperative to successful offshore outsourcing projects. In addition, our own research highlights certain capabilities that suppliers and clients should develop, the governing structures that they need to put in place and the bonding activities that they need to promote and make time for. Although offshore outsourcing brings its own distinctive issues, it is the case that the principles for running any ITO or BPO venture also apply to offshoring and offshore outsourcing arrangements. However, offshoring is increasingly part of most deals of any significant size, so it becomes necessary to see and manage outsourcing within a global context.

The main objectives of this book

This book offers a broad perspective on various issues relating to the sourcing of IT-enabled business processes and services in a national and global context. Its key objectives are to:

- Assess the impacts of global sourcing on business
- Assess the risks and benefits for firms engaging in sourcing activities
- Devise a plan to outsource a process or service from a client viewpoint
- Devise a plan to offer services from a supplier viewpoint
- Ensure sustainability over the life cycle of an outsourcing relationship
- Raise awareness to recent developments in the global sourcing arena such as captive strategies and innovation potential.

This book therefore examines both the client's and the supplier's involvement in sourcing relationships by emphasising not only the capabilities that each side should develop prior to entering a relationship but also the potentials that they should develop as a result of their interactions with each other.

Key definition: Sourcing

The field of sourcing is replete with jargon and acronyms. For example, the terms *bestshoring* and *rightshoring* have become recent buzzwords, widely used by managers but poorly defined by the professional press and academic publications. Even more worrisome is the inaccurate use of the terms *outsourcing* and *offshoring* by both managers and academics. Although these terms and others are defined in Chapter 1, we offer this explanation of *sourcing* from the outset: Sourcing is the act through which work is contracted or delegated to an external or internal entity that could be physically located anywhere. It encompasses various insourcing (keeping work in-house) and outsourcing arrangements such as offshore outsourcing, captive offshoring, nearshoring and onshoring.

Clearly, almost all firms are engaged in some way in sourcing activities, and each of them has developed a sourcing arrangement that suits its particular needs.

The structure of the book

The book is organised into 12 chapters in three key parts. Chapters 1 to 4 are about *making a sourcing decision*, Chapters 5 to 7 about *building sourcing competencies* and Chapters 8 to 12 about *managing sourcing relationships*. Some chapters can be read as a stand-alone body of knowledge (e.g., Chapters 1, 11 and 12), while others are more connected with other chapters.

Chapter 1 provides a historical perspective on outsourcing and offshoring, the marketplace and the incentives for firms from around the globe to tap into sourcing opportunities. Chapter 2 focuses on sourcing models for client firms and how to make sourcing decisions. Special attention is given to sourcing models based on Internet delivery of products or services that are becoming increasingly popular, such as cloud services and crowdsourcing. It also examines the sourcing arrangements available according to the nature of work outsourced. Chapter 3 considers geographical location in sourcing decisions and the factors that both client and supplier companies should consider when deciding on where a particular activity should be located. Chapter 4 continues the examination of country attractiveness, however, by focusing on the characteristics of Western countries. This chapter also discusses backsourcing of IT and business processes.

Chapter 5, which begins Part II, provides an overview of the supplier's landscape by examining supplier configurations, including multisourcing, and the role of intermediaries. It also discusses the core capabilities suppliers should develop to maintain their competitive position and to ensure their ability to provide quality services to their clients. Chapter 6 considers the supplier selection strategy from a client's viewpoint. This includes the evaluation of vendors, the outsourcing arrangements, the retained organisation capabilities and legal issues. Chapter 7 examines the notions of expertise and knowledge in sourcing relationships from both the supplier and client perspectives and discusses issues related to the knowledge transfer process.

Chapter 8, which begins Part III, considers the outsourcing life cycle and its key activities from a client's perspective. It also provides an overview of key transition issues. Chapter 9 addresses the key challenges that both client and suppliers face regarding governance of outsourcing relationships. Chapter 10 focuses on the management of globally distributed teams from a sourcing relationship perspective. Chapter 11 explores the role that captive centres play in a firm's global sourcing strategy and, consequently, the strategies a firm can pursue regarding its captive centre. It also discusses Shared Services Centres that present another form of insourcing or captive solution. Finally, Chapter 12 discusses one of the emerging topics in outsourcing – the potential to achieve innovation through outsourcing engagements – and provides a practical framework consisting of six steps to help client companies to incorporate innovation in their outsourcing strategy.

part I

Making a Sourcing Decision

chapter 1

Overview of the Global Sourcing Marketplace

With the advent of globalisation and heightened levels of competition, many organisations are having considerable difficulties in developing and maintaining the range of expertise and skills they need to compete effectively. The emergence of American, European, Japanese and other Asian multinationals has created a competitive environment requiring the globalisation, or at least semiglobalisation, of corporate strategy. Moreover, with developments in information and communication technologies (ICT), firms do not have to be large multinationals to compete globally. These developments have led many companies to turn to various sourcing strategies such as outsourcing, offshoring, offshore outsourcing, nearshoring and onshoring. Therefore, this chapter focuses on:

- The key terminologies used in the sourcing literature
- The background of global sourcing
- The key drivers, benefits and risks of global sourcing
- Market trends and future developments in global sourcing.

Definitions

- *Sourcing* is the act through which work is contracted or delegated to an external or internal entity that could be physically located anywhere. It encompasses various insourcing (keeping work in-house) and outsourcing arrangements such as offshore outsourcing, captive offshoring, nearshoring and onshoring.

- *Outsourcing* is defined as contracting with a third-party supplier for the management and completion of a certain amount of work, for a specified length of time, cost and level of service.
- *Offshoring* refers to the relocation of organisational activities (e.g., information technology, finance and accounting, back office and human resources) to a wholly owned subsidiary or an independent service provider in another country. This definition illuminates the importance of distinguishing whether the offshored work is performed by the same organisation or by a third party. When the work is offshored to a centre owned by the organisation, we refer to a *captive* model of service delivery. When the work is offshored to an independent third party, we refer to an *offshore outsourcing* model of service delivery. And when organisational activities are relocated to a neighbouring country (e.g., US organisations relocating their work to Canada or Mexico), we use the term *nearshoring*.

These definitions include various sourcing models: for example, staff augmentation, domestic and rural sourcing, crowdsourcing, cloud services, microsourcing, bundled services, out-tasking and shared services (terms explained in Chapter 2). In addition, there are various common buzzwords such as *best-sourcing* (or *best-shoring*, *right-shoring* and *far-shoring* (as opposed to nearshoring), usually coined and used by supplier companies. Finally, there is also the backsourcing trend, which implies bringing work back in-house.

Global Sourcing Background

The global IT outsourcing (ITO) market has increased each year since 1989, when global ITO was only a US$10 billion market. On conservative estimates, by the end of 2013, the global outsourcing contract value for business and IT services was about US$648 billion (business process outsourcing (BPO) US$304 billion, ITO US$344 billion) and by the end of 2014 exceeded US$700 billion. On some estimates the market will see a 4.8% compound annual growth through to the end of 2018 as more is outsourced and new service lines and delivery locations are added (Bhimani and Willcocks, 2014).

Looking at the global BPO and IT services market by region, in 2013 North America was 42% of the market, Europe, Middle East and Africa (EMEA)

34%, Japan 10%, the rest of Asia Pacific 9% and Latin America 5%. However, for the first time, in 2014 growth in outsourcing services in Europe exceeded growth in the USA.

Not surprisingly, spending on IT consulting topped any other function outsourced by leading multinationals in Western economies when working with a third-party service provider. Figure 1.1 depicts the distribution of expenditures in 2014 by the leading 150 multinationals in the UK and the USA on various ITO and BPO functions when working with suppliers.

While outsourcing has accelerated, we have also seen growth in the area of shared services and captive centres. Figure 1.2 depicts the distribution of outsourcing expenditure on shared services per function in 2014.

The main driver for outsourcing is still cost reduction; however, we have witnessed growing attention by client firms to other objectives such as access to skills and flexibility in how human capital is utilised. Figure 1.3 offers an insight into the drivers for outsourcing in 2014.

While, during 2014, many wondered whether automation and backsourcing (also known as re-shoring) would see the erosion of offshore outsourcing, in practice offshore outsourcing has been growing worldwide. Within the overall outsourcing figures cited above, offshore outsourcing exceeded US$100 billion in revenues in 2013 and is estimated to grow at 8–12%

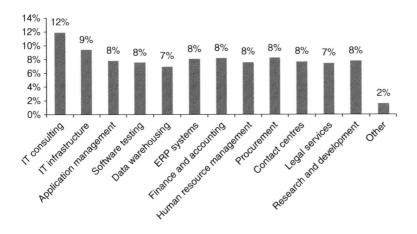

FIGURE 1.1 **Distribution of outsourcing expenditures by ITO and BPO functions when working with suppliers**
Source: Survey by Loughborough Centre for Global Sourcing and Service, 2014.

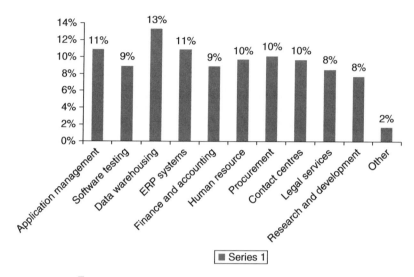

FIGURE 1.2 / **Distribution of outsourcing expenditures by ITO and BPO functions when working with shared service centres and captives**
Source: Survey by Loughborough Centre for Global Sourcing and Service, 2014.

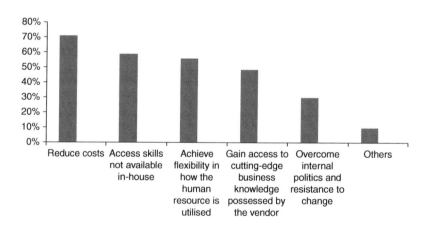

FIGURE 1.3 / **Main drivers of outsourcing**
Source: Survey by Loughborough Centre for Global Sourcing and Service, 2014.

per year from 2013 to 2018 (Willcocks et al., 2015). This strategy has always appeared promising in terms of the reduction of costs as certain organisational activities would be moved to an independent service provider in a country with favourable conditions. In more recent years, clients have pursued a cost-plus agenda when offshore outsourcing, and for large multinationals, offshore outsourcing increasingly has to fit into a larger global sourcing strategy that mitigates risk and links different sourcing options in a coordinated manner. The USA is a major player in the offshore outsourcing of IT and business-process applications. However, offshore outsourcing has appeared to be gaining momentum in Europe, where the UK is the lead consumer of such services. We cover offshore outsourcing in more details in Chapters 2 and 3.

Drivers, Benefits and Risks of Global Sourcing

The growth of global sourcing has been attributed to many factors. First, technological advances in the telecommunications industry and the Internet have shrunk space and time and have enabled the coordination of organisational activities at the global level. Other reasons are as follows: the supply of skilled yet low-cost labour in countries such as India and the Philippines and subsequently now over 125 further locations; investments in infrastructure; an improved business, economic and political climate in a number of developing countries; and the standardisation of IT processes and communication protocols that contribute to the efficiency of inter-organisational activities.

Along these lines, many countries have invested heavily in improving their telecommunications infrastructure, which is essential for electronically transmitted services. For example, Barbados has had a fully digitalised communications system with direct international dialling since the beginning of the 1990s. Jamaica constructed its Digiport, with a 20,000-telephone-line capacity and speeds of 1.5 Mbps. Furthermore, many countries have provided tax advantages to attract offshoring. For example, Bulgaria offers a 10% flat enterprise tax rate that is dropping to 0% in areas with high unemployment. In Jamaica the Digiport BPO free trade zones are tax free. South Africa offers government and provincial grants for job creation through attracting offshore work to the country and in 2014 made its immigration laws more supportive of the industry. Other countries like China, Morocco, Egypt and Kenya have invested heavily in business parks and in ways of supporting offshore industry growth. Chapter 3 deals with such issues in more detail.

Global sourcing may offer several benefits associated with the advantages of outsourcing in general. A company may reap significant cost advantages through the creation of economies of scale, access to the unique expertise of a third party and the reduction or stabilisation of overhead costs. In addition, a company may benefit from outsourcing by concentrating on core activities, organisational specialisations, or by focusing on achieving key strategic objectives. More specifically, a strategy of building core competencies and outsourcing the rest may enable a company to focus its resources on a relatively few knowledge-based core competencies where it can develop best-in-the-world capabilities (Quinn and Hilmer, 1994; Lacity and Willcocks, 2012). Concentration on a core business may allow a company to exploit distinctive competencies that will lead to a significant competitive advantage.

Another major benefit of outsourcing is that it can give the organisation access to the supplier's capabilities and innovative abilities, which may be expensive or impossible for the company to develop in-house (Quinn and Hilmer, 1994).

Even more important, a network of suppliers can provide any organisation with the ability to quickly adjust the scale and scope of its production capability upwards or downwards, at a lower cost, in response to changing demand. In this way, outsourcing can provide greater flexibility (McCarthy and Anagnostou, 2003). Furthermore, outsourcing can decrease the product or process design cycle time if the client uses multiple best-in-class suppliers that work simultaneously on individual components of the system, as each supplier can contribute greater depth and sophisticated knowledge in specialised areas and thus offer higher quality inputs than any individual supplier or client can (Quinn and Hilmer, 1994). On this basis, having several offshore centres can provide around-the-clock workdays. In other words, development and production can take place constantly by exploiting the time difference between different countries.

While firms seek to reduce costs and access skills and ideas from outsourcing engagements, it is not always clear whether value is appropriated from such relationships. Oshri and Kotlarsky (2009) examined value in outsourcing to conclude that the vast majority of client firms are in the dark when trying to measure and quantify the return on their outsourcing investments. In fact, less than half of the firms studied (43%) have attempted to calculate the financial impact of outsourcing to their bottom line, indicating that the financial benefits are difficult to quantify (51%). When asked about cutting back or bringing back operations in-house, executives sited 'unclear value for money' as the main driver (see Figure 1.4).

Adopting sourcing strategies poses several other disadvantages. Loss of critical skills or overdependence on an outside organisation for carrying out important business functions may evolve into significant threats to a company's well-being. Also, security and confidentiality of data can become major issues for many companies. Another major issue is losing control over the timing and quality of outputs since these will be undertaken by an outside supplier: the result may be a poorer quality of the final product or service, and this may sully a company's image.

The following case illustrates the challenges companies such as BSkyB face when pursuing a sourcing strategy. It highlights the responsibility both client and supplier hold when signing an outsourcing contract and the implications for both parties when things go wrong.

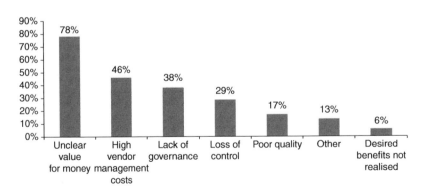

FIGURE 1.4 ╱ **Main drivers for cutting back or bringing back outsourced services**
Source: Oshri and Kotlarsky, 2009.

BSkyB: The Bumpy Road of Outsourcing

In 1983, Rupert Murdoch purchased Satellite Television, a company founded in 1981 by Brian Haynes, and renamed it Sky. After years of competition between British Satellite Broadcasting (BSB) and Sky, the two companies merged on 30 October 1990, to form BSkyB. By 2007, BSkyB had become the UK's largest independent broadcasting operation, supplying a broad range of programmes, channels and services to more than ten million people around the world.

In 2000, BSkyB was looking for a company that would redesign and implement a new Customer Relationship Management (CRM) system for that would be the heart of its business. The system needed to be built around Chordiant Software and run on Sun Microsystems hardware. BSkyB's contact centres in Livingston and Dunfermline in Scotland would use the new CRM system.

To achieve this objective, BSkyB conducted a competitive tender exercise to find a supplier that would be able to meet its criteria. Several bidders emerged during the tendering process, including PricewaterhouseCoopers and Electronic Data Systems (EDS). In the end, EDS was chosen as the supplier for the CRM system.

EDS had been founded in 1962 by Henry Ross Perot, a former salesman from IBM who came up with the idea that besides delivering computer equipment, IBM should also deliver electronic data processing services to its customers. When IBM rejected the idea, Perot resigned and founded his own company, EDS. In 2008, Hewlett-Packard (HP) acquired EDS, which now delivered a broad range of infrastructure technology, applications and BPO services. In 2009, EDS changed its name to HP Enterprise Services.

The initial idea was that EDS would provide BSkyB with a technically advanced solution that would make a valuable contribution to BSkyB's drive to lead innovation in customer service and maintain Sky Digital's industry-leading levels of customer retention. BSkyB's customers would be able to access account, billing and other information and services by phone, the Web or the television service itself.

On 30 November 2000, BSkyB and EDS signed a contract estimated at a value of £48 million. As there was uncertainty about the cost of this work (due to the uncertainty regarding the amount of work that needed to be done), BSkyB employed EDS on a time-and-materials basis. EDS stated that it would be able to go live in nine months and complete delivery in 18 months. However, just five months later, in March 2002, BSkyB terminated its relationship with EDS because, according to BSkyB, EDS did not fulfil its contractual obligations. BSkyB switched to in-house development, and the residual work was taken over by BSkyB's subsidiary, Sky Subscribers Services Ltd.

By 2004, BSkyB had invested over £170 million; in addition, its IT department had budgeted £50 million over the next four years to complete the implementation. By March 2006, BSkyB had successfully completed the project after spending £265 million.

Back in 2004, BSkyB initiated legal action against EDS, citing that EDS had not been honest during the competitive tender about its resources, technology and the methodology it planned to use in order to deliver the system within the defined time frame and within budget. BSkyB claimed that it would have probably chosen PricewaterhouseCoopers for the work if EDS had not given a false sales pitch in which it overestimated its capabilities. EDS, for its part, claimed that the most critical element in this project was that BSkyB did not specify the project properly and that it did not know exactly what BSkyB wanted or needed. In October 2007, the trial started at the High Court in London and was concluded in July 2008. On 26 January 2010, 18 months after the end of the trial, the High Court ruled on the dispute between BSkyB and EDS (now part of HP). It found that EDS had been deceitful when it claimed that it had carried out an accurate analysis of the time needed to complete the delivery and go live and when it claimed that it was able to deliver the system within the agreed-to schedule. According to the Court, the CRM manager for EDS had known that it was not possible to finish the project according to schedule and that there had not been an accurate analysis of what needed to be done. In addition, BSkyB proved that EDS had violated the contract. BSkyB was, therefore, awarded damages up to the liability cap set out in the contract. In addition, the Court stated that the responsibilities for deceitful misrepresentations that were not described in the contract were not accurately excluded by the same contract.

One major outcome from this trial was that BSkyB was able to prove that EDS had made a deceitful sales pitch, so the liability cap was not applicable. On 3 February 2010, the Technology and Construction Court ordered EDS to pay an interim payment of £200 million for damages.

Additional outsourcing risks are associated with organisational changes. For example, outsourcing is usually followed by changes in organisational structure with redundancies and layoffs. Research and experience indicate that outsourcing effectively signals to employees their employer's intention to initiate a change that may involve deskilling and redundancies (Kakabadse and Kakabadse, 2000). Such initiatives can generate internal fears and employee resistance.

Moreover, as Hendry (1995) highlights, outsourcing can be associated with problems related to the company's ability to learn because it can increase insecurity among the workforce and decrease its motivation, reducing employees' willingness to question and experiment. There are fears as well that interactions among skilled people in different functional activities, which often lead to unexpected new insights or solutions, will become less likely (Quinn and Hilmer, 1994).

With regard to offshore outsourcing, Rottman and Lacity (2006) offer a comprehensive list of risks associated with such ventures. These include different kinds of business, legal, political, workforce, social and logistical risks (see Table 1.1).

TABLE 1.1   Offshore outsourcing risks

Risk category	Sample risks
Business	No overall cost savings Poor quality Late deliverables
Legal	Inefficient or ineffective judicial system at offshore locale Intellectual property rights infringement Export restrictions Inflexible labour laws Difficulty obtaining visas Changes in tax laws that could significantly erode savings Inflexible contracts Breach in security or privacy
Political	Backlash from internal IT staff Perceived as unpatriotic Politicians' threats to tax US companies that source offshore Political instability within offshore country Political instability between USA and offshore country
Workforce	Supplier employee turnover Supplier employee burnout Inexperienced supplier employees Poor communication skills of supplier employees
Social	Cultural differences Holiday and religious calendar differences
Logistical	Time-zone challenges Managing remote teams Coordination of travel

Source: Adapted from Willcocks and Lacity, 2006.

The Future of Outsourcing and Offshoring

Drawing on a number of the authors' research streams, we can identify ten trends for the future of global sourcing markets.

Trend 1: Spending will continue to rise in all global sourcing markets, but BPO will overtake ITO

We have already seen how, following the long-term growth trend, ITO and BPO expenditure is set to rise continually in the 2012–2018 period. The interesting feature is that BPO is and will grow at a faster rate than ITO, with BPO expenditures rising across the board in areas such as the human resources function, procurement, back-office administration, call centres, legal, finance and accounting, customer-facing operations and asset management.

BPO is outpacing ITO because many executives recognise that they under-manage their back offices and do not wish to invest in back-office innova-tions. Suppliers are rapidly building capabilities to reap the benefits from improving inefficient processes and functions. IT provides major underpin-ning for, and pay-off from, reformed business processes. Thus, many of the BPO deals will encompass back-office IT systems. This is also evidenced by the shift in strategy of traditional IT suppliers like IBM and HP to provide more business-process services. Suppliers will increasingly replace clients' disparate back-office IT systems with Web-enabled, self-serve portals.

There have been some high-profile backsourcing (i.e., returning services in-house) cases in recent years: Sainsbury in 2005, Santander in 2012 and General Motors in 2013, for example. Although these cases have drawn the attention of the media, they have never represented a dominant trend towards backsourcing. The most common course of action at the end of a contract continues to be contract renewal with the same supplier. The typical pattern seems to be that a quarter of contracts are retendered and awarded to new suppliers, and only a few are backsourced.

Trend 2: The ITO and BPO outsourcing markets will continue to grow through multisourcing

Although ITO and BPO spending is increasing, the average size of indi-vidual contracts and the duration of contracts has been decreasing. For example, the Everest Group found that, among the ITO contracts signed in 1998, 24% of contracts were worth more than US$400 million and 33% of contracts were worth between US$50 and US$100 million. In 2005, only 11% of contracts were worth more than US$400 million and 57% were worth between US$50 and US$100 million. Concerning contract dura-tion, the Everest Group found that 37% of contracts signed in 1998 were more than nine years in duration compared to 18% in 2005 (Tisnovsky, 2006). According to a Gartner report from December 2009, in 2009 only six megadeals (contracts with a total reported contract value exceeding US$1 billion) were signed, with an average term of seven years, which is lower than the nine-year-average term in 12 megadeals signed in 2008. These trends continued across the 2008–2014 period, initially as responses to the recessionary climate but then as part of long-term trends in buying behaviour, which includes a reduction in the number of suppliers while pursuing the advantages of multisourcing.

Multisourcing is becoming the dominant practice, and its overall growth is driven by client organisations that are signing more contracts with more suppliers. Although multisourcing helps clients access the best suppliers and mitigates the risks of relying on a single supplier, it also means increased transaction costs because clients must manage more suppliers. In addition, suppliers themselves incur more transaction costs: they must bid more frequently because their contracts are shorter; they face more competition because smaller deals mean that more suppliers qualify to bid, and they need to attract more customers in order to meet growth targets.

Trend 3: Global clients will view India primarily as a destination for excellence rather than a way to lower costs

Many US and UK clients initially engaged Indian suppliers to provide technical services such as programming and platform upgrades. As these relationships matured, US clients assigned more challenging work to their Indian suppliers. For example, a US retailer first engaged an Indian supplier to help with Y2K compliance. As the relationship matured, the retailer assigned development and support tasks for critical business applications to the supplier. This retailer and other satisfied clients said, 'We went to India for lower costs, but we stayed for quality.'

Indian suppliers have also been taking actions to move themselves up the BPO value chain into complex BPO work and management consulting activities. At the same time, this has become a critical strategic move as the cost advantages India enjoyed in the early 2000s have eroded in the face of labour cost rises, higher labour attrition rates (by 2014 running at 25% or higher in many outsourcing arrangements) and increasing competition from cheaper locations (see Chapters 3 and 4).

We believe that India will remain the ITO and BPO powerhouse and will continue to have 65% or more of the global market over the next five years. However, Indian suppliers are going to have to work hard to be recognised among the top suppliers of higher added value areas of complex BPO and consulting.

Trend 4: China's investment in ITO and BPO services signals promise . . .

China invested US$142.3 billion in ICT in 2006, which it hoped would pay off in terms of its ability to compete globally in the offshore services market. Its long-term ITO and BPO future is expected to be strong (Lacity et al., 2010). The ITO and BPO supplier landscape is changing quickly with some of the suppliers finally setting global footprints, such as Pactera.

C A S E   S T U D Y

Pactera Technology International: An Emerging Global Chinese Player

by Ken Schulz

Pactera was formed in 2012 with a Merger of Equals (MOE) between leading China-based software outsourcing firms VanceInfo Technologies Inc and HiSoft International Ltd. This created the largest IT services and outsourcing firm headquartered in China with over 23,000 employees.

China Pioneers: 1995–2010

Prior to the MOE, VanceInfo already had a 17-year history, having been launched in 1995 by Chris Chen with 25 employees. VanceInfo secured IBM as its first major client by helping Big Blue localise its OS/2 operating system for the China market. VanceInfo began work for Microsoft in 1997 and in 2001 acquired Fuji Xerox as a client. As China's economy continued to expand, VanceInfo established multiple client-dedicated offshore development centres, investing together with clients in IT-product development and software R&D services, forging long-term partner relationships.

Current Pactera President David Chen joined Chris Chen to lead VanceInfo forward, and following ten years of steady growth to nearly 1,000 employees in 2005, the firm received funding from Silicon Valley VC Doll Capital Management and local VC Legend Capital in 2005, with another Silicon Valley firm, Sequoia Capital, joining a second round in 2006. The VC expertise and capital fuelled growth for the company, leading VanceInfo to list on the New York Stock Exchange in 2007.

Newly listed company VanceInfo grew to become China's largest software outsourcing company focused on the US and EU markets, with a marquee client base including Citigroup, Microsoft, IBM, Oracle, HP, Expedia, TIBCO and many other leading Fortune 1,000 companies.

HiSoft International Ltd was founded in Dalian, China, in 1996. Before 2006, HiSoft generated most of its revenues from clients in Japan. HiSoft's strategy was to leverage demand for China-based outsourced IT services from multinational and domestic corporations in China. Approximately one third of HiSoft's clients were Fortune 500 companies, representing over half of the company's revenue. Of its clients, 60% were from the USA and Europe, 30% from Japan and 10% from China.

HiSoft's first overseas subsidiary was established in Tokyo in August 2002. The same year, it established a US presence in Atlanta and New York. From 2007 to mid-2012, HiSoft successfully expanded to serve clients in the USA, Europe, China and Australia, helped by a series of overseas acquisitions.

HiSoft raised US$74 million during its IPO on NASDAQ in 2010. Around the time the company was planning to go public, it recruited a former executive of Hewlett-Packard China as its CEO: Tiak Koon Loh, still serving as the current Pactera CEO.

Market Consolidation: 2010–2014

One of HiSoft's primary strategies was to increase business for existing clients while building business with Chinese companies. With fresh capital from the IPO, HiSoft's geographic expansion and onshore capabilities upgrade strategy continued with the purchase of IT consulting firms NouvEON in the USA and BearingPoint in Australia.

VanceInfo held similar aspirations to move up the IT services value chain. Most Chinese domestic ITO companies operate at the lower end of the value chain, employed in coding, testing and other low-end value-added sectors. This lower end has smaller barriers to entry, as projects can be completed with lesser experienced employees including lower cost new graduates. At this low end of the chain, competition is fierce and profit margins have become increasingly tight.

At the other end of the spectrum, higher-end IT services and software outsourcing are subject to higher entry barriers. Competition is less crucial in this market, and it is often more a case of not finding sufficiently experienced personnel than competing with other foreign and domestic firms.

The importance of offering a full spectrum of services by addressing the high end of the market in addition to services targeted at the lower end was one of the factors driving VanceInfo and HiSoft to combine in late 2012 to form Pactera. Pactera believed there to be a lot of space for development at the high end, particularly in certain industry verticals and dependent on the ability to seize first-mover advantage in China. The company believed that players with a clear vision, international focus, innovation and a strong high-end business would grow fastest, and their market share would continue to expand.

The company is now positioned to benefit over the next decade, not just in the outsourcing industry but also in IT consulting services as China's economy continues to expand rapidly and companies seek more sophisticated IT systems to support growth. For example, Pactera supported Microsoft by helping to launch the Azure cloud platform in China.

Pactera is currently heavily reliant on its overseas client base, with nearly 40% of its revenue coming from USA-based customers and another 20% from Europe and overseas Asia-Pacific-based clients, while seeking to develop its relations with China domestic companies.

In servicing clients, the drive to increase quality while simultaneously lowering costs is also pushing Pactera to diversify the location of service delivery centres and offices. The strategy for the company emerged from the ground up, with government support being a significant factor. As ITO grew, national conferences were held and local governments gave financial support and other benefits, thus lowering costs to the company.

Going Global: The Future Outlook

In March 2014, a consortium led by US private-equity giant Blackstone Group acquired Pactera for around US$600 million. The Blackstone Group acquisition of Pactera was widely thought to be due to several key factors including the following: Pactera's relatively international management team that aligned well with the Blackstone Group; Pactera's ability to quickly enhance its growth rate by merging; and Pactera's position as the largest software outsourcing company in China and leading IT service provider in a rapidly developing and promising market.

Goals for Pactera following privatisation include becoming a leading global IT service enterprise with the largest scale in China while maintaining the leading position in China's outsourcing services. With competitive large-scale Chinese enterprises targeting multiple markets beginning to expand globally, the company also seeks to become the number one IT partner for Chinese customers expanding into international markets.

Privatisation might also help Pactera to complete its strategic transformation from an outsourcing service provider to an IT services player that provides a fuller spectrum of offerings including consulting, solutions and outsourcing services. Transformation requires time, money and resource support to balance short- and long-term development.

Privatisation is also expected to help accelerate the pace of the company's vertical transformation, as Pactera also seeks to focus on key industry verticals such as Banking, Financial Services and Insurance (BFSI), travel and technology, with strong aspirations to become the top-ranked service provider in the Chinese domestic banking IT solutions market by 2015.

The Chinese service outsourcing sector is still facing major challenges. Even in 2014, language barriers, cultural barriers and fears over losing intellectual property remained obstacles for the executives, who often preferred to access the vast Chinese talent by setting up captives and shared services (Oshri, 2014). The Chinese government and Chinese business sectors are well aware of these barriers and are seeking ways to address them. For example, the Chinese government invested US$5 billion in English-language training to target the ITO and BPO markets. Subsequently the Chinese national and provincial governments have made additional investments to develop the services industry. Given their similar size of populations, India and China have remarkably different records on offshore outsourcing, with India, attracting over ten times more than China in the global revenues. Unlike India, China does not have one focused marketing body for the country and relatively little assistance for would-be investors.

Trend 5: Developing countries beyond India and China will become important players in the global business and IT services market

In 2014, there were over 125 countries with operational ITO or BPO offshore sectors, and we see this number rising, albeit slowly, over the next five years. We also see a deepening and widening of services at many of these locations, as they seek competitive advantage in the global marketplace. Many US clients already use Central American suppliers for Spanish-speaking business processes such as help desks, patient scheduling and data entry. Synchronous time zones are another favourable factor for US firms looking to Central or South America for sourcing.

In Western Europe, organisations will increasingly source IT and business services to suppliers located in Eastern Europe. For example, the Visegrad-Four countries (Czech Republic, Hungary, Poland and Slovakia) offer Western European firms closer proximity, fewer time-zone differences and lower transaction costs than Asian alternatives.

In Africa too, many countries are actively seeking to become players in the global ITO and BPO markets. North Africa already exports IT services to Europe. One interesting study examined five Moroccan IT suppliers that provided services to clients in France as early as 2003 (Bruno et al., 2004). The common language, similar time zone and cultural capability make

Morocco attractive for French organisations seeking to outsource. South Africa is also exporting IT and BP services, primarily to UK-based clients. South Africa appeals primarily to UK-based clients because of the similar time zone, cultural similarities, English-speaking capabilities and good infrastructure. Even some sub-Saharan countries are building part of their future economies on IT (Willcocks et al., 2015).

Trend 6: Large companies will give application service provision a very strong second look, as it becomes cloud services

Many thought that application service provision (ASP) had died with the dot-com bust. But through cloud computing, small and medium enterprises (SMEs) and large organisations are increasingly buying into the proposition of renting applications software, infrastructure, applications, services and storage over the Internet. A few large multinationals, for example, Proctor & Gamble and Johnson & Johnson, have been leading the way in developing cloud-ready policies and developing and harnessing their own and service-provider capability to move to the cloud. By 2014, many SMEs, especially those 'born in the cloud' had adopted various forms of cloud computing services. Many large organisations want Net-native applications (proprietary applications designed and delivered specifically for Internet delivery) that are available only through software as a service (SaaS) delivery (e.g., Salesforce.com). Large organisations may also finally be ready to abandon their expensive proprietary suites for cheaper SaaS and cloud alternatives. Furthermore, SaaS providers may well have got the message by 2015 that clients want customised services, even if the products are standardised. The need for customised services actually increases the service providers' viability because they can generate profits by charging for value-added services.

Trend 7: Outsourcing will help insourcing ... to an extent

As organisations become smarter at outsourcing, they also become smarter at insourcing. In-house operations are facing tough competition in nearly every area and can no longer assume they will retain their monopoly status with the organisation. As a result, in-house operations are adopting the techniques of the market. While this book is about outsourcing and offshoring, it should be recalled that about 60% of IT work and about 80% of back-office service work is still managed in-house. Clearly there is still plenty of room for outsourcing expansion. And, also clearly, in-house operations will need to become much more competitive in their service offerings against what the burgeoning services market can offer.

Nevertheless during the 2013–2014 period, against the outsourcing growth trend we pointed to earlier, there were increasing examples of moving some work back in-house. Automation may help this trend much more over the next five years. However, such insourcing will be impeded by a supply shortage of talent within developed countries, particularly for IT skills. The USA is not alone in this. Nearly every research report suggests that other developed countries will suffer a shortage of domestic IT workers within the next five to eight years. The shortages in developed countries will be caused by the gap between a strong demand for domestic IT workers and a dwindling supply due to the lingering effects of declining enrolments into IT education and the future effects of the retirement of the 'baby boomers'. At the moment, however, it is not clear how the numbers will work out. Certainly the demographics suggest that the supply of IT and back-office workers will be much higher in what the USA and European countries would consider offshore outsourcing locations; though, of course, multinationals also have the option of building offshore captive sites there. The development of offshore locations and their labour pools could also help and is already supporting the growth of in-house captives (see Chapters 3 and 4).

Trend 8: Nearshoring will become more prevalent

Compared to offshoring to remote locations, the benefits of nearshoring include lower travel costs, fewer time-zone differences and closer cultural compatibility. The economic and management logics suggest a lot more nearshoring. The transaction costs for offshoring are not always obvious, but when they come to be noticeably large, then nearshoring becomes an obvious alternative. Nearshoring is about proximity not just in terms of geography but also culture, institutions, time zone, languages, religion and ethics. For these reasons for the UK, for example, South Africa could be considered almost a nearshore location, despite the two countries being over 11 hours apart in flight time. More conventionally, Canada, for example, is a significant nearshore destination for US clients. Some analysts argue that US clients could have lower total costs with nearshoring to Canada than with offshoring to India.

The Czech Republic, Poland and Hungary are significant nearshore destinations for Western Europe. Clients in Western Europe are attracted to Central and Eastern European suppliers for many of the same reasons that the USA is attracted to Canadian suppliers: familiarity with language, cultural understanding, minimal time-zone differences and low labour costs. However, Central and Eastern Europe may be more attractive for BPO than ITO because, while these countries provide an excellent general education, at the moment there are far less IT and engineering graduates than in India.

Nearshoring will also become more prevalent as part of client and supplier strategies to 'best-shore', that is, to find the optimal mix of locations for the dynamic portfolio of work they need to carry out.

Trend 9: More companies will sell their captive centres or create virtual captive centres

While it is widely recognised that Western companies are setting up sites offshore, there is an emerging trend that might be called 'The GE Effect'. General Electric (GE) may not have been the first US footprint in India, but certainly Jack Welch's enthusiasm for India made it acceptable for other CEOs to locate back offices there. GE established General Electric Capital International Services (GECIS) as a captive centre in India in 1997. In the winter of 2004, it sold off 60% of GECIS to two equity companies: Oak Hill Capital Partners and General Atlantic Partners. A year later, the name was changed to Genpact, and it is now one of the top ten BPO or ITO suppliers in India. Some have called GE's approach 'the virtual captive centre' because GE still maintains primary equity holding. With a virtual captive centre, the company owns the physical operations, but staff are employed by a third-party supplier. Presumably the virtual captive centre offers the best of both worlds: the client investor maintains strategic control while the supplier attracts, develops and retains local talent.

Among US clients there have been several examples of organisations selling their captive centres. Beyond the anecdotes, in 2007 the Brown-Wilson Group conducted a survey of 18,272 clients, which found that selling

captive centres may be a significant trend. Respondents from large organisations were more likely than those in mid-sized businesses to investigate
selling. The main reasons for selling captive centres were as follows:

- The captive centre was built to protect data and intellectual property,
  which is no longer viewed as a threat if provided by a third-party
  supplier
- Senior executives are no longer committed to captive centres
- It is no longer necessary to keep decision-making authority in-house
- Third parties are now able to handle complex processes.

There is a difference between the ITO and BPO captive centres: companies
are much more likely to set up captive centres for BPO than ITO. According to Oshri and van Uhm (2012), what has been happening to captives
is quite dynamic – both in selling and setting up a new one. We expect
this trend to continue over the next five years. In 2010, there were nearly
500 captive centres in 34 countries, employing over 440,000 professionals
(Oshri and van Uhm, 2012). Since then client companies have sought to
build global business services (GBS) – a dominant trend during 2014 –
and this development has boosted the interest in establishing captives
offshore, as part of their hybrid global sourcing portfolio (Willcocks et al.,
2015).

Trend 10: SMAC impacts outsourcing . . . in the longer run

We are regularly asked about the likely timing and impact of digital innovations such as social media, mobile Internet, business analytics and cloud
(SMAC) on outsourcing. Taking a broad view, we predict that, in combination and together with advanced robotics, the Internet of things and the
automation of knowledge work, these technologies will lead to the founding by 2025 of most organisations as fundamentally digital operations and
significant reliance on the cloud. But how do these developments affect
outsourcing over the next five years?

As we have seen, outsourcing will continue to grow, and the embed-
dedness of existing contracts signed for anything between three and
ten years will slow down the new technology impact. But outsourcing
will increasingly change its character, as suppliers themselves adopt these
technologies and build and offer services based on them. We will see a

number of disruptors impact the traditional outsourcing scene more force-fully. Cloud platform suppliers like Amazon, Google, Microsoft and IBM will move up the value chain with more automated platforms. Software-as-a-service could become a dominant sourcing model in certain areas such as employee performance management, indirect procurement, payroll and benefits administration, as clients move to self-help through managed services.

Automation (also known as robotic process automation) will have signif-icant impact on outsourcing industry. Generally speaking, work can be classified into four types: routine manual, routine cognitive, non-routine manual and non-routine cognitive. Of these, it is believed that routine manual work could be automated in the near future and routine cognitive work follows suit. Non-routine cognitive work is likely to be automated through the application of Big Data and business analytics, and non-routine cognitive work is also somewhat automated with the use of algorithms. What does this add up to? A recent study suggests that, just looking at the USA, about 47% of jobs are under serious threat of automa-tion over the next ten years (Frey and Osborne, 2013). If this scenario is correct, then client companies will be able to significantly reduce the number of employees, for example, not by outsourcing but by automat-ing. Meanwhile outsourcing suppliers may try to combat this by offering cheaper automated solutions of their own. The likely outcome over the next ten years is to see a slowing down of outsourcing growth among ser-vice providers, who will be moving increasingly from labour arbitrage to automated service offerings.

Summary

In this chapter, we have explained the key terminology relating to global sourcing and provided an extensive review of past, current and future trends in global sourcing. It is clear that more and more firms have intro-duced business solutions relating to global sourcing to access scarce skills, reduce costs and streamline operations. Furthermore, interest has been growing rapidly in outsourcing business processes. The success rate of outsourcing has been mixed, because outsourcing benefits are not easily won and managements on both client and supplier sides face multiple risks and challenges on the path to successful outcomes. Meanwhile SMAC and related technologies are going to have a long-term significant impact on outsourcing, which will see outsourcing still grow but make more automated service propositions.

chapter 2

Sourcing Models: What and When to Outsource or Offshore

Clients are facing a large variety of alternatives to choose from when making sourcing decisions, which means that they need to take into account a number of considerations to be able to make the right decision. This chapter focuses on sourcing models for client firms and how to make sourcing decisions. In particular, it covers the following topics:

- Sourcing models
- Factors to consider when making a decision about outsourcing and offshoring
- The most suitable processes for outsourcing and offshoring.

Overview of Sourcing Models

Various types of global sourcing models have emerged. The major distinction among these models lies in whether the function is performed by a subsidiary business unit (BU) of the firm or an external supplier (or by both, as a joint effort) and also whether the function is performed on the firm's premises (i.e., on-site) or off-site, which can be onshore (in the country where the organisation is located), nearshore (in a neighbouring country) or in an offshore location. Figure 2.1 provides an overview of the most popular sourcing models, which is followed by a more detailed explanation.

Ownership		Third party	Insourcing *Staff augmentation*	Onshore outsourcing *Domestic supplier, 'rural sourcing'*	Offshore/nearshore outsourcing *Foreign supplier*
	Buy				
	Hybrid	Joint venture		Co-sourcing	Offshore/nearshore development centre **Build-operate-transfer**
	Make	In-house	Internal delivery	Shared services	Captive centre (*e.g., R&D*); **Captive shared services**
			On-site	Onshore (same country)	Nearshore/offshore
				Off-site	

Location

FIGURE 2.1 / Overview of sourcing models

Insourcing: This sourcing model is based on managing the provision of services internally, through buying in skills that are not available in-house, on a temporary basis. This is usually achieved through staff augmentation (also referred to as *body-shopping*), a sourcing model that implies that staff are supplied to clients on demand, at a pre-agreed rate. Most large outsourcing suppliers and management consultancies offer staff augmentation services.

Domestic outsourcing: This is based on contracting with a third party situated in the same country as the client organisation for the completion of a certain amount of work, for a specified length of time and at a certain cost and level of service. Domestic outsourcing implies that the supplier is in close proximity to the client. Alternative terms for this sourcing model are *home-shoring* or *rural outsourcing,* which involves sending the work to lower wage, usually rural, regions within the home country. This trend is popular in the USA, Israel, India and several other countries.

Offshore-outsourcing: This model implies contracting with suppliers based at an offshore location (which usually means in a developing country and separated from the client by an ocean).

Impact sourcing: This is a new sourcing model that is based on dividing work into small tasks ('micro-work') and sending it to centres in developing regions where employees complete it. It aims to promote economic growth in developing regions (Gino and Staats, 2012).

Out-tasking: This is outsourcing on a small scale. It usually implies ongoing management of and support for selected packaged applications. Out-tasking is popular with local suppliers; however, it can also be provided from offshore locations (in particular, if the supplier is a global company such as IBM).

Captive or *in-house sourcing*: A strategic choice to locate organisational activities within a wholly owned subsidiary in another country. Captive sourcing models offer *basic, shared, hybrid* and *divested* captive options (these are discussed in detail in Chapter 11).

Build–operate–transfer (BOT) models: The client contracts with an offshore or nearshore service provider to execute an outsourcing arrangement whereby the supplier will build and operate the service centre (e.g., a call centre or any other business process) for an extended period of time. The client retains the right to take over the operation under certain conditions and certain financial arrangements.

Joint venture in the outsourcing or offshoring context: This is a partnership between a client firm and an offshore supplier whereby the parties contribute resources to the new venture. Many of the offshoring joint ventures have a BOT component built into the agreement.

Shared services: This is an operational approach of centralising administrative and business processes that were once carried out in separate divisions or locations, for example, finance, procurement, human resources and IT. A shared service centre can be a captive centre or outsourced to a third party. With the increasing popularity of the shared services model, we believe it deserves a more detailed explanation.

Shared services imply the consolidation of support functions from several departments into a stand-alone organisational entity whose objective is to provide services as efficiently and effectively as possible. When managed well, shared services can reduce costs, improve services and even generate revenue. A shared service can take various forms of commercial structure such as unitary, lead department or joint initiatives. *Unitary* refers to a single organisation that consolidates and centralises a business service, and a *lead department* is an organisation that is consolidating and centralising a business service to share with other organisations. *Joint initiatives* are set up by two or more organisations that have reached an agreement to build and operate shared services. Similar to outsourcing arrangements, shared services can be run onshore, nearshore or offshore. More about shared services can be found in Chapter 11.

Sourcing Models Based on Internet Delivery

Sourcing models based on Internet delivery of products or services that are becoming increasingly popular are *cloud services* and *crowdsourcing*. In practice, each of these high-level sourcing models can be implemented in different ways, in terms of specific operational and commercial aspects of service provision. Below we describe the key principles of these two Internet-based sourcing models and give examples of how these models have been adopted by client firms.

Cloud computing services

Cloud computing is defined as a 'model for enabling ubiquitous, convenient, on-demand network access to a shared pool of configurable computing resources (e.g., networks, servers, storage, applications and services) that can be rapidly provisioned and released with minimal management effort or service provider interaction' (Mell and Grance, 2011). In the global sourcing marketplace, cloud computing has taken the form of *cloud services* (or *cloud computing services*) such as IT resources, business applications, infrastructures or platforms which are delivered on demand, using public, community, private or hybrid infrastructures. The metaphor of the cloud draws on how the Internet is depicted in computer network diagrams and represents an abstraction of the complex infrastructure it conceals. In other words, cloud computing allows users to access technology-enabled services on the Internet without having to know or understand the technology infrastructure that supports them. Nor do they have much control over it.

The key benefit of cloud computing is that it provides on-demand access to supercomputer-level power, even from a smartphone or laptop. Enabling massively scalable services characterises cloud computing. For example, those who log on to Facebook or search for flights online are taking advantage of cloud computing. They are connecting to large volumes of data stored in remote clusters or networks of computers. Google is another example of cloud computing.

The key properties of cloud services are as follows (Armbrust et al., 2009):

- Pay-as-you-go usage of the IT service
- The service is on-demand, able to scale up and scale down
- Access to applications and information from any access point
- Abstraction of the infrastructure so applications are not locked into devices or locations
- The ability to create the illusion of infinite capacity.

Cloud services can be hosted and configured for single or multiple client organisations and even hosted privately within the organisation or provided over a virtual private network (VPN). There are four basic types of cloud infrastructures[1] that characterise cloud-deployment strategies:

- *Private clouds*, which are operated solely for the use of a single organisation servicing multiple consumers (e.g., business units) within the organisation
- *Community clouds*, which are operated for the exclusive use of a specific group from organisations that have shared concerns (e.g., mission, security requirements, policy and/or compliance considerations)
- *Public clouds*, which use cloud infrastructure available for the use of the general public (i.e., referred to as public network)
- *Hybrid clouds*, which combine the infrastructure of two or more clouds (public, community and private) that remain unique entities but are connected in such a way that enables data and application portability.

The main distinction between cloud infrastructures is in the restrictions regarding the specific group of consumers who can access the cloud (i.e., one organisation, cross-organisational community or public). In terms of the ownership of the infrastructure, any type of cloud may be owned, managed and operated by a business, academic or government organisation, a third party, or some combination of these, and it may exist on or off premises (NICT, 2011).

While many organisations were initially reluctant to use cloud services, the general public have embraced them in the form of social media platforms, such as Facebook, Twitter, LinkedIn, Pinterest and YouTube, among others. Consumer demand for easy-to-use, intuitive, accessible applications – accessed via a browser – has spread upwards through many organisations as employees expect the same ease of use from their employer's in-house systems.

In recent years, ongoing economic challenges and the need to improve efficiency, streamline operations and cut costs have prompted the large-enterprise world to pay serious attention to cloud computing, even those that previously believed cloud services to be the preserve of smaller and medium-sized organisations.

While the primary driver for corporates to investigate cloud computing has tended to be cost savings, many have come to realise that the cloud promises a lot more in the form of operational efficiency, reduced waste and increased business agility, partly because clients can begin to unburden themselves of the onerous on-premise software and hardware upgrade cycle.

Cloud services also rely to a large extent on virtualisation, and this breaking apart of monolithic on-premise infrastructures and dispersing them across networks in the form of hosted solutions and virtualised systems carries its own economic advantages, even if some dyed-in-the-wool IT strategists feel threatened by the reduction in their personal domains.

That said, legitimate concerns remain, especially around data security and public cloud infrastructures. At the root of the problem is the misleading terminology. Rather than being somehow 'out there' worldwide, cloud services actually reside in hardware – data centres – that are located on land and are, therefore, subject to national laws, including those laws concerning data hosting, processing and transfer in both the client and supplier territories. Therefore, privacy and confidentiality become a concern, especially when clients use service providers in a different country, where the local law may allow the government of that country to access certain data stored on hosted servers.

These issues have become particularly relevant in the wake of the Snowden case and other revelations concerning the National Security Agency monitoring data and communications. Various countries, including the USA and India, mandate government oversight of data that are hosted, processed or transferred within national borders, under national security regulations (such as the US Patriot Act).

There are also security implications of a different kind inherent in supplier lock-in. Being reliant on any single supplier to host data remotely and, potentially, also computing platforms and core business applications means being a hostage to that supplier's fortunes, good customer relations, employees and internal security regime.

But with the growth in cloud services, it has become evident that there is increased demand for enterprise cloud solutions among clients that might once have only considered traditional outsourcing options. The enterprise cloud solution market has entered a high-growth phase and holds considerable potential for enterprises and suppliers alike. But in order to capitalise on that potential and ensure the delivery of true business value, client organisations need to learn more about the following points:

- The maturity of the IT industry in its support of enterprise cloud solutions
- The attractiveness of the cloud-based market for suppliers
- The factors enabling and influencing the adoption of cloud over traditional on-premise solutions
- How enterprise solution suppliers add value – and plan to add value – to customers through their cloud-based offerings.

Furthermore, it is important to consider who the different actors are and their roles in the cloud marketplace. The National Institute of Standards and Technology (NIST) has developed the NIST cloud computing reference architecture (Mell and Grance, 2011) that distinguishes between five major actors and specifies their roles in the delivery and consumption of cloud services. These roles (described in Figure 2.2) can be used as a tool for discussing the requirements, structures and operations of cloud computing.

Cloud-based sourcing models

In terms of commercial sourcing models, what is generally known is that cloud services are far from being a single-template solution. Typically, there are three main forms: Platform as a Service (PaaS), Infrastructure as a Service (IaaS) and Software as a Service (SaaS). These can be delivered

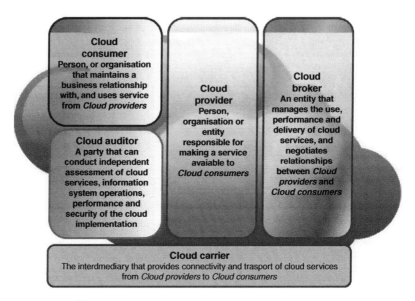

Cloud consumer
Person, or organisation that maintains a business relationship with, and uses service from *Cloud providers*

Cloud auditor
A party that can conduct independent assessment of cloud services, information system operations, performance and security of the cloud implementation

Cloud provider
Person, organisation or entity responsible for making a service avaiable to *Cloud consumers*

Cloud broker
An entity that manages the use, performance and delivery of cloud services, and negotiates relationships between *Cloud providers* and *Cloud consumers*

Cloud carrier
The interdmediary that provides connectivity and trasport of cloud services from *Cloud providers* to *Cloud consumers*

FIGURE 2.2 / **Actors in the NIST cloud computing reference architecture**
Source: Mell and Grange, 2011.

over public, community, private or hybrid infrastructures and can also be combined to create various forms of Business Platform as a Service (BPaaS) offerings.

- *PaaS* provides a development platform for developing end-user solutions. Google's App Engine and Microsoft Azure are examples of this.
- *IaaS* supplies storage and processing capabilities as services over the network. Capacity is pooled and made available to handle workloads that range from application components to high-performance applications. Amazon's cloud is an example of an IaaS platform.
- *SaaS*, meanwhile, provides a complete application as a service on demand. The software runs in a/the cloud and may service multiple end users or client organisations. The most widely known example, and a pioneer of the model, is Salesforce.com; although, it now also provides a platform and an ecosystem of hosted business applications. A number of other solutions like Microsoft Office 365 and Google Apps offer a range of day-to-day business applications. Apple's own walled-garden approach offers an alternative ecosystem, used by millions of consumers. Many types of software are well suited to the SaaS model

for customers with little interest or capability in software deployment but with substantial computing needs. The model can be applied within different segments of the market. At the higher end of the market, suppliers may offer applications such as Enterprise Resource Planning (ERP), CRM, and e-commerce, as well as selective industry-specific solutions. Low-end applications include solutions for small and medium enterprises that the users can easily configure.

Different commercial cloud models offer different types of cloud services which can be consumed in multiple ways. Some examples of the services requested under different models and usage scenarios are included in Table 2.1.

On-premise vs. cloud solutions

With the growing maturity of cloud services, most organisations face a dilemma about whether to continue investing in on-premise solutions. One of the main challenges is technology legacy and the internal support structures that have grown up around it over many years. Many senior IT strategists now accept that, given the opportunity to start from scratch, many would do things very differently. The challenge for those IT strategists, therefore, is to become more business and information focused.

A key differentiator between traditional on-premise solutions and cloud computing is control. On-premise solutions give clients complete control over their assets – licensing issues aside – while leaving them with capital outlay and support headaches. By contrast, the cloud model demands a different mindset by expecting the client to relinquish some control and potentially share assets in exchange for greater scalability, more rapid deployment and reduced costs. Lock-in is an issue here, as has already been explored.

Some organisations adopt a hybrid approach where the solution spans both on-premise and cloud elements. Many organisations retain core/critical systems and applications in-house, while pushing non-critical and replicable business process tasks outside of the organisation. In this way, cloud services are analogous to many clients' attitudes to outsourcing. Other organisations preserve their current IT assets on premise while investing for their future needs in the cloud.

TABLE 2.1   Cloud consumer and cloud provider activities

Service models	Examples of services available	Cloud consumer activities	Provider activities
SaaS	ERP, billing, sales, CRM, collaboration, HR, email and office productivity, content management, social networks, financials, document management	Uses application/service for business process operations	Installs, manages, maintains and supports the software application on a cloud infrastructure
PaaS	Business intelligence, application deployment, database, integration, development and testing	Develops, tests, deploys, and manages applications hosted in a cloud system	Provisions and manages cloud infrastructure and middleware for the platform consumers; provides development, deployment, and administration tools to platform consumers
IaaS	Service management, platform hosting, storage, compute, backup and recovery	Creates/installs, manages and monitors services for IT infrastructure operations	Provisions and manages the physical processing, storage, networking, and the hosting environment and cloud infrastructure for IaaS consumers

Source: Based on Mell and Grance, 2011.

Maturity of cloud solutions: Client and supplier perspectives

Oshri and Kavari (2013) interviewed 32 users and 34 suppliers of enterprise cloud solutions to establish their views about the maturity of the market, their satisfaction with the range of services and the value gained from them. Understanding the interviewees' views about each of the cloud computing models was of particular interest.

Maturity and satisfaction

Firms were asked to identify the current cloud market maturity level within each of the main service models to determine if they were mature enough to be used in an enterprise environment. The findings demonstrate that the level of maturity varies depending on the service model.

Over 98% of respondents indicated that they believed SaaS to be above the 'infancy' stage, with 55% positioning it as mature. Approximately 88% of respondents positioned IaaS above the infancy stage, with a majority (61.5%) indicating that it was still in the growth phase and was not mature as yet. PaaS was voted the most immature of the three, with over one quarter (26%) of respondents believing it still to be in its infancy.

Client organisations were overwhelmingly satisfied with their SaaS solutions, with over 90% of them describing themselves as 'Satisfied' or 'Very satisfied'. Both IaaS and PaaS received about 60% 'Satisfied' or 'Very satisfied' ratings. This implies that the perceived level of maturity has a direct impact on the supply and consumption of cloud services in the enterprise market – not surprisingly, perhaps. Put another way, organisations seem healthily resistant to hype.

Business, data and financial factors

Client organisations were asked to rate how business and financial factors influenced their choice of cloud-based enterprise solutions. Generally speaking, client organisations and suppliers shared the same perspectives on most business and financial considerations. However, the research showed that while suppliers believed that scalability was one of the key influences on the adoption of enterprise cloud services, client organisations did not share this view very strongly.

Firms were asked to rate the other business factors enabling and hindering the adoption of enterprise cloud solutions. Both client organisations and suppliers rated cost management as one of the key influencers of the adoption of cloud solutions. Interestingly, while clients perceived productivity to be a key element, suppliers did not share this view. The top factor hindering enterprise cloud adoption was information security, while the least important factor was performance.

Firms were then asked to rate the factors that added value. The research revealed that suppliers overestimated the importance of experimenting with new ideas; client organisations needed persuading that hard business outcomes would be delivered.

It is understandable why suppliers might choose to focus on obvious enterprise concerns like cost and innovation during the initial stages of cloud adoption. However, the enterprise cloud market has matured to a stage where other business drivers have equal, if not more, weight in an enterprise's decision-making process. Suppliers need to refocus their marketing efforts to better align with these changes in customer attitudes and behaviour.

On security, suppliers need to be open and honest about the security regimes they provide. Due diligence is essential for clients, who should also discuss with potential suppliers what both sides can do to implement better data security. And on supplier credibility, suppliers need to move away from the use of generic references to bolster their credibility. It has become clear that enterprises need recommendations from a trusted source.

Organisations that plan to include cloud as part of their IT portfolio need to have a comprehensive IT and business strategy in place to deal with the differences that they will encounter on their journey to the cloud. The whole organisation will need to be trained to adopt best practices on ensuring data security.

Since security and lack of confidence in the supplier are the two main factors hindering cloud adoption, client organisations need to have a robust vetting and selection process where they review and validate the credentials of their potential cloud services supplier.

The following case discusses the various challenges faced and approached by Global Pharma with regard to their cloud computing strategy.

C A S E   S T U D Y

A Global Operating Model That Exploits Cloud Computing Services[2]

by Mark Skilton

The global pharmaceutical market is a multibillion-dollar dynamic worldwide business ranging from consumer healthcare products to advanced medical devices and biotechnology research. Many aspects of the marketplace are interconnected by the need for constant research and rapid market trials through to dynamic scaling up and down of collaborative product manufacturing and diverse distribution supply chains to deliver to residential, wholesale and retail marketplaces. The industry is regulated through regional and global governance standards, ranging from patent laws for products and drug licensing through to compliance standards including the US Food and Drug Administration (FDA), as well as specific health data protection laws such as the US Health Insurance Portability and Accountability Act.

The Global Pharma company competes in these conditions through a wide and expansive organisational structure spanning 100,000 direct employees; 250 BUs operating in the Americas, Europe, Middle East, Asia Pacific and South American markets; and a wide partner channel ecosystem network. Its products span consumer health care, medical devices design, manufacture, distribution and biomedical product research and commercialisation.

The following operational capabilities are essential to Global Pharma:

- The ability of front-end business operations to adapt and offer products and services quickly in response to market and consumer demand
- The ability to create research patents and rapidly move research to market test trials
- The ability to build operational cost efficiencies into the infrastructure through shared services
- Rapid movement of existing and new business operations and resources to locations that would enable (i) flexible market entry and withdrawal, (ii) to build and expand capacity and shrink and remove capacity as needed and (iii) to pursue market opportunities
- Strong security and compliance partitioning and controls over BUs
- Partner networks to enable effective collaboration and yet guard security compliance and corporate societal values
- The development of brands and pricing strategies across diverse market geographies to exploit patents and market

buying behaviours for long-term shareholder value in the brand and revenue share.

Global Pharma's IT hardware and software assets and staff are consolidated into regional data centres connected by a corporate global network. A small central corporate IT function coordinates policy and strategy, which is largely distributed down to the BU-based IT functions to meet local market and business service requirements. The use and development of the business applications and infrastructure are focused onshore by region. Large-scale corporate systems are developed in each data centre, and some are replicated across other regional data centres. Significant investment in virtualisation has addressed the operational efficiencies of the data centre as the pharmaceutical market environment continues to change rapidly. At present, because of the cultural and organisational diversity, regional BUs own IT strategy and delivery.

Steps Towards Adopting Cloud Computing

In 2009, the Global Pharma IT board saw that many of pharmaceutical industry characteristics aligned well with the capabilities found in cloud computing. This resulted in a cloud strategy plan and assessment of current investments in data centres and a number of strategic pilots to test public, private, and hybrid cloud solutions and to learn more about cloud technology and business models. By the middle of 2010, these investigations had focused on a complete global private cloud and recommended developing pilots to accelerate the design of the private cloud data-centre solution.

In terms of an operating model, moving to cloud computing redefines the need for each region and BU to develop certain types of IT service onshore. Common services hosted in a secure private cloud-based data centre provide the possibility for many BUs to move to an offshore shared model that Global Pharma saw as an opportunity to improve its organisational efficiency. While agility in individual markets and BUs was still essential to competitiveness in Global Pharma's specific markets, Global

Pharma sought to support this by targeting cloud computing services for specific business activity needs.

Global Pharma developed a vision of an operating model using cloud computing:

- Flexible front-end IT services to enable the IT function to support rapid business demand in disparate dynamic markets
- Alignment of IT modernisation programmes of data centres, networks and applications to become on demand and with shared cost efficiencies
- Coordinated modular data centres and service centres for operating efficiencies from a one-to-many service for BUs.

Defining the Right Type of Cloud Operating Model

Given the strategic decision to move to private cloud computing, Global Pharma had already invested extensively in infrastructure virtualisation technology and a global data centre network. Cloud computing, however, introduced the need for a modular infrastructure. The plan of work by the end 2010 was to modernise the infrastructure with modular data centres and networks, enabling a new operating model for IT resources and software applications to align with business capacity needs across the global operation and to deploy to meet specific BUs.

In the distributed user groups in Global Pharma's BUs, there was a range of business processes that could be supported by common administration services such as email, storage and collaboration. These were candidates for shared services. Other specific services defined for each BU or as strategic platforms were mission critical and differentiating for the company. Hosting these business activities required cloud infrastructure services to be dedicated to these services and the potential assembly of specific application services to be put together to meet differentiated service levels.

Thus, in parallel with the modular data-centre concept, the analysis of corporate and BU enterprise software applications hosted in the modular data centre identified different types of business activities that were grouped into portfolios of cloud computing services that could be moved to a cloud computing environment. Business activities that represented commodity services across many user groups in one-to-many fashion (such as email and content management) and did not require much data storage and consumption of computing power were grouped into horizontal cloud services. Specific high-resource intensive business activities (with high computing power and data storage consumption) that included both one-to-many and one-to-one niche-specific services for markets were grouped into vertical cloud services. Business activities that involved collaborative business transactions that were common across BUs but more complex and more resource intensive than commodity services (e.g., the general functionality of customer relationship management and enterprise resource planning) were grouped together as candidates for a shared service cloud-based computing environment:

- Business activities for horizontal cloud services (one-to-many): email, market trial tests, storage, enterprise portals, content management and human capital management
- Business activities for vertical cloud services (one-to-one and one-to-many): engineering, research simulation and processing, business intelligence, niche enterprise resource planning, customer relationship management (industry specific) and supply chain management (planning and scheduling)
- Business activities for shared cloud services (one-to-many): global enterprise resource planning, customer relationship management (online stores), supplier relationship management, product life-cycle management and global supply chain management.

Impact of Cloud Services on Global Pharma

As a result of the modular approach that created data centres and services for common cross-BU services, specific high-resource intensive business activities and specific business capability platforms hosted in the cloud were given to alternative data centres. To manage these cloud services, Global Pharma created employer competency centres for skills, training and investment programmes. Other competency groups were set up to support common shared services around specific technologies such as Microsoft, Oracle and SAP.

Furthermore, the movement to modular data centres and the grouping of business activities into classes of cloud application services enabled support for business activities to be managed between onshore and offshore cloud data centres, where permitted. Moreover, the migration of existing applications and services to cloud-based data centres required changes in service management practices. Existing service centre operations dedicated to specific BUs needed to develop cross-BU cloud services and align to specific cloud platform service support needs.

Because compliance issues related to data movements across borders prohibited the use of offshore cloud data centre services, Global Pharma faced difficulties in using public cloud.

Issues Hampering Forward Movement for Global Pharma

Global Pharma faced a number of issues related to cloud computing. At the strategic level, Global Pharma needed to amend its business strategy to maximise the benefits from cloud computing and incorporate cloud computing strategy into the business strategy. At the operational level, Global Pharma struggled to decide what operations and business processes should be moved to public, private or hybrid cloud options, and how the global operating model needed to change to get the benefits of cloud computing. In addressing these issues, Global Pharma identified specific challenges:

- *Managing multiple clouds and required capabilities*: If Global Pharma chose a private cloud, it needed to recognise that running a cloud service as a supplier was different from consuming a cloud service. The skills required for the transformation are more complex, because an understanding of all of the components of cloud architecture does not typically reside in just one supplier. The BU stakeholders also needed to identify generic services (those used across different functions and BUs) to build the one-to-many usage patterns to enable a return on the investment from the cloud and avoid fragmentation and multiple clouds.

• *Offshoring in the cloud*: Global Pharma was already operating in an onshore and offshore distributed model enabled through its data centres. However, the move to distributed cloud-hosted business services enabled one location to distribute a business activity to another region. Locations of business activities that became business services still needed to be controlled for compliance and security management for the regional and BU.

• *Security and operational concerns*: Specific security and compliance issues for the US FDA and data controls such as Safeharbor Knowledge Solutions, which prohibits medical data movement off-premise and offshore, and Federation of Security access to supplier partner networks that need multiple identity and authentication control had to be handled appropriately. Partitioning specific business activities for FDA security compliance into specific data centre domains was one approach to contain a dedicated cloud resource to focus performance and security controls of critical systems. This required specific cloud rules for control and access. Alternatively, Global Pharma could consider partitioning applications into different cloud services types – for example, an FDA application cloud, an ERP cloud, a Microsoft cloud, or an Oracle cloud to support specific supplier licensing and performance issues.

• *Outsourcing, in-house or hybrid service delivery*: With a private cloud, Global Pharma would become a service provider delivering on-demand services to its own BUs. An alternative to doing everything in-house would be the use of third parties. However, it was not clear how these third parties could participate as alternative private clouds. In particular, how would third-party outsourcers with cloud data centres be certified for pharmaceutical company use? And how would external private clouds be integrated with internal company private clouds?

- *Payment structure and licence reengineering*: The licensing issue was not clear. The use of pay-as-you-go consumption models of applications and infrastructure resources would not necessarily be compatible with existing licensing based on usage per user instance. If this is virtualised and not specific to a physical instance of hardware, the software licence model breaks down. Alternatives might be found through reseller licence models or licence pooling for the corporation. How would individual suppliers need to be handled on a case-by-case basis? How would umbrella contract agreements for existing supplier software licences be affected if they are moved to a cloud-based hosted environment?

- *Stakeholder engagement*: In distributed user groups in the Global Pharma BUs, a range of cloud services needed to be defined for each BU and market-facing operation. Focusing on common services versus variations of service required the involvement of many different stakeholders from these groups to build the one-to-many opportunities that cloud can support.

The cloud service provider also had to address some issues. If Global Pharma decided to create a private cloud, the internal unit delivering the cloud services and any third parties had to clarify the following issues:

- *Alignment of modular business services with demand*: The use of modular business activity (service) hosted in specific data centres required control and demand forecast planning of capacity availability. Demand aggregation and request management processes needed to accommodate a shift to a catalogue-style provisioning model. This included a portal strategy for self-service. From Global Pharma's perspective, the cloud provider (or the internal unit providing services in the private cloud) had to be able to forecast shifts in demand in order to meet that demand. From the cloud provider's perspective, the ability to forecast demand capacity is essential to ensure the service was able to meet operational demands.

- *Alignment with modular business services and supply capacity*: The standard operating environments hosted as various templates for cloud resources needed to be aligned with the types of applications and usage patterns for the allocated capacity. This introduced new operating practices for traffic and load balancing.
- *Power efficiencies and facilities certification*: Efficiency of power consumption in cloud computing can be affected by a large-scale burst in demand. In certain circumstances, the power demand in the cloud data centre needed to be planned to be available to prevent insufficient energy to support operations. And efficient green energy and certification of services are as essential in cloud operations as in conventionally managed hosting.

Crowdsourcing

Crowdsourcing is the act of taking a job traditionally performed by employees and outsourcing it to an undefined, generally large group of people in the form of an 'open call' (Howe, 2008). This sourcing model has been widely adopted in the open innovation movement (e.g., by Innocentive, TekScout, IdeaConnection, and many other open innovation marketplaces and communities). A large number of new business ventures have emerged through crowdsourcing, mainly by creating an opportunity for anybody to submit an idea (examples are products such as photos to iStockphoto.com or T-shirt designs to Threadless.com) and let the community of users or potential buyers decide whether a particular creation is worth buying. Crowdsourcing projects rely on the contributions of individuals or a collective of people who are not necessarily motivated by monetary incentives. Psychological motivations, such as self-fulfilment, sense of contribution and the pleasure of solving problems are other motivation factors, no less important than monetary rewards. The following case study describes the crowdsourcing phenomenon and provides examples of crowdsourcing firms.

Crowdsourcing

by Onook Oh and Rajiv Kishore

The Crowdsourcing Phenomenon

With the development of Web 2.0 technologies, entrepreneurs are continually creating and experimenting with innovative e-business models. One of the recent e-business models that has gained popularity and recognition in a short span is crowdsourcing. This business model harnesses the potential of a heterogeneous and globally dispersed online crowd to meet a variety of business needs. As with any new major business development, crowdsourcing has spawned a new and emerging vocabulary including terms such as 'prosumers' (producers + consumers) or 'produsage' (production + usage). A key implication of these new coinages is that consumers are no longer passive buyers who simply consume end products. Rather, they are active 'prosumers' who directly or indirectly participate in co-creating the goods and services they consume. As a result, the line between producer and consumer indeed becomes blurry in the crowdsourcing phenomenon.

Crowdsourcing may be best understood as a variant of the outsourcing phenomenon, in that both sourcing mechanisms utilise resources from outside the organisational boundaries to meet internal business needs. However, a major difference between the two sourcing mechanisms is that, while traditional outsourcing relies predominantly on a handful of established professional services firms, crowdsourcing turns to a much larger heterogeneous, online crowd of individuals to meet their internal business needs. The main driver that made reaching to a multitude of potential virtual workers and crowdsourcing possible is the collection of Web 2.0 technologies that enable individuals to actively participate and engage in co-creation activities through the 24/7 interconnected virtual technological environment. Furthermore, a crowd of individuals that is highly connected through this technological environment makes it possible for organisations to aggregate individual profiles and create a large virtual workforce of varied skills sets that they can search and match for meeting specific business needs and then contract with specific individuals all in real time.

Examples of Crowdsourcing Firms

InnoCentive: The Oil Spill Recovery Institute (OSRI) was formed to find ways to remove oil from contaminated areas in response to the catastrophic 1989 Exxon Valdez oil spill in Alaska, and it continues to be engaged in cleaning up all the remaining oil from affected areas. While dozens of barges have diligently pumped oil from iceberg cracks into barge tanks, the mixture of pumped water and oil quickly freezes to a sticky state, making it difficult to separate oil from water. In 2007, OSRI posted a challenge on the InnoCentive website. Within two weeks, a cement expert, John Davis, came up with a simple solution that surprised OSRI scientists. John applied tools and techniques widely used in the concrete industry. The concrete industry uses a vibration tool to keep cement from becoming solid during massive cement pours. John's solution was to attach a long pole and insert it into the oil recovery tanks and to vibrate this pole to prevent oil and water from freezing. Using this simple vibrating tool, OSRI could remove oil from water, and the challenge solver, John, was rewarded US$20,00.

The InnoCentive website is comprised of seekers and solvers. Seekers – corporations or non-profit organisations – can post their Research and Development (R&D) challenges to InnoCentive's open innovation marketplace website. Each challenge has a solution submission deadline and is assigned a cash reward ranging from US$5,000 to more than US$1 million. Any registered InnoCentive solver can enter the online project room to gain access to the posted challenges and work on any project that he or she may want to solve. The seeker reviews submitted solutions after the deadline, awards the announced cash reward to the best solver and pays an agreed commission to InnoCentive.

Launched in 2001, InnoCentive has posted more than 1,650 external challenges and achieves a premium challenge success rate of 85%, using the above-described crowdsourcing model. In contrast to technology services firms working with a handful of highly skilled scientists and researchers, InnoCentive is working with 300,000 anonymous solvers from nearly 200 countries.[3] To solve problems, InnoCentive is using the crowd's collective creativity and the power of scale of the knowledge community. InnoCentive counts Proctor & Gamble, Boeing, DuPont, LG and other large and famous brand names as its seeker customers.

Cambrian House: Michael Sikorsky raised US$10.1 million from 2006 to 2007 for his new venture firm, Cambrian House Inc. As a Web 2.0 platform-based crowdsourcing start-up, his vision was to create 'low-cost software quickly'.

The first video game, Gwabs, took a volunteer team six months from concept to finished product and cost US$200,000. Producing it with in-house staff, says Sikorsky, 'would have taken 50% longer and cost three times as much'.[4]

In the initial phase of its growth, Cambrian House hosted and developed a mass crowdsourcing community. During that period, Cambrian House mixed an open-source software development model with a traditional company format and was able to attract about 50,000 members and more than 7,000 ideas from the crowd.[5] Cambrian outsourced market research, product design and development to this community and focused only on project management, sales and marketing. With transparent compensation schemes and respect for its community members, Cambrian utilised the collective knowledge of online community members in a creative and cost-effective way.

The product development process at Cambrian worked as follows[6]: any individual could submit his or her idea for a fresh, new software to CambrianHouse.com. Then Cambrian community members discussed, researched and voted on that idea. On a regular basis, Cambrian issued 100 Cambros (Cambrian's virtual money) to the individual who submitted the best idea. This individual could form a project team using Cambrian community members. Cambrian on its part created a demo website for the selected idea and conducted market research using Google's pay-per-click advertising. Using Google analytic tools, Cambrian analysed market demand by gathering statistical information: 'How many people are searching for your idea right now?', 'How many visit your site?', 'Do they ask for more information?', 'Would they pre-order your product?'. If the idea showed market demand, they invested in the project themselves, otherwise they cancelled it. Once the project was completed and was put into production for public use, Cambrian took 50% of the revenue generated for project management, sales and marketing. Each contributor to the project received 'royalty points' for as long as the product generated revenue.

Cambrian had been developing a crowdsourcing technology platform since its launch to enable its own crowdsourcing model. It shifted its strategy around 2008 and started offering its crowdsourcing technology platform named Chaordix™as 'crowdsourcing technology in a box' to new industries and enterprises wishing to bring crowdsourcing to their own businesses. The Chaordix platform provides much more enhanced functionality for crowdsourcing than just in the area of software development, and Cambrian partners can now use this platform for generating team insights, product innovation, brand innovation and business model innovation through business-to-business collaboration.[7]

OhMyNews: For many newspaper companies, the web is simply another channel to deliver and/or sell their news content created by professional journalists. Launched in February 2000, a Korean online news media company, OhMyNews (www.ohmynews.com[8]), innovated the way in which news content is created and delivered to consumers. As an online newspaper, this company finds and generates news content through voluntary citizen reporters instead of professional journalists. The founder, Yeonho Oh, says that he 'wanted to start a tradition free of newspaper company elitism where news items are evaluated based on quality, regardless of whether it came from a major newspaper, a local reporter, an educated journalist, or a neighbourhood housewife'.[9]

Starting in 2000 with 727 voluntary citizen reporters, OhMyNews had more than 40,000 citizen reporters in 2005 and more than 78,000 in 2014 out of South Korea's total population of 46 million. Typical citizen reporters write a story or two per week. Once the story is submitted online, it remains as a 'Saengnamu' article before being accepted by the OhMyNews copyeditor team. During this period, intensive screening takes place, such as for sentence construction, checking for factual errors and the value of the news and the copyediting process by professional internal editors. When an article is approved, citizen reporters can monitor the number of readers' clicks or comments and collect monetary rewards in a virtual 'tip jar'.

In the OhMyNews business model, readers are not passive consumers of news content. They are both active producers and consumers. This citizen reporter model turned out to be quite effective, as it can deliver the same news content much faster and with a unique perspective. However, high-quality news content does not come for nothing. OhMyNews has designed and implemented unique quality management programmes to produce high-quality news contents. To enhance their news quality, OhMyNews actively involves its citizen reporters in online conversations. For citizen reporters' news to be placed as a headline, they have to persuade OhMyNew's frontline copyeditors. Also, OhMyNews organises regular seminars for citizen reporters to help write high-quality news and to give copyright advice. OhMyNews was so successful that in 2005, nearly 70 citizen reporters contracted to write books. In May 2006, OhMyNews was invited as a special guest to Google's Zeitgeist media forum in London, along with world-renowned media companies such as Reuters and Le Monde. This model of citizen reporting is now being adopted by mainstream news media organisations owing to its unique value proposition. CNN has developed a community of iReporters (http://ireport.cnn. com), who provide first-person accounts of breaking news in areas where it does not have its own professional reporters at the time.

Online crowdsourcing environments and marketplaces[10]

Similar to the emergence of large numbers of business-to-customer and customer-to-customer online marketplaces that bring together buyers and sellers (e.g., Amazon and eBay), online marketplaces for sourcing customised products and services have emerged. Such marketplaces allow customers to contract a supplier (an individual or a company) to develop and deliver a product or service based on the customer's specific needs. Different from online auctions such as eBay and uBid and e-malls like Amazon, which sell ready goods, sourcing marketplaces provide clients a suitable supplier for a product or service delivery. Marketplaces such as Freelancer, Elance, Guru and oDesk[11] serve as intermediaries that provide legal and project management support in the form of standard contracts that include copyright protection, payment protection and basic project management stages to facilitate interactions between clients and suppliers who are essentially members of the crowd. Registered crowd members can be individuals or firms. This sourcing model is usually suitable for relatively small and well-defined tasks such as website design, the development of specialised applications or software development to implement small product features, proofreading or indexing. Clients and suppliers rely exclusively on online interactions and usually never meet face-to-face.

Online crowdsourcing represents a somewhat unknown slice of the global sourcing landscape. *Online sourcing environments* (OSE) are online spaces where buyers and suppliers of services can meet, offer and apply for jobs; carry out project-related tasks; and conduct financial transactions.

All OSEs have three main stakeholders: buyers, suppliers who form the 'crowd' and (online) platforms. Buyers are companies or individuals who come to OSEs because they are interested in outsourcing a part of their workload. Historically most OSE buyers have been small – usually entrepreneurs and small firms with fewer than 100 employees, mostly from English-speaking countries. Suppliers are also represented primarily by small service firms and individuals, with the latter being either moonlighters or independent professionals. They participate in OSEs to market their skills and services to potential buyers. The population of suppliers is more geographically distributed than that of buyers, yet the USA still contributes a significant portion. In addition, certain countries have become somewhat specialised in specific project types – for example, India, Romania and Pakistan dominate the IT category. The third stakeholder is the intermediary, the marketplace itself, which takes the shape of an *online platform*. These are the websites that provide an environment where buyers and suppliers can interact.

A new project in an OSE usually starts with the buyer formalising its work needs and converting them into project requirements. These requirements are then communicated to suppliers typically in the form of a job, project (a request for bid) or competition announcement. The buyer selects a supplier to work on the project. This may be done on the basis of proposals (bids) submitted by suppliers or an actual project deliverable submitted as a part of a competition or contest. Once the job is awarded, the buyer oversees its completion and, when the final deliverable is deemed acceptable, pays the supplier for services rendered. The final step in the buyer workflow is to rate the supplier and, sometimes, provide additional qualitative feedback on the project.

Suppliers register with OSEs by building a personal profile. Most OSEs today allow rich supplier profiles that include personal and contact information, educational and employment history, job history on the platform and, in many cases, skill evaluation data (tested or self-reported). Once the profile is in place, the supplier can start searching and applying for relevant job or project announcements.

The mechanics of the application process may vary from one online sourcing marketplace platform to another, but usually it is set up as either a reverse auction or a competition. Once selected, the supplier starts working on the project. The work is usually facilitated by the platform, which provides communication, collaboration and project management tools. Once the job is completed, the supplier collects the payment and provides feedback on the buyer.

We distinguish three main types of OSEs: *directories*, which provide listings of projects, supplier profiles and contact information, but where deals are usually done offline; *marketplaces*, which connect buyers and suppliers and facilitate their interaction throughout the entire sourcing life cycle; and *communities*, which aim to build a network of talented and skilled individuals in a particular field, such as creative design or computer programming. Their key characteristics are summarised in Table 2.2.

Boundaries among the three OSE types often blur or change over time. For example, a platform may start out as a directory, but over time, features are added with the objective of gradually evolving into a marketplace. Similarly, some platforms in the marketplace category are starting to adopt elements from the community category. For example, marketplace platforms Elance and oDesk have made significant efforts to engage with and foster the community of suppliers (e.g., both platforms maintain blogs and are active on Twitter).

Kaganer et al. (2012) summarise four major types of crowdsourcing platforms that provide financial incentives: facilitator, arbitrator, aggregator and governor models. The *facilitator* refers to crowdsourcing platforms (e.g., Elance and Freelancer) that provide relatively transparent mechanisms for both project initiators and suppliers (crowd members) to view each other's expertise, credibility and past experience in order to make decisions. In a facilitator contract, usually the client is expected to select one supplier who can be an individual or a firm. The fees are agreed between the client and the supplier in advance, before the supplier commences the project. With respect to the *arbitrator* model, suppliers compete with each other and provide deliverables that they decide to submit without an advanced promise of a payment (e.g., crowdSPRING). The project initiator only selects one deliverable that best fulfils its need and only the wining supplier gets paid. The *aggregator* model usually engages with a large number of suppliers to deliver a huge amount of simple, repetitive tasks and there is no coordination need among suppliers (e.g., CrowdFlower). For each supplier, the payment procedure is the same as with the facilitator model. In the governor model (e.g., Trada), the crowdsourcing platform provides project governance by employing a combination of human project managers and a sophisticated software-enabled framework for monitoring and coordinating individual tasks. *Governor* platforms provide a thicker layer of project governance, including

TABLE 2.2 Characteristics of online sourcing environments

	Directories	Marketplaces	Communities
Main focus or objective	Help buyers discover suppliers by providing supplier listings with profile and contact information	Connects buyers and suppliers of services throughout all stages of the workflow	Helps members (i.e., suppliers) develop professionally through community interaction and paid client (i.e., buyer) engagements
Nature or structure of deals	Deals are done offline; the platform is not involved	Deals are done online, usually through a reverse-auction type of process; the platform is involved in both legal and financial aspects of the deal	Deals are done online and usually structured as contests or competitions; the platform is involved in both legal and financial aspects of the deal
Platform's role in facilitating buyer–supplier interaction	No buyer–supplier interaction takes place on the platform; buyers may have an option of posting projects online, but all the ensuing activities take place outside of the platform	The platform facilitates buyer–supplier interaction with a focus on project completion	The platform facilitates buyer–supplier interaction with a focus on learning and community building
Revenue model	Advertising, sponsorship	Project commission paid by suppliers; buyers and suppliers may sign up for premium membership	Project commission/fee paid by buyers
Platform examples	Infolancer, Chinasourcing	Elance, Guru, oDesk, Freelancer	crowdSPRING, TopCoder (Direct)

collecting project requirements from the client, breaking them up into micro-tasks, coordinating completion and sequencing individual tasks, conducting supplier certification and ensuring the quality of the final deliverable (Kaganer et al., 2013). Furthermore, there is the *campaign* model which refers to those firm-initiated campaigns engaging external workforces to achieve particular business purposes (e.g., Bonabeau, 2009; Whitla, 2009). Usually the firm creates a dedicated online space (supported by a crowdsourcing platform) for the campaign. The crowd gets involved in the campaign in the form of competitions. Unlike the arbitrator model, there are usually multiple ranked winners getting the rewards. For example, LEGO®learns from consumers' creativity through maintaining its own platform CUUSOO to invite players to design their own toys. Such a model is frequently used for marketing, R&D and customer-research-related business purposes (Whitla, 2009).

Why do buyers come to OSEs?

OSEs afford buyers instant global reach. Neither buyers in search of talented people nor suppliers are bounded by their region or country. Buyers benefit from low costs that result from global supplier competition. The differences in bids submitted to the same project description are usually due to lower wages and costs in the supplier countries or regions. OSE programmers in India, Bangladesh and Pakistan usually submit bids that are much lower than those by their competitors in wealthy nations.

Another advantage OSEs offer to buyers is the ability to quickly launch and scale up projects. Once a buyer posts a project, it is common to get 20–30 proposals from suppliers within the first two or three days. For larger projects, OSEs can help buyers mobilise the supplier community to start working in parallel on the individual tasks comprising the project. Community-type platforms like crowdSPRING and TopCoder do an especially good job at that.

Finally, buyers can take advantage of an established framework provided by OSEs for initiating and managing the sourcing projects (i.e., a comprehensive suite of online tools and services that help buyers manage all aspects of the sourcing relationship).

What challenges do OSE buyers face?

Trust is key to any successful buyer–supplier relationship, especially in OSEs that lack personal contact and face-to-face interaction, with cross-cultural and language differences creating additional obstacles. A buyer needs to have confidence that the supplier it selects will complete the project on time and that the final deliverable will be of acceptable quality. The buyer also needs to be assured that, in case problems arise, effective mechanisms are available within the platform to address the issue. Thus, trust must be established at two levels: the supplier level and the platform level.

At the supplier level, the general strategy has been to make the OSEs more transparent, to open up communication channels between the buyer and supplier and to provide tools to monitor project progress. For example, in the early years of OSEs, suppliers had anonymous user profiles and aliases instead of real names. Over time, OSEs realised that this approach was counterproductive in terms of helping the parties build trusting relationships. Today most platforms allow suppliers to build rich profiles providing detailed personal and contact information, educational and employment history, skill evaluation scores and often a portfolio of previous work. In addition, to make up for the lack of personal recommendations common in traditional offline environments, platforms have introduced sophisticated rating systems and feedback mechanisms. Buyers can also see a complete history of projects the supplier has worked on, along with earnings and project completion statistics.

With respect to opening up communication channels, platforms like Elance and oDesk offer built-in online communication services, including chat, discussion forums, Web conferencing and phone integration. These tools can be used to interview a supplier at the selection phase or facilitate collaboration between the two parties throughout the project. Similarly, many platforms now offer project management tools enabling buyers to establish milestones and link payments to milestone completion.

Fostering trust at the platform level is based on the idea that since it is virtually impossible to ensure the trustworthiness of each individual supplier in a global context, the platform itself should become the guarantor that buyers will trust. Two primary mechanisms are used to accomplish this goal. The first includes initiatives seeking to reduce the perception of risk for the buyer. Escrow accounts (the project payment is held by the platform until the work is completed and approved by the buyer), arbitration services and mandatory intellectual property agreements for suppliers provide the most common examples.

The second mechanism focuses on grooming the supplier pool. Here, the rationale is that by weeding out poor suppliers and promoting high-quality ones, the platform will build up a trustworthy reputation for itself. For example, Elance encourages all buyers to take advantage of its project management module. Once the critical mass of projects goes through the module to create some benchmark history, a platform-wide monitoring system can be established to identify and warn suppliers who regularly underperform.

Can outsourcing suppliers benefit from crowdsourcing?

Crowdsourcing offers several potential benefits to outsourcing suppliers, among them an alternative to the on-site-offshore model. This next generation of outsourcing which is associated with the 'human cloud', a virtual, on-demand workforce (Kaganer et al., 2012), is enabled through crowdsourcing platforms. As large companies such as Microsoft,[12] IBM,[13] GE[14] and Google[15] have started experimenting with crowdsourcing, its growing popularity has stimulated a range of mixed reactions in the outsourcing community. Some established suppliers are ignoring the fact that an 'unknown workforce' is delivering jobs that could have been contracted to them. Others realise the increasing competition and are attempting to utilise this virtual on-demand workforce for their benefit. In particular, during the economic downturn, when reducing headcount across global delivery centres was seen as one of the obvious solutions to reduce costs, especially fixed costs, a possibility to tap into a global talent pool and employ required skills on demand created an interesting proposition for established service providers.

While the expected economic benefits of this proposition are significant, it is not clear what effort is required from established IT service providers to be able to successfully leverage crowdsourcing. Kaganer et al. (2012) suggest, for example, that the organisational challenges associated with the human cloud require new management models and skills from the contracting organisation (the buyer). Putting this perspective into the outsourcing context, Nevo and Kotlarsky (2014) argue that service providers engaging in crowdsourcing need to develop new capabilities to successfully utilise crowdsourcing in delivering services to their clients. Based on data collected from focus groups with crowdsourcing leaders at a large multinational technology organisation, the new capabilities that were identified stem from the need of the traditional service provider to assume a 'client' role in the crowdsourcing context, while still acting as a 'supplier' in providing services to the end-client (for a detailed discussion of new capabilities, see Nevo and Kotlarsky (2014)). Overall, the combination of 'client' and 'supplier' capabilities would enable a primary supplier to manage the three stakeholder groups that play an important role in crowdsourced projects:

1. *The client* who is ultimately the most important stakeholder, with client buy-in needed to ensure their satisfaction. Not all clients that contract a specific organisation may agree to have (parts of) their work crowdsourced.
2. *Internal team members* who need to design, facilitate and manage crowdsourced work, as well as integrate the crowdsourced deliverable into the services delivered to the end-client.
3. *The crowd* who need to have appropriate support (e.g., infrastructure) from the primary service provider, and feel motivated to respond to crowdsourcing calls.

Considerations for Outsourcing and Offshoring

An activity can be sourced as an overall set of processes or as smaller parts of it. The tasks and business processes that can be outsourced or offshored vary. In order of increasing complexity, they are as follows:

- Low-cost simple back-office functions such as infrastructure and data management
- Customer-facing services such as call centres or help desks and telemarketing
- Business functions such as human resources, finance, and accounting, and procurement
- Strategic knowledge-intensive processes, such as business intelligence, market research, and various R&D activities.

Using the scope of outsourcing as a criterion (i.e., the degree to which a process is managed internally or by a third party), we distinguish three models:

Total outsourcing, which refers to transferring more than 80% of a function's operating budget to external providers

Total in-house sourcing, which refers to retaining the management and provision of more than 80% of the function's operating budget within the organisation

Selective outsourcing, which refers to sourcing selected functions to external parties while managing 20–80% of the function's operating budget internally.

Along these lines, Metters (2008) suggests that offshoring and outsourcing decisions should be seen as a spectrum rather than as distinct categories. With regard to the offshoring decision, Metters explains that, initially, it may appear categorical as a process performed either in the home country or offshore. However, Metters also emphasises degrees to the level of offshoring that are related to the amount of risk a firm undertakes. For example, we could consider a US firm that would like to lower the costs of a back-office process related to keying in handwritten English text to a computer system. Modern information and communication technologies enable the performance of this process from various remote locations in a more cost-effective way. In the decision relating to where to offshore, a number of factors may play significant roles, depending on the company's business model. Metters focuses on the case of electronically transferrable services and identifies labour costs, cultural distance from the data source and quality of infrastructure as some of the most important factors to consider when making offshoring decisions.

If we take into account the labour costs of clerical workers, the most favourable cost alternative is offshoring the process of keying handwritten English text to a computer system to China. As illustrated in Figure 2.3, China is the most attractive destination for a US customer

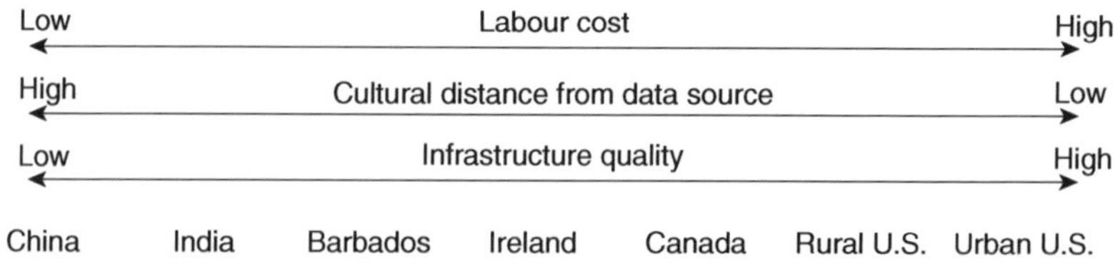

Low	Labour cost	High
High	Cultural distance from data source	Low
Low	Infrastructure quality	High

China   India   Barbados   Ireland   Canada   Rural U.S.   Urban U.S.

FIGURE 2.3 / **Spectrum of single-facility offshoring choices for a US customer**
Source: Metters, 2008.

in terms of labour costs. However, non-English-speaking Chinese workers use character recognition rather than understanding English as a language. For this reason, undertaking this process would require two or even more employees to independently key characters and ensure that the process is performed correctly. Another choice might be India, where English-speaking Indians would perform the keying. This choice would entail higher wages than in China, but only one-fifth the level of US wages. Furthermore, this choice would entail a relatively lower level of language and cultural barriers between the client and the supplier organisation. An even more expensive option might be to offshore the process to Barbados, where English is the prevalent spoken language and salaries are 20–50% of the US levels. Another option might be to offshore (more precisely, to nearshore) the work to Canada, where wages are lower relative to the USA yet higher than the other destinations mentioned. A further option might be using homeshoring or rural outsourcing by sending the work to lower-wage rural regions within the US. Finally, the firm can engage in offshoring to multiple destinations and perform the same process within different facilities around the world. On this basis, the cost of labour, the cultural distance and the quality of infrastructure are the most relevant factors in the choice of an offshoring option.

In contrast to electronically transmitted services, viewing offshoring options as a spectrum is more complex if we consider non-electronically transmitted services such as manufacturing. For such processes, factors such as tax regimes, tariffs and government regulations make costs highly specific rather than general.

Identifying the Right Processes for Outsourcing and Offshoring

Factors influencing the suitability of processes for outsourcing and offshoring

Understanding the core of each sourcing model and what it has to offer is of vital significance for engaging in effective sourcing strategies. However, in the case of outsourcing and offshoring, it is of equal importance to identify which processes should be transferred to another supplier (domestic or offshore) or another country as part of the business of a captive centre.

According to Metters (2008), firms typically consider activities for outsourcing or offshoring that are not critical for the company's operations or holding on to its competitive advantage. The reason is that when a task is being outsourced, the institutional knowledge concerning the task is also leaving.

The scale of the process is also important in deciding if outsourcing is an appropriate solution. The costs associated with searching and selecting an appropriate supplier, establishing service-level metrics, creating and managing the contract, monitoring the ongoing outsourcing relationship and enforcing the contract may be significant. In the case of offshoring, these costs are even more significant because of the complexity of these ventures. However, a process can also be too large for outsourcing to be effective. When a process is too large, outsourcing may represent only an additional layer of management, thus complicating operations and adding costs.

Processes that are being influenced by rapidly changing technologies constitute good candidates for outsourcing, unless they are critical to the company's business model and operations. The reason is that small in-house units have a relatively limited capability to keep up with the rapidly changing technological environment. Firms that dedicate themselves to these activities (such as IBM, Accenture, Infosys and Tata Consultancy Services) can be more innovative because they specialise in this business.

Furthermore, outsourcing (or insourcing) is appropriate for activities that have a high degree of variance – for example, an activity which requires 50 people one day and only ten the next. Hiring 50 people for this activity when they are only occasionally needed constitutes a significant cost for the firm. An outsourcer can mitigate this variance by serving several countercyclical clients.

With regard to offshoring, Aron and Singh (2005) note that most companies do not make decisions systematically and rigorously enough and in fact repeatedly make at least one of three fundamental mistakes. First, although many companies spend time choosing countries, cities and suppliers and put significant effort into negotiations, they do not spend time evaluating which processes should go offshore and which should not. It appears that most companies have difficulty in distinguishing core processes that they must control, critical processes that they must buy from expert suppliers, and commodity processes that they can outsource.

Second, most organisations do not fully consider the risks associated with offshoring. Financial managers and senior executives make calculations in relation to the costs and benefits of offshoring without taking into account that, after signing the deal, the supplier might gain an upper hand. Most outsourcing customers appear to disregard any risks related to the power relation between the two partners and make choices that eliminate the savings from outsourcing.

Third, a number of companies do not understand that outsourcing is not an all-or-nothing choice; rather, there is a range of sourcing models that they can follow.

Metters (2008) suggests that processes that require substantial levels of communication between the client and the supplier do not constitute good candidates for offshoring. Time-zone differences, language and other sorts of communication barriers can shrink the benefits of offshoring. However, Aron and Singh (2005) appear to be more concerned with how processes are ranked in terms of their value to the organisation. They suggest that there must be a careful consideration between business processes that constitute good candidates for offshoring and those that do not. Processes that are important for the creation of value should not be offshored.

Along these lines, Aron and Singh (2005) suggest that executives should rank organisational processes along two dimensions: their potential for value creation and for value capture. More specifically, executives should consider how crucial a process is in the creation of customer value compared to other processes. Furthermore, they should consider the extent to which each process enables the organisation to capture some of the value created for customers. For the processes that are ranked high, such as working capital management and cash-flow forecasting, offshoring is not suggested. Processes that are ranked lower (e.g., payment authorisation and invoice verification) appear better candidates for offshoring.

It is important to note that one of the two dimensions can be more important for certain industries or specific companies. In this case, rankings must be calculated taking into account the relative weight of each of these dimensions. Ranking all of the company's processes creates a value hierarchy that reflects which processes should go offshore and which should not. The higher the rank of a process is, the more crucial its role is to the company's strategy, and thus the less it should be considered for offshoring or outsourcing.

Having identified activities that are outsourcing candidates, Willcocks et al. (2002) suggest evaluating whether the market can service the requirement. If the market is not cheap, capable or mature enough, then the organisation will need to seek a largely in-house solution. Table 2.3 captures the major elements for consideration and plots the cost efficiencies and capabilities the market can offer against carrying out the activity internally.

TABLE 2.3   Strategic sourcing by market comparison

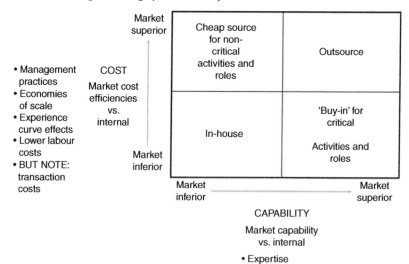

Where the market can carry out a task cheaper and better, then outsourcing is the obvious decision. As an example, Federal Express provides customer delivery for Dell. Where the market offers an inferior cost and capability, then in-house sourcing will be the best alternative. Where the market offers a better cost deal, then this should be taken, but only for processes that are not critical for value creation and value capture. Where the market offers superior capability but at a premium price above what the in-house cost might be, there may still be good reasons for buying in or close partnering with the third party, not least to leverage and learn from their expertise, and apply it to processes with higher potential for value creation and value capture.

Impact of operational and structural risks on outsourcing and offshoring decisions

Another aspect to consider while deciding which processes can be off-shored or outsourced is related to two major types of risk that companies face: *operational risk*, which refers to the danger that processes will not function properly and operate smoothly after offshoring, and *structural risk*, which refers to the danger that the relationship between clients and suppliers may not work as expected. With regard to operational risk, it is of great significance to evaluate the extent to which processes can be codified and measured. Aron and Singh (2005) distinguish transparent, codifiable, opaque and non-codifiable processes.

- *Transparent processes* (e.g., transaction processing, telecollection and technical support) can be clearly measured in terms of quality and are the tasks that can be fully codified. Consequently, the operational risk of offshoring and outsourcing in this case is very low.
- *Codifiable processes* can be measured to some extent in terms of the quality of their execution, and most of the work can be codified. If firms can measure the quality of the final outcome to a satisfactory extent (e.g., for customer service and account management), then the operational risk of offshoring and outsourcing becomes more manageable. However, if measuring the final outcome is not possible (e.g., for processes such as equity research, yield analysis and litigation support), then the operational risk becomes very high.

- *Opaque processes* can be codified in terms of the work being done, but the quality of the process outputs is difficult to measure (e.g., for processes such as insurance underwriting, invoice management, and cash flow forecasting). Although the risks of offshoring these processes are moderate, companies can monitor the work being done and inspect samples to ensure that the outcome meets their expectations. This, however, could be rather troublesome and expensive. If a company can specify how the supplier should do the work, it can lower the risk of offshoring by establishing a performance-based reward system and penalties.
- *Non-codifiable* processes, as the term implies, cannot be codified; examples are supply chain coordination and customer data analysis. In addition, often they cannot be measured in terms of the quality being achieved (such as pricing and working capital management). For this reason, such processes usually carry a high amount of operational risk. If an organisation chooses to outsource such processes, it should closely supervise the supplier's work.

The ability to monitor work and the precision of metrics used to measure process quality define the degree of structural risk that outsourcing presents to a client firm (Aron and Singh, 2005). For example, transaction processing and insurance claims processing are typically easy to monitor, with precise metrics to measure their quality. Therefore, these activities present low structural risk. Activities like product design and research and development are high risk, because it is difficult to monitor outcomes and challenging to define a precise quality metric.

While engaging in an outsourcing relationship, most companies assume that their supplier will behave in a collaborative way. This is not necessarily true, however, even in the case of companies that are buying services from captive centres that they own. For example, structural risk may arise because a supplier does not update the processes of performing certain tasks, does not invest in employee training and does not hire the most qualified people. Another problem is that service providers often exert much less effort in getting the work done than they originally agreed to. Structural risk also arises when contractual terms are altered after clients have handed over processes to suppliers. Once a company has handed a set of processes to a supplier, it is not easy to take it back in-house at short notice. Suppliers are aware of this and thus may use their power position to demand higher prices.

It is also important to consider that when firms source processes that require the transfer of a large amount of knowledge, they have to invest time and effort to pass this knowledge on to the supplier's employees. Furthermore, some processes take a long time to stabilise when they are offshored. In both cases, the cost of switching suppliers is very high.

Nonetheless, structural risk can be mitigated in a number of ways. First, firms must establish contractual clauses that will impose on the supplier the obligation to continue to deliver the service at a certain price after the contract's expiration date. Usually this period is 150% of the time that it would take for the supplier to deliver output that matches the organisation's requirements and quality standards. Furthermore, companies should try to split their business between two or more suppliers. Working with multiple suppliers provides a strong element of power for a company for at least two reasons. First, if a supplier underperforms, it becomes easier to transfer the work to another supplier that is already executing the same processes. Second, working with multiple suppliers will generate a competitive climate among them that, if managed carefully, can become very beneficial for the client in terms of price and the quality of service delivered. (We discuss sourcing models that use multiple suppliers in Chapter 5.)

Aron and Singh (2005) suggest that firms should base their outsourcing and offshoring decisions on the assessment of operational and structural risks. For activities that present high operational and structural risks such as corporate planning, they recommend executing such activities in-house and onshore. For activities that present moderate operational and structural risks such as supply chain coordination, they suggest outsourcing carefully, using extended organisation offshore, and monitor closely in real time. (*Extended organisation* is a hybrid organisational form where the client company specifies the quality of services it wants and works closely alongside suppliers to get that quality by managing the suppliers carefully and monitoring the agents' work to ensure that things are done properly.) Activities with low operational and structural risks such as transaction processing are suitable for outsourcing to offshore service providers. Table 2.4 provides the full spectrum of organisational

TABLE 2.4   Choosing location and organisational form

Operational risk				
HIGH	**Outsource to service provider located nearby (nearshore)** *Litigation support*	**Set up captive centre nearby or onshore** *ReyD, design*	**Execute process in house and onshore** *Pricing, corporate planning*
MODERATE	**Oursource to offshore service provider over time** *Insurance claims processing, customer support*	**Oursource carefully, using 'extended organisation' offshore, and monitor closely in real time** *Supply chain coordination*	**Set up captive centre offshore** *Equity research*
LOW	**Outsource to offshore service provider** *Data entry, transaction processing*	**Outsource carefully, using 'extended organisation' offshore** *Telecollection, technical support*	**Outsource carefully, using 'extended organisation' offshore, and conduct frequent process audits** *Customer data analysis market research analysis*
	LOW	**MODERATE**	**HIGH**

Structural risk

Source: Aron and Singh, 2005.

forms and locations and several examples of activities suitable for each combination of operational and structural risks (each being low, moderate and high).

Complex and problematic business processes

In addition to the value-creation and value-capture criteria that certain processes present, as well as the relative operational and structural risks in outsourcing, Aron and Clemons (2004) suggest that the complexity of pro-cesses plays a significant role in offshoring decisions. They provide a useful set of criteria for evaluating process complexity that can help executives make appropriate sourcing decisions:

1. The codifiability of the data that must be transferred so that the process can be performed by the external party in a reliable way and with adherence to the required quality standards
2. The amount of training that must be provided to the employees of the supplier so that they become competent in performing the work
3. The cost of monitoring performance levels
4. The difficulty in assessing managers' level of confidence that their quality assessments will be accurate and reliable
5. The desired educational level for the employees of the supplier
6. Revenue per supplier working on the assigned task
7. Number of sub-tasks associated with the task
8. A single overall measure of task complexity used to assess the accuracy of ratings and the weight associated with different factors.

Taking a different perspective, Puryear and Detrick (2006) suggest that the main problem with offshoring is that many managers regard it as a panacea for operational processes. Instead of diagnosing and correcting deficiencies, many managers seek to move the problems somewhere else. In most cases, however, this tactic is counterproductive. For this reason, the authors suggest that before considering offshoring, firms should determine the factors that inhibit performance. To address such inhibitors, they suggest the following three strategies:

1. *Revamp business processes.* Increased complexity is a fundamental factor causing organisational deficiencies and poor performance. Offshoring is not always an answer to the problem. Managing complexity and eliminating unnecessary complications can bring significant cost reductions, without engaging in the risks of offshoring. This is what the Brother International Corporation did when dealing with its problematic front-line call centre operations. The company received approximately 1.8 million calls on an annual basis, which took too long to process. To make matters worse, customer profiles were lost in online databases, and representatives were able to resolve fewer than half of the queries from new customers. However, instead of misdiagnosing the problem as a

simple customer service problem that could be solved by offshoring it to an external cost-efficient party, executives tried to 'dig deeper'. They discovered that solving the issue of managing customer complaints could actually benefit the organisation if the insights gained with regard to their customers' profiles and tastes could be shared and used to improve marketing and product design. For this reason, they did not consider offshoring call centre operations, but instead decided to improve them. The division consolidated paper manuals into an online directory and integrated its records into a CRM database. Within a year, product returns had dropped by one third and the time needed to resolve customer problems dropped by 43 seconds on average. The new CRM enabled the company to capture insights with regard to its customers that it used in the development of its new products and marketing strategies.

2. *Reinforce credibility and trust.* Sourcing strategies often mask dysfunctional relationships between departments and BUs. For this reason, it is important to make sure that different divisions and units within an organisation are collaborating effectively and that their goals are aligned. For example, at the brokerage firm Charles Schwab, IT had long been viewed as a source of competitive advantage. But while the IT budget remained strong, pressure to deliver new applications meant less spending to update infrastructure and reduce complexity. Over time, the firm's IT efforts drifted. When a major two-year initiative to develop a new portfolio management system failed, trust in IT plummeted. In response, the company launched a business-led IT project in 2004 geared to restructuring the IT infrastructure. The alliance and collaboration between the business and the IT department was fundamental for the effective execution of the project.

3. *Find the scale-economy sweet spot.* Contemporary organisations can benefit significantly from the consolidation of activities to the regional or global level. For example, one global financial services company reduced its cost structure significantly by consolidating its scattered customer service centres. The company had to deal with a host of inconsistent procedures across its centres. However, the standardisation of the technology and the connection between the locations by a routing software boosted both efficiency and customer satisfaction. The overall savings of the company reached US$200 million.

Summary

This chapter reviewed key models for making decisions regarding outsourcing and offshoring. Although many dimensions must be considered, firms are mainly concerned with the following: which parts of the business to outsource and to what locations. This chapter brings together the considerations regarding these two questions, to offer a comprehensive analysis of the options available for firms.

chapter 3

Country Attractiveness for Sourcing

This chapter discusses the maturity of various geographical locations worldwide and the factors that clients and suppliers take into account when deciding on their offshoring and offshore-outsourcing strategies. We focus on the following aspects:

• An overview of sourcing destinations
• Criteria for selecting locations
• The advantages of nearshoring as a sourcing option.

An Overview of Sourcing Destinations

Both clients and suppliers consider sourcing destinations but with different goals in mind. Suppliers are interested in locations where they can set up global delivery centres. Client companies are interested in outsourcing a range of possible activities, or in setting up captive facilities abroad, typically for R&D, shared services or customer support to service their own organisation or their customers.

Together with India, which currently attracts over 65% of ITO and over 43% of the BPO market (Willcocks et al., 2015), Brazil, Russia and China (referred to as BRIC economies) are considered the most attractive (tier 1) sourcing destinations for ITO and BPO. This is mainly because of the scale of services, available skills and the maturity achieved with regard to sourcing activities. Suppliers as well as captive centres based in these countries, in particular in India, tend to move up the value chain, departing from specific and repetitive tasks that are usually captured by new entrants – the so-called tier 2 and tier 3 countries. By 2015, over 125 offshore locations have been providing ITO and BPO services for more than five years and are seeking to mature their service capabilities.

A range of reports suggested the BRIC offshore ITO/BPO market share as 65% to 70% for India, and the rest almost equally divided between China, Russia and Brazil. According to NASSCOM (2012), ITO/BPO export revenue (excluding hardware) for India would exceed US$69 billion in 2013, serviced by about a 2.2 million workforce. This represented a growth of 16.3% on 2011. The BPO segment was expected to grow by 12% to reach US$16 billion in 2012 (NASSCOM, 2012). Brazil was next as the most frequent nearshore destination, mainly for US-based large companies. However, Brazil and China could have done more to leverage their potential, while Russia, despite a lack of government support, was succeeding in finding high value but niche work. This still remained true as of 2014 (Willcocks et al., 2015).

Reports concerning non-BRIC countries suggested global market share of around 15% in 2012. In BPO, the Philippines BPO industry earned US$11 billion in 2011 (Punongbayan & Araullo Report, 2012). In the same year, the Philippines ITO/BPO industry employed 638,000 full-time employees representing a 22% increase from 2010. Non-BRIC locations vary in areas of specialisation and offering. Some non-BRIC locations offer nearshoring opportunities; for example, the Czech Republic for Germany or Mexico for the USA. Further, India and China, between 2012 and 2015, have been turning to non-BRIC locations for some solutions, for example to secure lower costs or labour availability. As at 2015, among the top contenders globally and for different markets were Romania, Bulgaria, Poland, Slovakia, the Czech Republic, Belarus, Morocco, Tunisia, Costa Rica, Mexico, Venezuela, Vietnam, Egypt (despite the 2011 'revolution') and the Philippines. Non-BRIC locations also offer different risk-reward ratios, and, given Indian dominance, have sought to identify niche offerings – by service, geography or industry. For example, South Africa has gone down the niche route, leveraging not only contact centres as an area of specialty but also multiple location attractiveness factors.

The relative attractiveness of BRIC and non-BRIC countries as sourcing destinations is dynamic. Their attractiveness needs to be understood in the context of long-term global sourcing trends and the current global economic climate. In this regard, spending will continue to rise in all global sourcing markets through recessionary as well as growth periods, but spending on BPO will overtake spending on ITO within the next five years. BPO expenditures will be in areas such as the human-resource function, procurement, back-office administration, call centres, legal, finance and accounting, customer-facing operations and asset management. In line with this trend, a highly competitive global services market presents opportunities for countries that can offer the right mix of costs, skills and reliable service (see the trends in Chapter 1).

Emerging sourcing destinations are trying to differentiate their offerings from BRIC countries and from their tier 2 and tier 3 rivals when competing for a contract. For example, Egypt has promoted itself as a low-cost destination for call centres that specialise in European languages. Dubai and Singapore present their IT security systems and legal systems as an advantage, particularly with regard to the outsourcing of high-security and business-continuity services. South Africa stresses its reputation for services in contact centres and hopes to transfer this into more complex BPO work. The Philippines, a former US colony, stresses its long cultural ties with the USA and the excellent English skills of its population to attract English-speaking call centres. Morocco is trying to attract French-speaking European clients to set up call centres, while Central and South American Spanish-speaking countries seek to establish call centres that can provide services to the Hispanic market in the USA (Reinhardt et al., 2006). In fact, recent studies have shown that some non-BRIC destinations have sought to, and have been successful in, competing with BRIC by positioning their specialised skills sets in particular areas and often by offering lower costs than other potential destinations (Kotlarsky and Oshri, 2008; Willcocks et al., 2015).

While second- and third-tier outsourcing destinations are improving their position, India has continued to gain volume in the area of ITO and BPO services over the 2011–2015 period. Many global clients (large multinational corporations) view India as a centre of excellence for ITO and BPO and not merely as a low-cost destination. Many US and European clients initially engaged Indian suppliers to provide technical services such as programming and platform upgrades (e.g., to help with compliance at the turn of the century). However, as these relationships matured, Western clients assigned more challenging work to Indian suppliers, such as development and support tasks for critical business applications.

However, India and, to a lesser extent, China, Brazil and Russia have now, for a number of years, been experiencing upward pressure on wages, combined with rising, and sometimes high, labour attrition. There is in fact a war for talent within each of the BRIC countries, which suppresses the key factors that made these countries attractive destinations for outsourcing in the first place. For example, many firms from India and China have relocated offshore activities from these countries to more attractive locations. And major Indian suppliers such as Tata Consultancy Services (TCS) are setting up global delivery centres in China, mainly because the supply of engineering skills and the proficiency in English has significantly improved in recent years in China.

To put these views into context, China's US$142.3 billion investment in ICT in 2006 aimed at improving its competitive position in the offshoring service market. Willcocks and Lacity (2009) predicted that China's ITO and BPO service capabilities would become strong, and by 2014 its ITO/BPO revenues probably exceeded US$7 billion. However, the main ITO and BPO suppliers in China are either large US-based suppliers like Accenture, Capgemini, Dell, HP and IBM or large India-based suppliers like Genpact, Infosys and TCS. Still, similar to the development of the Indian services supply base, many Chinese suppliers do not want to compete solely in terms of low-level technical skills. Now they are trying to address the full range of the service value chain, such as Pactera, featured in Chapter 1.

Nevertheless, many client organisations are cautious of China's ITO and BPO services because of language and cultural barriers and fears over losing intellectual property (IP). The Chinese government and business sectors are well aware of these barriers and are seeking ways to address them. For example, the Chinese government is investing US$5 billion in English-language training to improve the marketability of the ITO and BPO services from China. In 2009, the Chinese government redressed the lack of attention to the services outsourcing industry by establishing 23 service outsourcing cities and numerous outsourcing hubs such as Henan Outsourcing Park (Oshri, 2014).

Developing countries other than India and China are becoming players in the IT services market. Many US clients already use Central American suppliers for Spanish-speaking business processes such as help desks, patient scheduling and data entry. Synchronous time zones are one of the drivers for US firms that outsource work to Central or South America. Furthermore, access to skills and scale are two factors that clients consider in their assessment of attractive locations. In this regard, Brazil has the advantage of a large population, the innovative creativity of its engineers and government programmes supporting the outsourcing industry; while Chile and Uruguay, for example, have exploited their time-zone advantages, back-office proficiencies and government incentives to attract outsourcing work.

While South America is emerging as an attractive destination for offshoring and offshore outsourcing, today organisations from Western Europe are increasingly sourcing IT and businesses services to suppliers located in Central Eastern Europe (CEE). Among the key drivers of such a trend are the closer proximity to the supplier, limited time-zone differences and lower transaction costs than those incurred through using Asian alternatives. Furthermore, research on captives (Oshri, 2011; Oshri and van Uhm, 2012) shows that the CEE region is becoming a popular nearshore captive destination for Western European clients. In particular, Bulgaria, the Czech Republic and Hungary have attracted large numbers of R&D centres, making them a hub for business innovation and high-value, knowledge-intensive professional services.

In sub-Saharan Africa, several countries are actively seeking to become players in the global ITO and BPO markets. These countries, for example, Botswana and Kenya, have quickly established their economies partly on the competitiveness of IT and IT services. Another example is South Africa, which is exporting IT and business services primarily to UK-based clients, because of similar time zones, cultural similarities, English-speaking capabilities and a good infrastructure. Mediterranean North Africa already exports IT services to Europe. For example, Moroccan IT suppliers are attractive for clients in France because of the common language, similar time zone and cultural capability.

Criteria for Selecting Locations

Selecting a location is one of the major challenges organisations face when making offshoring and outsourcing decisions. A decision to relocate a business function or set up a new captive facility (for clients) or delivery centre (for suppliers) abroad is based to a great extent on the attractiveness of the sourcing location. Several frameworks for selecting offshoring and offshore-outsourcing destinations are set out in the academic and professional literature to help managers assess the attractiveness of countries and regions. All of these frameworks consider costs, business environment, availability of labour resources and specific skills. Some frameworks (e.g., Carmel, 2003; Farrell, 2006) are more detailed than others (e.g., A.T. Kearney's three factors) in terms of the factors they consider when comparing potential sourcing locations. We compared and combined factors identified in several offshore destination evaluation frameworks, primarily developed in practitioner-oriented literature, to define criteria we are using for evaluating country attractiveness (Kotlarsky et al., 2013). We describe these factors in Table 3.1 and discuss them in detail below, providing an example of how each of these factors can be used to compare the attractiveness of several non-BRIC tier 2 countries for the sourcing of IT services and BPO. Examples in this chapter are based on the recent ten-country study by Willcocks et al. (2015) covering India, Philippines, South Africa, Poland, Morocco, Malaysia, Kenya, Sri Lanka, Egypt and Northern Ireland. (More examples related to the attractiveness of Western countries based on research by Oshri and Ravishenkar (2014) are included in Chapter 4.)

Factor 1: Costs

Companies considering outsourcing IT or business processes typically compare a range of costs, including labour costs (average wages for skilled workers and managers), infrastructure costs (unit costs for telecom networks, Internet access and power, office rent) and corporate taxes (tax breaks and regulations and other incentives for local investment), across potential outsourcing locations. In addition, they are now also looking at value-added dimensions for how they might benefit over time.

TABLE 3.1   Factors for assessing country attractiveness for outsourcing and offshoring

Factor	Description	Sources
Cost	• **Labour costs** (average wages for skilled workers and managers) • **Infrastructure costs** (unit costs for telecom networks, Internet access and power and office rent) • **Corporate taxes** (tax breaks, regulations and other incentives for local investment)	Carmel and Tija (2005) Doh et al. (2009) Farrell (2006) Bardhan and Kroll (2006) Heeks and Nicholson (2004)
Skills	• **Skill pool** (the size of the labour pool with required skills). Required skills may include technical and business knowledge, management skills, languages and the ability to learn new concepts and innovate. The **scalability of labour resources** in the long term (i.e., the ability to supply sufficient labour resources to handle growing demand) is a major issue to consider when choosing a sourcing destination. An indication of the scalability of labour resources in a country is the growth in the number of graduates with desired skills from year to year. Countries that offer scalability of labour resources are also more likely to keep wages relatively low due to the constant supply of new graduates • **Supplier landscape** (the size of the local sector providing IT services and other business functions). For clients looking to outsource IT or business processes, it is imperative to evaluate the vendor's landscape in terms of the general skills set (or capabilities) and competencies of vendors	Carmel and Tija (2005) Doh et al. (2009) Bardhan and Kroll (2006) Farrell (2006) Zaheer et al. (2009) Heeks and Nicholson (2004)
Business and living environment	• **Government support** (policy on foreign investment, labour laws, bureaucratic and regulatory burden, level of corruption) • **Business environment** (compatibility with prevailing business culture and ethics) • **Living environment** (overall quality of life, prevalence of HIV infection, serious crime per capita) • **Accessibility** (travel time, flight frequency and time difference)	Carmel (2005) Hahn et al. (2009) Farrell (2006) Bardhan and Kroll (2006) Zaheer et al. (2009) Heeks and Nicholson (2004)

(continued)

TABLE 3.1 Continued

Factor	Description	Sources
Market potential	• Attractiveness of the **local market** (the current gross domestic product and its growth rate) • Access to **nearby markets** (adjacent region)	Farrell (2006)
Risk profile	• **Security issues** (i.e., risks to personal security) and **property-related** issues, such as fraud, crime and terrorism) • **Disruptive events** (including the risk of a labour uprising, political unrest and natural disasters) • **Regulatory risks** (the stability, fairness and efficiency of the legal framework) • **Macroeconomic risks** (such as cost inflation, currency fluctuation and capital freedom) • **Intellectual property** risk (strength of the data and IP protection regime)	Doh et al. (2009) Hahn et al. (2009) Farrell (2006) Bardhan and Kroll (2006) Zaheer et al. (2009) Heeks and Nicholson (2004)
Quality of infrastructure	• **Telecommunication and IT** (i.e., network downtime, speed of service restoration and connectivity) • **Real estate** (both the availability and quality) • **Transportation** (the scale and quality of road and rail networks) • **Power** (the reliability of power supply)	Carmel and Tija (2005) Doh et al. (2009) Farrell (2006) Bardhan and Kroll (2006) Zaheer et al. (2009) Heeks and Nicholson (2004)
Cultural compatibility	• **Key characteristics of the national culture** (how they are similar or different to the cultures of the target markets) • **Business culture** (expectations and behaviours at a workplace and employer–employee relationships)	Carmel and Tija (2005) Hahn and Bunyaratavej (2010) Farrell (2006) Hahn et al. (2009) Bardhan and Kroll (2006) Zaheer et al. (2009) Heeks and Nicholson (2004)

Source: Kotlarsky, Levina and Kuraksina, 2011.

EXAMPLE: Comparing Costs

Cost is invariably in the top three reasons cited by clients for offshoring. However, cost is not a simple equation. One commonly used measure is the direct operating cost per full-time employee. In the 2014 study of nine countries in direct competition with South Africa, India, the Philippines, Malaysia and Egypt led, while, in 2012, only Poland and Northern Ireland were more costly than South Africa across its selected skills base (Willcocks et al., 2015). However, the declining value of the Rand had made South Africa increasingly less expensive in 2013, 2014 and 2015. For the African locations, in 2014, labour costs in Morocco were higher than Egypt and Kenya but lower than in Europe and about half the labour costs in its major market of France. However, all ten locations were subsidised to some degree through tax allowances and government/regional incentives for inward investment. A further factor is infrastructure. Here, especially in telecommunications, historically South Africa had lagged behind its major competitors, but the gap has narrowed considerably over the last four years.

On cost comparison, several other factors are pertinent. The first is cost dynamism. India and the Philippines have been experiencing erosion in their cost advantage due to scale and accelerating demand, creating skills shortages that drive up labour costs. One result is these countries outsourcing and offshoring work themselves, for example to Egypt, Sri Lanka and China in order to stabilise labour costs. Another response is the rise of cheaper second-tier locations (e.g., Katowice, Poznan and Wroclaw in Poland; Davao, Sta. Rosa, Cebu, Pasig, Quezon and Mandaluyong City in the Philippines).

A further factor is hidden costs. For example, there was a widespread shortage of middle management and team leadership skills on the supplier side in many of the ten locations studied in 2014. The point here is that dealing with such shortages costs time, money and sometimes productivity. Clients also often fail to factor into their cost equations the cost of their own management of offshoring arrangements. On one analysis, the management costs of domestic outsourcing fall between 4% and 8% of contract value, but this moves to 12–16% with offshoring arrangements.

Factor 2: Skills

This factor encompasses the skill pool (the size of labour pool with required skills) and the supplier landscape (the size of the local sector providing IT services and other business functions). Required skills may include technical and business knowledge, management skills, languages and the ability to learn new concepts and to innovate.

Labour resources

The scalability of labour resources in the long term (i.e., the ability to supply sufficient labour resources to handle growing demand) is a major issue to consider while deciding on a sourcing destination. An indication of the scalability of labour resources is the growth in the number of graduates with desired skills that the country is able to produce each year – for example, technical and business knowledge, management skills, languages and the ability to learn new concepts and innovate. Countries that offer scalability of labour resources are also more likely to keep wages relatively low due to a constant supply of graduates.

For companies considering expansion to offshore or nearshore locations, it is important to evaluate the gap between desired and available skills. Furthermore, these companies should assess the efforts by various stakeholders to bridge such skill gaps, for example, through various specialised in-house training programmes.

Supplier landscape

Clients looking to outsource IT or business processes must evaluate the supplier landscape in terms of the skills set (or capabilities) and competencies of suppliers. In this regard, clients should assess each supplier's ability to respond to their ongoing needs (a delivery competency), radically improve service in terms of quality and cost (a transformation competency) and be willing and able to align its business model to their values, goals and needs (a relational competency). Countries that have suppliers able to demonstrate such competencies to clients are in a better position to attract those looking to outsource high-value, complex, knowledge-intensive and strategic activities. The supplier landscape combines both local and international suppliers that have a presence in the country (e.g., have set up a delivery centre). The maturity of suppliers in a country can be assessed based on 12 capabilities that are grouped into three key areas of competencies: relationship, transformation and delivery (mentioned above and discussed in further detail in Chapter 5).

EXAMPLE: Comparing Availability of Skills

Skill pools can be difficult to assess, and numbers can be confusing. Poland and Northern Ireland have well-developed education systems and are generally strong in sciences, technology, engineering and business, and accessible to the vast majority of the indigenous population. This contrasts with less accessibility and the lower levels of English/other language proficiency in several African and Asian countries we studied. Thus, while Poland's population is much smaller than, for example Egypt, the Philippines and Morocco, the percentage of the population being educated and becoming a highly skilled workforce is much higher. However, graduate numbers still do not compare with India, the Philippines and Egypt. The labour pools of Poland and Northern Ireland remain limited and could come under pressure quite quickly in the face of growing demand, though Northern Ireland was actually losing BPO work in recessionary conditions through 2011–2013.

The scalability of labour resources in the longer term is a major issue for client companies to consider when deciding on an offshore and outsourcing destination. Countries that offer scalability of labour resources are more likely to relieve pressure on skills shortages and rising wages through taking active measures to provide a constant supply of school leavers and graduates.

The number of graduates produced annually by any country is one indicator of how scalable the labour pool for the country will be in the long run. India is the offshore powerhouse in terms of ITO, BPO back office and voice and is trying to gain major traction on higher value BPO work. India's universities produced 4.4 million new graduates in 2012, with almost 16% focusing on science and technology. These figures were even higher for 2013 and 2014. However, reports by McKinsey and NASSCOM suggest that only around 30% of graduates are readily employable. For this reason, in the last six years major suppliers like Infosys and TCS have set up and run very large pre-employment training programmes. India has a prevalence of English-language skills (on some estimates 20% of the population in 2014), but accent and quality are mixed. Adult literacy runs at 54% of the population. In 2012, India added 230,000 employees to its 2.8 million ITO/BPO workforce, still more again in 2013 and 2014. Pressure on skills and wages are pushing Indian suppliers and captives to second-tier locations, and also to other cheaper locations abroad. On call centres, India has an 800,000 workforce but has seen some repatriation to the UK and USA in the last three years over service quality issues, changes in the cost equation and some moves to other offshore locations.

The study of the Chinese economy skills-base by Oshri (2014) reported that China produced 6.8 million graduates in 2013 with about 65% in science and engineering but only 16% in business studies. This research led to the conclusion that the lack of management skills in the Chinese ITO and BPO sector hinders its internationalisation.

Egypt has over 330,000 graduates (from all disciplines) every year and 31,000 of these have degrees in technology, science or engineering. Egypt has 'multi-linguinity', with over 25,000 graduates annually from Cairo alone able to speak English and other major European languages. Like several other locations, however, Egypt has struggled to build requisite middle-management BPO skills.

In South Africa, the annual supply of high-school leavers exceeds 227,000. Graduates and post-graduates have exceeded 140,000 annually in recent years, with 51% in science, engineering technology and business, the rest in humanities and social sciences. South Africa added 370,000 proficient English speakers to the workforce in 2011, compared to 4.4 million in India and 450,000 in the Philippines. Other locations had smaller additions, the next in size being Malaysia with 160,000 and Egypt with 70,000. South Africa is also strong in legal, accounting and business skills, which support offshored legal-process and financial-service operations.

For the Philippines 82% of work is voice contact, primarily to the USA (though it has services offered in 18 languages). The rest of ITO/BPO services include finance, accounting, medical transcription, human resources and IT. Filipino residents are considered to speak a more 'American-style' version of English than their Indian counterparts. In 2011, the Philippines officially overtook India as the world's offshore call centre capital. By 2014, the BPO industry employed over 640,000 people and the figure is expected to rise eventually to 1.3 million, provided the key skill creation challenges are addressed. Like India, the Philippines, as a mature, large destination experiencing growing demand, faces challenges in skills shortages, retention of talent, as well as rising labour costs. Some government action has been taken to address the skills issues.

Sri Lanka has an adult literacy rate of 91%. Sri Lanka uses English as a unifying language, primarily in government. English is spoken by about 10% of the population. With few skills problems, BPO resources in Sri Lanka are very affordable. Junior non-voice workers with limited experience collect just 7% of what a comparable employee would earn in the USA. More skilled employees, with five to nine years' experience can expect to earn US$8,300, 15% of US wages. Historically Sri Lanka has provided skills and expertise in IT development, accounting and some legal back-office work. Given the strong educational standards in legal and accounting qualifications, there are real opportunities to increase the scale of operations and grow the offshore accounting and legal-process outsourcing market, especially with the cost competitiveness Sri Lanka can offer against its neighbour, India. Sri Lanka is particularly well endowed in IT skills with over 120 software development firms, with estimated exports exceeding US$75 million by 2014. Sri Lanka is emerging and quickly gaining momentum in the outsourcing market because of its proximity to India. Its labour pool is exponentially smaller than India's, but Sri Lanka aimed to create 30,000 new jobs in the ITO/BPO industry between 2013 and 2018.

Kenya is at a relatively early stage in development as an offshore location but has satisfactory skills in IT, English and to some extent certain forms of knowledge process to support further foreign investment in its ITO/BPO growing industry.

Morocco is providing skills to support nearshore operations for European-based companies such as Dell, Deloitte, HP and Attento. Morocco offers well-trained human resources, and for voice BPO has strong capability in French and Spanish, as well as English. For offshore development, Morocco is positioned well to get a good share of the European offshoring IT market. It has a large pool of skilled human resources in the region where banks, computer and insurance companies could become major clients. Its business parks host more than 100 multinationals, and its policies, private sector and government target growing a workforce of more than 90,000 people by 2017 in the outsourcing field, concentrating on shared service centres, non-voice BPO, voice BPO and ITO.

Malaysia has a literacy rate of 92%, a workforce size of over 12 million, with over 180,000 graduates entering the labour market annually, 54% with science and technology backgrounds. English speakers make up 28% of the population. Its education and training programmes support IT, financial and accounting and general back-office process outsourcing activity.

Finally, the ten-country study found widespread shortages of middle-management and team-leadership skills on the supplier side in offshore locations. This was also as true in the more mature locations such as the Philippines, India and Sri Lanka (though not Northern Ireland and Poland) as in the emerging locations of Kenya and Egypt.

Factor 3: Business and living environment

This factor considers governance support (policy on foreign investment, labour laws, bureaucratic and regulatory burden, level of corruption), the business environment (compatibility with prevailing business culture and ethics), the living environment (overall quality of life, prevalence of HIV infection, serious crime per capita) and accessibility (travel time, flight frequency, time difference).

EXAMPLE: Comparing Business and Living Environment

The governments of all ten comparison countries favoured foreign investment, relaxed labour laws to some extent and tried to reduce some of the regulatory and bureaucratic burden. Corruption is perceived by clients as an issue in some countries, including China. Most governments understand that and some have pursued strong action to eradicate this, in order to support an emerging or mature BPO industry. However, particularly in developing countries without strong detection and regulatory agencies, corruption is not always easy to police. The Transparency International's Corruption Perceptions Index regularly reports on this issue, but if you look at these from 2009 to 2014, they show a somewhat changing picture almost from year to year. Generally Northern Ireland, Malaysia, Poland and South Africa tend to score better; India and Morocco less so, while the Philippines, Egypt, Sri Lanka and Kenya less so again. However, these are general country indicators rather than specifically for the BPO sector in the country where governments need to attract inward investment and choose to act more strictly.

Following this last point, business environments can be made compatible with foreign clients' standards and culture through setting up carefully controlled business environments in which to operate. We see this with India's and Morocco's business parks, for example. Egypt has made great efforts to develop such business environments around several of its major cities. As business environments, Malaysia, South Africa, Northern Ireland and Poland tend to be more compatible with their target markets. Sri Lanka, like India, has some strong cultural compatibilities with its UK market historically.

On living environment, South Africa, Northern Ireland, Malaysia, then India and the Philippines were perceived as most attractive, and Kenya the least attractive. Of course, accessibility – in terms of travel time, accessibility and time difference – depends on the client. From a UK perspective, South Africa has great accessibility, a compatible time zone and tolerable travel time: the same is true for Poland and Northern Ireland. South Africa is still attractive from an Australian perspective, but not for the USA. Countries like Morocco and Egypt play into smaller nearshore niches that give them advantages on accessibility. Meanwhile, India has so many diverse customers around the globe, inevitably there are going to be trade-offs on accessibility. Not surprisingly, the Philippines scores more highly on accessibility with its mainly US-based customers.

Factor 4: Quality of infrastructure

Quality of infrastructure includes telecommunication and IT (network downtime, speed of service restoration, connectivity), real estate (availability and quality), transportation (scale and quality of road and rail network) and power (reliability of power supply).

EXAMPLE: Comparing Quality of Infrastructure

All ten locations claimed high-quality infrastructure, but in practice there are large variations across the sample. On telecoms and IT, it is difficult to run an offshore location as a business proposition without reliable, fast, relatively cheap technology with low downtime, fast restoration of service and good connectivity. Most popular outsourcing sites (cities) in India and Philippines have achieved this as have several locations in Morocco, Malaysia, South Africa, Northern Ireland and Poland. Sri Lanka has a relatively good record, while Kenya is still building its capability but now has good access to a steady telecom connectivity. In Poland and Northern Ireland, quality of telecoms and IT infrastructure is comparable with that found in the UK and France. Malaysia has advanced IT and telecom facilities. In our other North African and Asian countries, it is common to find an advanced IT infrastructure in business parks and large cities but a very limited IT infrastructure in rural areas – or none at all. The

Philippines stands out as having a particularly good telecoms infrastructure with a reliable domestic and inter-island service because of the US military bases there.

The cost of real estate can be an unpleasant surprise in some offshore locations. Mumbai and Bangalore in India, for example, are no longer cheap. In practice, renting commercial space in Mumbai can cost higher than in downtown New York. As a country, and specific cities therein, grows their offshore market, inevitably real-estate prices rise, as is recently happening with Poland. The Philippines still has low real-estate costs (Manila is ranked second lowest in Asia after Djakarta) and also has special economic zones in several cities. Real-estate costs do vary across the other locations, with Malaysia, Poland and Northern Ireland being at the higher end, followed by South Africa which is in fact cheaper than the Philippines. Sri Lanka and Kenya are at the lowest end, and Egypt and Morocco are protected somewhat when business parks are utilised.

Transportation and power tend to be at their most efficient and reliable in Poland, South Africa, Northern Ireland and Malaysia. There are variations in the Indian experience depending on the city location. Road and transportation generally in the Philippines is fairly low quality, on a par with, for example, former Russian states, as is the reliability of power supply; though, as in India, in some cases the BPO sector operates in protected conditions created by service providers themselves. Morocco tends to have better transport and power facilities than Egypt, though Egypt has been upgrading extensively over the last three years. Of our ten locations, Sri Lanka and Kenya are at the bottom end on these factors.

Factor 5: Risk profile

This factor assesses security issues (risks to personal security and property-related issues, such as fraud, crime and terrorism), disruptive events (risk of labour uprising, political unrest, natural disasters), regulatory risks (stability, fairness, efficiency of legal framework), macroeconomic risks (cost inflation, currency fluctuation and capital freedom) and IP risk (strength of data and IP protection regime).

EXAMPLE: Comparing Risk Profile

When making offshoring decisions, companies have been typically driven primarily by cost, skills availability and service factors. But since 2008, and through the Arab Spring and after, risk has taken on a heightened significance in their BPO calculations. Events have driven this, for example: Egypt's BPO activity being stalled by unexpected political and social events and natural disasters affecting Bangkok's business attractiveness. Suppliers are also aware that clients in recessionary USA and Western Europe cannot be guaranteed. By establishing a presence in new offshore locations, a supplier can improve the cost and skills proposition, making it more competitive in its existing markets. But the supplier can also spread risk by establishing a local presence to seek secondary markets within the new region.

Risks can be on a country scale but can also be limited to specific locales within a nation. Terrorism has had a high profile in India, Sri Lanka, Egypt, Northern Ireland and more recently Kenya. But much of this has been historical, and surprisingly small in scale despite media magnification. Except for Sri Lanka, which has recently ended a 30-year long civil strife in its north-west region, it would be possible to point to similar levels of terrorism in the UK and Spain, for example. More critical are risks to personal security from fraud and crime, and this tends to vary by region and city within each country, and also by neighbourhood within each city. In our ten locations at least, the BPO industries tend to be located in quite well-protected areas.

Some countries are more prone to natural disasters than others and this can affect location attractiveness. Japan, for example, regularly experiences earthquakes, and Mumbai has seasonal torrential rain. Less anticipatable are political risks: Egypt followed by Kenya and Sri Lanka being the highest risk countries. Malaysia, Northern Ireland and Poland are countries with the lowest disruptive-event risk among the ten countries studied. Morocco remained largely unaffected by the Arab Spring of 2011, while South Africa's labour unrest in 2012–2013 should be put in the context of a relatively stable democratic state and economy. India and the Philippines are also considered relatively stable political entities for BPO purposes.

On regulatory risks, Northern Ireland, Poland and Malaysia have the best profiles; Kenya, and Egypt the worst, followed by Sri Lanka. India received some adverse comments on legal inefficiencies; while the Philippines, South Africa and Morocco are generally rated as meeting requirements. IP risk is rated as at its worst in Sri Lanka, Kenya and Egypt, followed by Morocco. There is divided opinion on India and the Philippines which may reflect their large market sizes, thus offering a diverse range of experiences on this issue. Northern Ireland and Poland are rated as better than requirement on this issue, likewise (though with a lower mark) South Africa and Malaysia.

Factor 6: Market potential

Market potential can be assessed based on the attractiveness of the local market (current gross domestic product and gross domestic product growth rate) and access to nearby markets (in the host country and adjacent regions). This may take one or more forms:

• Whether the local market is attractive for setting up a captive operation (client consideration) or delivery centre (supplier consideration) that would use local labour, infrastructure and resources
• Whether the local market is populated with sophisticated local service suppliers (client and supplier consideration)
• Whether the local or nearby market have the demand for outsourcing services (supplier consideration for setting up a service centre).

EXAMPLE: Comparing Market Potential

In terms of scale and range of services, India with a US$70 billion plus ITO/BPO annual revenue is easily number one in the captive and offshore-outsourcing market but is not so strong on supply to the host and nearby region. The Philippines is next with US$11 billion in revenues, and by 2012 had overtaken India as the biggest contact centre location by number of seats. From 2012 to 2013 there have been some moves away from India on call centres, but it still attracts such work and remains second in size and revenues. These countries now have major offshore industries and will use this as a basis to accelerate their growth over the next five years. Neither country will slow down. Indian suppliers are increasingly providing best-shoring models, mixing skills onshore (close to the customer), offshore and 'anyshore' in the search for optimal price points and labour skills pools. Both are attempting to move higher up the value chain into complex BPO, with India, indeed, seeking to rebrand itself as a business-process services country.

Given these advantages, the other eight countries tend to seek service niches in order to differentiate, gain new business and build momentum and scale. Sri Lanka gains 'overload' work from its neighbour India at a lower price point, but in 2014 was offering and gaining further momentum in software development, accounting and legal-processing services. Morocco will continue to be a relatively small but growing market, mainly nearshoring into Western Europe. Egypt has voice captives, and a small but growing IT services and BPO market, but its offshore future is temporarily on hold while political and economic instabilities work their way through. Malaysia is a second-tier outsourcing location with good cost competitiveness and English and technical skills. It looks to grow itself as an ITO/BPO location, has good infrastructure for captive operations but is still looking for its precise focus and market(s).

Through 2012–2014, Poland grew fast as a destination, especially for nearshore work from West Europe and large global suppliers. Its education dividend in technical and engineering skills and employable workforce gives it leverage in complex ITO/BPO work as well as more commoditised services. In time, cost pressures will emerge as a 'problem of success,' as we have already seen in India. Northern Ireland also has a strong employable ITO/BPO workforce and a less attractive price point and is likely to regain momentum in less recessionary conditions, taking advantage of its nearshore positioning with Europe and links with the USA.

The African countries in the 2014 sample were South Africa and Kenya. South Africa emerged as a rising offshore location with strongly differentiated services, high-quality contact capability, but still underplaying its potential strengths in financial services and legal process outsourcing and accounting. Kenya was still a start-up location with limited scale, able to deliver on IT and voice and some commodity back-office work, but needing several years of sustained investment and marketing to achieve the scale of any of the other locations.

C A S E   S T U D Y

The Giant Awakens: Sheen Software Systems Considers China for Offshore IT Outsourcing

by Erran Carmel

Frank Xin, the founder of Sheen-USA and his friend Zhang Chang were ordering dinner at M on the Bund, the stylish eatery overlooking the dazzling Shanghai riverfront. 'I'm bullish on China and particularly on Shanghai,' said Xin. His friend, Chang, a vice-president of Information Systems at a major Shanghai bank, was more careful.

> Look, Xin, as a friend, I think you're taking some major risks in setting up shop across the ocean. And this stuff about lightweight methodologies seems lightweight to me.

Frank Xin Goes to China

Xin had made up his mind that China was where his offshore-outsourcing unit would be located. He had monitored the recent emergence of the offshore-outsourcing industry in China. His deliberation was only on where and what form his Chinese operations would take. He considered Shanghai because of the buzz and because of some family ties in the city. Shanghai is a good strategic point to grow, he thought. And in answer to his own hesitations, he thought: 'If Shanghai itself continues to get expensive, I can move to one of the nearby cities with tech parks such as Suzhou or Hangzhou' [Each is 12 hours by train from Shanghai.].

Operations

Xin wasn't sure how to set up his China operations. He saw two options: setting up his own captive office that would be a subsidiary of Sheen-USA or partnering with an existing firm. In that arrangement, he would sign an agreement with a Shanghai firm whereby the Shanghai firm would allocate some of its staff to Sheen. Xin saw advantages to each. If he decided to lease an office, he had a number of choices. His first interest was in the software park in Pudang, a newly built area in eastern Shanghai. But the facility was already full. Pudang costs were very low for Shanghai, at 55 cents per square metre versus about 70 to 80 cents in the rest of the city. Being a member of the software park, even if Xin did not reside there, having a subsidiary in China would give his company other financial benefits: a tax holiday for the first three years (on profits) and a 50% reduction on taxes in the subsequent five years. Xin was not sure what profits would be allocated to his Shanghai office, though.

Xin began planning his offshore strategy by attending the 2003 Global IT outsourcing summit[1] in downtown Shanghai a few minutes' walk from the Bund. The two-day conference was one of the first in China that focused on offshore outsourcing. It was organised by the Shanghai Municipal Foreign Economic Relations and Trade Commission, the Shanghai Municipal and Formalisation Commission, the Shanghai Software Industry Association and several other organisations.

At the conference, the vice-mayor of Shanghai welcomed the attendees. About 200 people attended the conference, most of them from Chinese software companies. Several foreign firms had sent their representatives, including ADP-Asia and Siemens. Conference speeches included those by the heads of Microsoft China and Shanda (a leading computer-game maker based in Shanghai) and the CTO of WebEx, an American firm with R&D in Shanghai. The summit was covered in the next day's English-language *Shanghai Daily* with the headline, 'China's software outsourcing industry is expected to shorten its gap with India in about three years'.

By 2003, the China software market had been growing at a fast pace for several years. Unlike the Indian industry, which most see as its main competitor, China's industry enjoyed strong demand domestically from an economy that had been growing over the past decade at double-digit compound annual growth rate. Beginning roughly in 2000, Chinese firms had begun to set their sights on augmenting the domestic demand with foreign markets. In 2003, China was expected to export roughly US$1 billion in software and software services. The Shanghai metropolitan area accounted for roughly 12% of the total software exports. Shanghai was also home to software R&D centres for HP and Ericsson, as well as support centres and localisation centres for Microsoft and other multinationals.

Xin and His Company Sheen

Frank Xin was reflective of many global software entrepreneurs: as an 'overseas Chinese', he was able to bridge East and West. His home had been in Los Angeles for 15 years. Having grown up in Taiwan, he spoke Mandarin and could be understood in Shanghai, though he was having to master the local Chinese dialect. Prior to founding Sheen, he was at PeopleSoft.

Xin founded Sheen in 2000 to provide customised solutions for the business and entertainment industries. His large clients included Disney and 20th Century Fox, but most of his clients were small- and medium-sized enterprises. In all cases, the development teams assigned to projects were small and nimble – usually three to six technical staff. Most of his clients were local, but some were based elsewhere in California and the USA.

Sheen had four permanent employees and a dozen regular consultants and contractors brought in when needed. He ran a small, lean shop that relied on the combined technical abilities and sales abilities of the principals. 'My strategy is to grow,' said Xin, 'to capitalise on our strengths and the strengths of the Chinese.'

In Sheen's client engagements, the firm used its own adaptation of agile methodologies, also known as 'lightweight methodologies', the most famous of which is Extreme Programming (XP). The 'agile movement' is a reaction to the 'heavy' methodologies exemplified by the Software Engineering Institute's Capability Maturity Model (CMM), which emphasise controls and documentation, both of which are anathema to independent-minded programmers.

Xin said, 'We've found that most clients don't have the bandwidth to do full-blown systems analysis and design, so agile methodologies are better suited. Agile approaches are much better suited to more and better communication between client and developers with lots of end-user participation and small, nimble teams of developers. By working closer with the developer, the client gets over the xenophobia of working with the foreigner, the unknown.'

The other part of Xin's strategy was to use the strength of the Chinese. While the Indian outsourcing industry had mastered the factory approach of software production, the Chinese software industry was only slowly, and perhaps reluctantly, following that lead. About 20 Indian firms had attained the highest process standards of software development: CMM level 5. India's success was all the more noteworthy because its firms represented roughly 50% of all global firms that have attained this standard. 'When we bid against CMM level 5 Indian firms, how do we beat them? We have to offer something different,' reflected Xin.

Chinese programmers are educated in computer science programmes with a tradition of theory and algorithm development. Students coming out of this educational system are not interested in working in factory environments in which they are handed specifications. They want to work with the customer to solve problems. 'Agile programming is a much better fit to Chinese work culture than the stifling procedures embedded in the CMM,' said Xin.

One of the cornerstones of agile methodologies is tight team-work and close interactions between client and developer. Sheen's approach to teamwork was to place people at the client site as much as possible. Sometimes this could be for as much as half of the project duration. When the client wanted the team at its site for longer periods of time, this added to the project cost, and Sheen passes the cost to the client. 'In China, every-one wants to be their own boss, people are less conformative; so when you use agile methods, you allow everyone on the team to give feedback.'

The A. T. Kearney Global Services Location Index (2011), shown in Table 3.2, illustrates a different approach to assessing the attractiveness of a location for outsourcing and offshoring. Its approach provides a score for each factor (financial attractiveness, people skills and availability, and business environment), which are added up to create a final score. We believe that a qualitative assessment should be combined with a quantified approach to decide on the attractiveness of a location for outsourcing.

Finally, those who are comparing potential sourcing destinations must consider the influence of certain cities on such a decision. The rationale for this is that costs, availability of skills and infrastructure may vary significantly across cities within the same country. Even factors such as the environment, risk profile and market potential can present varying results when examined in each city of the same country. The Global Services Tholons Report (Vashistha and Khan, 2008) shows that comparing countries is superficial because 'no two cities of a country would be at the same level of skills maturity or offer the same cost advantage'. For example, some cities graduate more engineers; others more accountants. Therefore, sourcing decisions can be more accurate if the attractiveness of potential locations such as cities are assessed, rather than countries.

One approach to assessing the attractiveness of cities for outsourcing is that proposed by Farrell (2006), in which the scale and quality of workforce, business catalyst, cost, infrastructure, risk profile and quality of life are among the more critical factors. According to 2014 Tholons

TABLE 3.2   A.T. Kearney Global Services Location Index™, 2011

Rank	Country	Financial attractiveness	People skills and availability	Business environment	Total score
1	India	3.11	2.76	1.14	7.01
2	China	2.62	2.55	1.31	6.49
3	Malaysia	2.78	1.38	1.83	5.99
4	Egypt	3.10	1.36	1.35	5.81
5	Indonesia	3.24	1.53	1.01	5.78
6	Mexico	2.68	1.60	1.44	5.72
7	Thailand	3.05	1.38	1.29	5.72
8	Vietnam	3.27	1.19	1.24	5.69
9	Philippines	3.18	1.31	1.16	5.65
10	Chile	2.44	1.27	1.82	5.52
11	Estonia	2.31	0.95	2.24	5.51
12	Brazil	2.02	2.07	1.38	5.48
13	Latvia	2.56	0.93	1.96	5.46
14	Lithuania	2.48	0.93	2.02	5.43
15	United Arab Emirates	2.41	0.94	2.05	5.41
16	United Kingdom	0.91	2.26	2.23	5.41
17	Bulgaria	2.82	0.88	1.67	5.37
18	United States	0.45	2.88	2.01	5.35
19	Costa Rica	2.84	0.94	1.56	5.34
20	Russia	2.48	1.79	1.07	5.34
21	Sri Lanka	3.20	0.95	1.11	5.26
22	Jordon	2.97	0.77	1.49	5.23
23	Tunisia	3.05	0.81	1.37	5.23
24	Poland	2.14	1.27	1.81	5.23
25	Romania	2.54	1.03	1.65	5.21
26	Germany	0.76	2.17	2.27	5.20

(continued)

TABLE 3.2   Continued

Rank	Country	Financial attractiveness	People skills and availability	Business environment	Total score
27	Ghana	3.12	0.69	1.28	5.18
28	Pakistan	3.23	1.16	0.76	5.15
29	Senegal	3.23	0.78	1.11	5.12
30	Argentina	2.45	1.58	1.09	5.12
31	Hungary	2.05	1.24	1.82	5.11
32	Singapore	1.00	1.66	2.40	5.06
33	Jamaica	2.81	0.86	1.34	5.01
34	Panama	2.77	0.72	1.49	4.98
35	Czech Republic	1.81	1.14	2.03	4.98
36	Mauritius	2.41	0.87	1.70	4.98
37	Morocco	2.83	0.87	1.26	4.96
38	Ukarine	2.86	1.07	1.02	4.95
39	Canada	0.56	2.14	2.25	4.95
40	Slovakia	2.33	0.93	1.65	4.91
41	Uruguay	2.42	0.91	1.42	4.75
42	Spain	0.81	2.06	1.88	4.75
43	Colombia	2.34	1.20	1.18	4.72
44	France	0.38	2.12	2.11	4.61
45	South Africa	2.27	0.93	1.37	4.57
46	Australia	0.51	1.80	2.13	4.44
47	Israel	1.45	1.35	1.64	4.4448
48	Turkey	1.87	1.29	1.17	4.33
49	Ireland	0.42	1.74	2.08	2.24
50	Portugal	1.21	1.09	1.85	4.15

Note: The weight distribution for three categories is 40:30:30. Financial attractiveness is rated on a scale of 0 to 4, and the categories for people skills and availability, and business environment are on a scale of 0 to 3.
Source: A.T. Kearney Global Services Location Index™, 2011.

Top 100 Outsourcing Destinations Ranking among the top ten global outsourcing cities: six are in India and the others are Manila and Cebu City in the Philippines, Kraków in Poland (number eight) and Dublin in Ireland (number ten). It is interesting to think through how quickly this ranking is changing and ponder how dynamic the global sourcing environment has been – and will be. For example, in 2010 Kraków was among the top five emerging cities according to Tholons ranking of emerging destinations and in 2014 it is among the established destinations list. In a few years we will see several locations in Central and Eastern Europe that might well be promoted, but others demoted for running into cost and skills challenges.

Nearshoring and Beyond

Nearshoring is an activity in which a client outsources work to a supplier located in a foreign low-wage country and yet the supplier is close in distance and in terms of time-zone differences. Compared to offshore outsourcing, the benefits of nearshoring include lower travel costs, fewer time-zone differences and closer cultural compatibility. Canada, for example, is a significant nearshore destination for US clients. Indeed, some analysts argue that US clients can have lower costs when nearshoring work to Canada as compared with the strategy to offshore-outsource to India.

However, the question which remains is the degree to which distance matters (or not) in nearshoring, in comparison to the alternative to offshore. In their study of nearshoring, Carmel and Abbott (2007) argue that distance still matters and point to customers choosing the nearshore option to gain benefit from one or more of the following constructs of proximity: geographical, temporal, cultural, linguistic, economic, political and historical linkages.

Nearshoring represents a major way in which non-BRIC countries can compete with India for market share. The top Indian firms now offer a variety of location choices to their clients, which mitigates some of the currency costs incurred in uncertain markets. For example, India-based TCS can offer its British clients services that are 'farshore' (India), nearshore (Budapest, Hungary) and onshore from their offices in London, Nottingham or elsewhere. Another Indian firm, Infosys, has 'proximity development centres' and like other Indian firms has also refined its internal processes in mitigating time-zone difficulties (Carmel and Abbott, 2007).

Nearshoring may be part of a more complex outsourcing arrangement, in particular when the client firm is a multinational company that requires a supplier with a global presence to deliver services to business units based in different geographies. This can be illustrated through the example of the outsourcing contract between TCS and ABN AMRO (Oshri et al., 2007a). In this contract, TCS provided IT services to the bank from offshore locations (Mumbai and São Paulo), from nearshore locations (Budapest and Luxembourg) and from an onshore location (Amsterdam). The client and the supplier assessed the most appropriate location to provide services based on some of the criteria outlined above (e.g., availability of skills, language and cost). Our research suggests that clients and suppliers are increasingly moving to such an arrangement for either insourced or outsourced IT and business services (Oshri et al., 2007a).

Nearshoring is less likely to dominate the offshoring strategy in the coming years; however, it is going to be one component within the best-shoring strategy. According to numerous reports in the media, several regions have emerged recently as attractive for nearshoring such as Central and Eastern Europe (to Western Europe), Northern Africa (for French and Arabic speaking countries), the Caribbeans (to the USA east-coast), Southeastern China (to Japan and South Korea) and Central and South America (to North America).

Summary

This chapter has provided an extensive review of the factors that affect country attractiveness for outsourcing and offshoring. Through examples, the chapter has illustrated the comparative advantage of certain locations within the context of the nature of the function outsourced. As such contexts change, the attractiveness of a location may change as well. Country attractiveness also needs to be combined with a more granular analysis of city and regional attractiveness within each country.

4

The Attractiveness of Western Countries for Outsourcing Services and Backsourcing

In this chapter, we continue the examination of country attractiveness, however, by focusing on the characteristics of Western countries. We build on the country attractiveness framework presented in Chapter 3 which is generally suitable for the evaluation of developing countries and revise it to accommodate the value proposition of Western countries. We illustrate the use of this Talent-based, Value-adding and Advanced Sourcing (TAVAAS) framework based on the analysis of the UK. The attractiveness of Western countries for outsourcing services has become an important component in the firm's global business service portfolio as some services are provided from onshore or in some other cases services are brought back in-house from an offshore location. In this chapter, we therefore focus on the following aspects:

- A framework to analyse the attractiveness of Western economies for outsourcing services: the UK case
- A decision matrix to assess firm's propensity to invest in a Western economy
- Backsourcing IT and Business Processes.

The Attractiveness of a Western Economy for Outsourcing Services

Outsourcing: A new competitive regime

Outsourcing is in a new era: an era of value-adding services, innovation and transformation. An era that shifts competition to skills and expertise and that shapes the firm's strategic objectives on business transformation rather than technical solutions. As the outsourcing landscape is changing, so competition between countries for outsourcing work is reconstructing. It is no longer competition for low costs but a search for superior skills, both technical and managerial, that provide the strategic guidance and operational excellence needed in the 21st century.

As the outsourcing industry of ITO and BPO enters its fourth decade, a shift has taken place in terms of the value expected from large global players. Firms are shifting their attention from a single one-off cost reduction to seek ongoing value delivered through partnership and close ties. As part of this major shift in the outsourcing arena, firms are now paying more attention to the ability to work closely with the supplier on technical and business challenges and deliver innovation and transformational programmes as a key supplier selection criterion. Such changes in the outsourcing landscape offer great opportunities for countries that developed their outsourcing offerings around high-quality and value-adding services that are customer-centric enabled by advanced sourcing capabilities.

While such a strategic shift in the outsourcing landscape has been observed in the last five years, the tools to assess the attractiveness of high-talent and advanced sourcing capabilities of countries have not been updated. Indeed, several frameworks for country attractiveness have been offered in the existing academic and professional literature (summarised in Table 3.1 in Chapter 3); however, these tools have been designed to assist managers to assess the attractiveness of mainly low-cost countries with a highly specialising workforce. Oshri and Ravishankar (2014) modified the Farrell (2006) framework to fit the challenges that talent-based, value-adding countries such as the UK is facing in attracting outsourcing investments.

In the global sourcing marketplace, the UK has long been perceived as a lucrative outsourcing market. It is considered to be the second largest consumer of outsourcing services and a hub for leading global suppliers that provide end-to-end BPO and ITO services to UK- and Europe-based customers. However, the shift in value sought from outsourcing engagement is now positioning the UK as a contender for high-value outsourcing destinations.

We examine the UK position in light of the following three trends (reported in Oshri and Ravishankar, 2014):

1. The maturity of the outsourcing industry will drive more and more client firms to seek impact on business and strategic performance from their suppliers.
2. Client firms and suppliers will deploy complex sourcing models that will increase the importance of sourcing managerial capabilities, such as relationship management, against technical and delivery capabilities.
3. As growth through outsourcing is becoming a key strategic driver for partnership, locations with promising entry points to lucrative markets will become more attractive for outsourcing investments, such as the UK market as an entry point to the US market.

These trends change the nature of competition in the outsourcing industry, placing greater importance on the knowledge-base of the country, both technical and managerial skills, and on the trade opportunities a country may offer as entry points to other lucrative markets.

Talent-based, Value-adding and Advanced Sourcing (TAVAAS) capabilities country attractiveness framework

In order to assess the attractiveness of TAVAAS countries, such as the UK, the USA and Germany, we propose the following factors and their respective weights (Table 4.1).

In developing the weights per factor, both the demand and supply side of outsourcing services were considered. For example, we assert that client firms that seek high-quality service based on an advanced platform of sourcing capabilities are likely to consider costs as a less important factor than the availability and quality of skills. Similarly, supplier firms that invest in TAVAAS countries are more likely to attribute high importance to growth opportunities over the cost-base of the country.

TABLE 4.1 TAVAAS countries attractiveness framework

Factor	Categories	Weight
Costs		15%
	Average wage per skilled employee and manager	
	Average rental office space per square metre ($€/m^2/yr$)	
	Cost of telecom, Internet access (US$ per month)	
	Cost of power (Kw/H)	
Availability of skills		30%
	Size of the labour market	
	Quality of relevant delivery skills indicator	
	Quality of relevant sourcing management skills	
Environment		15%
	Corruption index	
	Quality of life index	
	Serious crime index	
	Accessibility to the country indicator	
	Corporate tax	
Quality of infrastructure		10%
	Network downtime	
	Availability of housing indicator	
	Quality of roads and rails indicator	
Risk profile		10%
	Personal security index	
	Natural disasters index	
	Political unrest index	
	Cost inflation index	
	Intellectual property indicator	
Market potential		20%
	Attractiveness of local market index	
	Leverage to promising markets indicator	
Total		100%

Source: Oshri and Ravishankar, 2014.

Based on data collected from various sources including interviews with key informants from leading suppliers and client firms, we have developed a perceptual map of the attractiveness of seven countries in Europe: the UK, Ireland, Germany, France, the Netherlands, Czech Republic and Poland (for a more detailed comparative analysis about these countries please see Appendix A). We report on data collected from various public sources and also offer expert opinion regarding some of the factors, in particular where public information was not available (included below in the example box).

EXAMPLE: UK Attractiveness Analysis

Cost

The UK is certainly positioned as a high-cost location, in particular as compared with the Czech Republic and Poland. However, the UK cost base is not significantly more expensive than Germany and Ireland. For example, the average wage per skilled employee in the UK is US$33,513 compared with US$41,170 in Ireland. The cost of telecommunications and power in the UK is lower than Ireland; however, corporate tax in Ireland (12.5%) is lower than the UK (20–24%) (Figures 4.1 and 4.2).

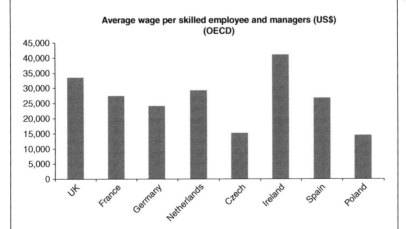

FIGURE **4.1** Average wage per skilled employee and managers (US$)

Source: Oshri and Ravishankar, 2014.

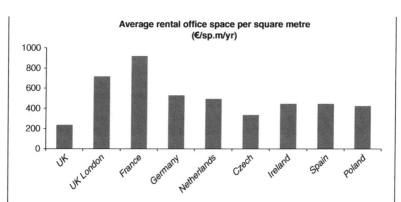

FIGURE 4.2 Average rental office space per square metre

Source: Oshri and Ravishankar, 2014.

Availability of skills

The UK is offering a highly skilled and well-rounded workforce that is capable of both managing and delivering outsourcing services. The supply of both technical and management talent from UK universities, combined with the extensive experience in outsourcing, positions the UK ahead of any other country in Europe. There is evidence that recent investment in the UK is mainly motivated by the highly skilled outsourcing management talent available in various parts of the country including the North East, Wales and Scotland. Further, the supplier landscape in the UK in terms of presence and scope of services has developed far more than in any other European country, reflecting the interest that suppliers express in making significant investments in the UK (Figure 4.3).

Environment

The environment in the UK is also attractive, mainly because of low levels of corruption, good quality of life and low levels of crime compared with other European countries. With 462 airports, the UK has one of the highest number of airports per capita in Europe, a positive indicator of country accessibility (Figure 4.4).[1]

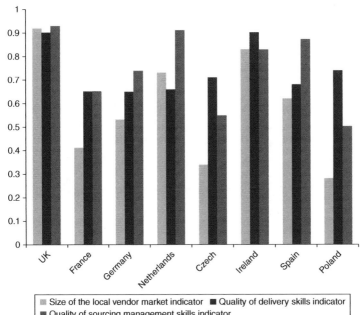

FIGURE **4.3** / **Availability of skills**

Source: Oshri and Ravishankar, 2014.

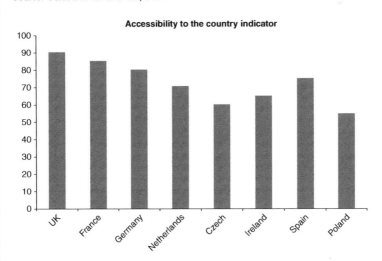

FIGURE **4.4** / **Accessibility to countries**

Source: Oshri and Ravishankar, 2014.

Infrastructure

The quality of the UK's infrastructure is moderate but well ahead of Poland and the Czech Republic and not too distant from other European countries. For example, the availability of real estate in the UK has scored 93.7 compared with only 65.9 in Ireland and 84.7 in Germany. While network downtime performance is below industry standards, the quality of housing in the UK is among the best in these European countries. The UK government has recently acknowledged the shortcomings with regard to broadband access and has massively invested in improving technological capabilities such as an upgrade to 4G and 5G technologies and the expansion of broadband usage across the UK (Figure 4.5).[2]

Risk

The UK offers a low risk profile (along with Ireland, Germany, France and the Netherlands); however, the UK's personal security indicator (80.2) is far better than Ireland (62.3) and nearly the same as Germany (86.6). The UK enjoys a moderate to low score on risk of labour strikes, on a par with Ireland but slightly better than the risk in Germany (Figure 4.6).

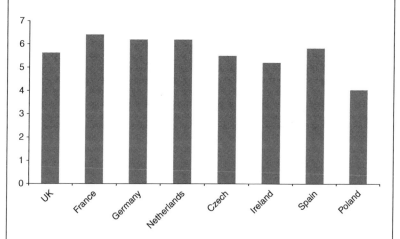

FIGURE 4.5 **Quality of overall infrastructure**

Source: Oshri and Ravishankar, 2014.

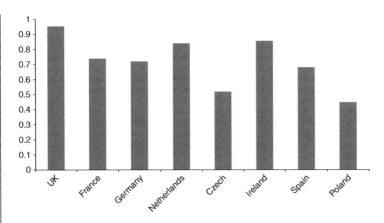

FIGURE 4.6 / **Access to nearby markets**

Source: Oshri and Ravishankar, 2014.

Market

The UK has the strongest market entry point in Europe. Among the reasons identified for the strong market attractiveness are the high service mentality and delivery system, the availability of language skills and the strong trade ties with the USA, which are considered leverage for many of the suppliers investing in the UK (Figure 4.7).

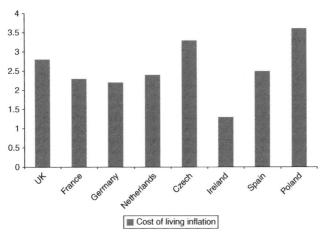

FIGURE 4.7 / **Cost of living inflation**

Source: Oshri and Ravishankar, 2014.

The Outsourcing Services Value Proposition of Western Economies

As the outsourcing of IT and business processes enters its fourth decade, a significant change has taken place. Client firms now seek to benefit from value-adding services and access to unique skills in their engagements with outsourcing suppliers. Innovation and business transformation have come to the fore when client firms and suppliers negotiate a contract, and success is assessed based on both operational excellence and strategic transformation. Talent management and supply of skilled employees capable of engaging in business solutions delivered through cutting-edge technology have become a critical source of competitiveness for suppliers. These critical skills are hard to develop and exploit, in particular in countries that have emerged only recently as attractive locations for outsourcing, such as Poland, the Czech Republic, Hungary, Spain, Egypt, South Africa and Morocco. Other locations, such as Brazil, Russia and China, have not managed to develop strong business innovation capabilities. As the outsourcing competitive landscape is changing towards higher value services, the traditional offshoring location will continue to compete on cost in an ever-search for cost reduction through automation and relocation to cheaper locations. However, countries with a strong talent position combined with an innovative and nimble economy will shift their value proposition towards value-adding services that command premium fees for higher value services.

The UK outsourcing landscape, as an example, is at the heart of this change. Being the second largest outsourcing market in the world, populated with sophisticated consumers of outsourcing services and a supply of technical and managerial talent, the UK has attracted top-tier suppliers to set up delivery centres and sales offices around the country. In this regard, Western economies such as the UK offer value proposition for suppliers and client firms around the following:

• A premium service mentality
• Large-scale, sophisticated outsourcing economy
• Supply of linguistic, technical and managerial talent
• Flexible workforce distributed around the country.

Opportunities for growth in Western economies such as the UK are also attractive. The UK ITO sector is one of the largest in the world and its BPO sector is growing fast. In particular, the contact centre sector has been attracting investments in recent years as client firms sought to benefit from access to talent in more affordable locations, such as the North of England, and in some cases have brought back their operations from offshore locations to the UK to improve customer experience.

Without doubt, the USA, the UK and Germany have maintained their competitive position in the outsourcing industry despite their disadvantageous cost position. While some European countries may be seen as more attractive on the cost side, other factors play a far more important role.

There are also opportunities for client firms to benefit from the Western economies outsourcing proposition. Client firms with extensive outsourcing experience that have developed a strong retained IT function (discussed in Chapter 6) and a sophisticated internal sourcing unit may consider backsourcing (also known as re-shoring or insourcing) part or an entire outsourced function. (We discuss backsourcing in depth in the following section.)

Making an investment decision is complex. To guide suppliers in their decision-making to invest in Western economies such as the UK, the USA or Germany, we offer a decision tool that considers the key factors affecting outsourcing FDI and a three-step assessment process.

Are you Prone to Consume or Provide Outsourcing Services in a Western Economy? A Decision-Making Tool

Step 1: Assess your Propensity to Invest in the UK

Using the decision matrix, please keep track of your score by carefully answering the questions below. If your answer falls within the description provided under 'Tend to invest in a Western economy', then you score the maximum points for this question. If your answer falls within the description provided under 'Do not tend to invest in a Western economy', then your score is zero. If your answer is somewhere between the two answers, please make a judgement regarding your score. For example, if your answer for the first question 'What is my value proposition?' is a combination of high-value services that drive innovation and cost reductions, then your score should be 4 or above (Table 4.2).

TABLE 4.2   A decision matrix to assess your propensity to invest in a Western economy

What is my ...	Tend to invest in a Western economy	Do not tend to invest in a Western economy
... value proposition? (7%)	High-value services that deliver innovation	Mainly cost reductions
... service mentality? (15%)	High quality, working closely with my clients	Mainly driven by SLAs, offshore-based
... governance philosophy? (6%)	Combination of transactional and relational approaches	Mainly transactional
... strategy to remain relevant in my market? (8%)	Innovate my business models and technological platforms	Mainly innovate my technological platforms
... strategy to growth? (10%)	Enter competitive and demanding markets to improve service quality as test-bed for more challenging markets	Avoid competitive and demanding markets; mainly focus on existing markets
... philosophy towards competition in the market? (5%)	Competition drives innovation and creates opportunities to differentiate	Competition destroys value and ability to command margins
... strategy to acquire global clients? (9%)	Set up global centres of excellence	Set up regional delivery centres
... strategy to acquire talent? (10%)	Talent comes at cost	Talent is cheaper in offshore locations
... strategy to talent management? (5%)	Offer a career path	Offer a job
... sourcing models strategy? (8%)	A combination of sourcing models to arrive in an optimal utilisation of assets	The application of those sourcing models that drive operational excellence
... risk mitigation strategy? (7%)	Investments in both high- and low-risk locations	Investments in mainly high-risk locations
... strategy to select a location to set up a new centre of excellence? (10%)	Evaluate multiple factors that weigh in growth opportunities, costs, infrastructure and risk	Mainly focus on costs

Step 2: Sum Up Your Score

Having scored each factor, total the scores to make a single score out of 100.

Step 3: Assess Your Propensity to Invest in a Western Economy

A score between 66 and 100 is past the tipping point to invest in the UK as a destination for outsourcing services. A score below 33 signals that you are unlikely to benefit from investing in a Western economy as a destination for outsourcing services. A score between 34 and 65 is in the area that requires additional analysis to understand your tendency to shift strategy and operations to deliver higher value, talent-based outsourcing services; however, without aligning the strategic vision with the operational strategy (Figure 4.8).

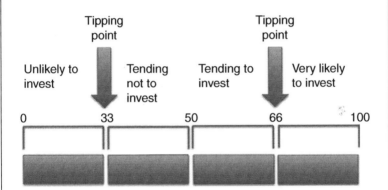

FIGURE 4.8 / A decision matrix to consider propensity to invest in a Western economy
Source: Oshri and Ravishankar, 2014.

/ Backsourcing of IT and Business Processes

Backsourcing concerns with bringing back in-house previously outsourced services. It is the reversal of a pre-existing outsourcing strategy and a re-aggregation of previously disintegrated internal capabilities (Wong, 2008). This sourcing strategy differs from insourcing where organisations retain the management and provision of services internally after carefully evaluating the external service market (Hirscheim and Lacity, 2000). Backsourcing may take different forms. For instance, backsourcing can range from bringing back a single business function such as helpdesk or call centre to a complete reversal of an entire business function such as R&D. The latter would be larger in scale, budget and more complex in nature than the former. The backsourcing process presents major challenges to organisations which include managing organisational change, re-transferring knowledge and other resources to develop new capabilities and competency (Ejodame and Oshri, 2014).

In the public's mind, backsourcing is often synonymous with the so-called 're-shoring' of jobs that have been outsourced to offshore locations. In particular, public dissatisfaction with offshore call centres is well known, and there have been demands from the customers of a number of companies for onshore-only services.

But there is much more to backsourcing than public irritation with those companies that appear to favour cost-cutting over customer service. Indeed, backsourcing goes far beyond customer contact roles and into the heart of IT and business process outsourcing.

Pulling back work: Background

In 2013, Oshri surveyed 200 large consumers of outsourcing services based in the UK and the USA. The study revealed that 44% of the sample has brought back services at one point or another (Oshri, 2014). Yet despite the fact that many client firms brought back some services, there has surprisingly been little academic research into backsourcing.

Indeed, the list of companies that have backsourced in over last 20 years is certainly getting longer. Among notable examples is that of American Airlines, which brought back its IT infrastructure from IBM in 2007 and JPMorgan Chase, which terminated its US$5 billion (£3.3 billion) contract with IBM in 2004, two years after signing it.

Others have followed suit. In 2005, Sainsbury's terminated an outsourcing contract with Accenture after five years of service; while McDermott International dropped what was supposed to be a ten-year global outsourcing deal with AT&T's professional services wing, taking back responsibility for the design, implementation and management of its IT.

More recently, both Santander and General Motors announced that they were repatriating work that had been offshored to India. Santander was one of many companies to be criticised for offshoring its customer service centres, leading customers to feel as though their loyalty was being devalued by the opportunity to cut costs. Table 4.3 provides an overview of major backsourcing cases and the reasons for the backsourcing.

The prevailing view of backsourcing has been that an informed decision was made after evaluating the facts, based on a desire for lower costs, higher value and/or better control and service. However, research shows that most organisations backsource as a passive reaction to a short-term problem rather than as a positive and considered sourcing strategy for the longer term.

Customer rebellion aside, pursuing backsourcing as a reactive, remedial strategy is risky. Some organisations should certainly consider backsourcing if they have made significant improvements to their internal capabilities, but others should avoid it if their in-house functions have not improved since outsourcing.

CASE STUDY

Backsourcing Cheque-Checking Services

Any cheque the bank receives needs to go through a cheque-clearing process. As part of the cheque clearing, there is a manual process in which a specialist checks whether the cheque has been tampered with by a fraudster. What kind of specialty would be needed to check cheques? (Think Leonardo de Caprio and the movie *Catch Me if You Can*). Just the same as many other Banks, EnglishBank needed to provide a complete cheque-clearing process. While some parts of the clearing process were kept in-house, the cheque checking was outsourced to GermanSupplier back in 2001. GermanSupplier built the capability to check cheques by manually examining the EnglishBank cheques and assuring EnglishBank that no fraudulent activity was suspected. In 2010, EnglishBank decided to backsource this function in-house. The main reasons for backsourcing the cheque-checking function was a consequence of an overall decision to bring core services back in-house, based on a perception that services performed in-house have a better customer satisfaction rate.

EnglishBank proceeded with the backsourcing process swiftly by applying its well-developed process-oriented skills to ensure that cheque checking could be done in-house. However, the bank stumbled when it came to a rather simple question: how do you recruit people who are capable of checking cheques?

EnglishBank thought this through and realised that it would not be possible to advertise a job description to perfectly describe the set of skills required. The approach taken in bringing back the function in-house and rebuilding this capability was based on the assumption that such skills could not be acquired from the market. Instead, the talent recruited for these positions should be carefully trained by setting up criteria as to when minimum proficiency in detecting fraud activity has been developed by an individual.

And this is what EnglishBank did. Indeed, new recruits underwent training in which a two-tier checking panel was created. Cheques were delivered to the first specialist, who carefully examined the cheques and filled out a report whether these cheques had been tampered with by a fraudster. Then, the same cheques were passed on to the second specialist, who examined the cheques, not knowing the opinion of first expert. As the specialists were checking the cheques, EnglishBank set up certain indicators to sense whether they had reached the proficiency needed in the long term. For example, EnglishBank recorded average levels of fraud the specialist detected and kept track on those to see if they changed over time. EnglishBank also paired specialists to check each other's outcomes and recorded those incidents when the first specialist failed to detect a cheque which was tampered with. Further, the bank recorded the overall incidents in which the first check of a fraud cheque went unnoticed and the trend over time. EnglishBank continued with this training until both the first- and second-tier specialists were in agreement with regard to fraud activity in the checked cheques, and the average number of mistakes had stabilised to an acceptable figure according to bank regulations. At this point in time, EnglishBank completed rebuilding the capability in-house, a process that took several months and some unusual approaches for training.

The main drivers for backsourcing

There are three major categories of reasons to backsource: contract problems, opportunities arising from organisational change and opportunities from external factors in the business environment. Cost considerations have been critical in some decisions, of course, as has the quality of the outsourced relationship, service or product. However, these last two factors suggest that due diligence may not have been properly carried out pre-contract.

One common reason to backsource is when the costs associated with outsourcing are substantially higher than originally planned, sometimes because of hidden costs that accumulate over time. Cost savings may also have been overestimated by the buyer at the outset or can disappear as the client ramps up outsourcing activities and its expectations of the outcome.

Another reason may be a gap between expected and actual service levels. However, recent studies show that organisations that backsource generally experience lower service levels and quality than those that switch outsourcing suppliers instead. In other words, the failure of one outsourcing relationship should not be interpreted as the failure of the outsourcing model.

A critical factor in some backsourcing decisions is the client's loss of control over functions that had previously helped create strategic value – for example, an in-house IT function that is later identified as having been a contributor to gaining or maintaining a sustained advantage in the marketplace. Several studies find that losing a competitive edge is the driver behind about 25% of cases.

Sometimes this loss of control makes client firms realise that they are locked into an outsourcing relationship with a supplier that 'knows better'

TABLE 4.3 Who backsourced: what, when and why

	Client	Supplier	Period	Size of deal	Contract problem/ cost	Change in strategy	Loss of control	Knowledge mismatch	IS role change	New executives
1	EE	T-Systems	2008–2013	US$685 million		◆			◆	
2	GM	HP	1997–2012	US$2.5 billion	◆	◆			◆	
3	Sandwell Council	BT	1998–2013	US$14 million	◆					
4	BAE	Logica	2012	-	◆					
5	Young's Sea Food	-	2013	-			◆		◆	
6	Philips	Philips China	2007–2012	-		◆				◆
7	Apple	Foxconn	2013	-		◆				◆
8	PacifiCare Health Systems	Keane Inc.	2002–2006	US$500 million		◆				
9	Prudential	Capgemini	2001–2006	£55 million	◆					◆
10	Sears, UK	Andersen Consulting	1996–2006	£344 million					◆	
11	UBS	Perot Systems	1996–2006	US$1.8 billion					◆	
12	Bedfordshire County Council UK	Hyder Business Services	2001–2005	£260 million		◆				

(continued)

TABLE 4.3　Continued

	Client	Supplier	Period	Size of deal	Contract problem/ cost	Change in strategy	Loss of control	Knowledge mismatch	IS role change	New executives
13	Sears Holding Corp.	CSC	2004–2005	US$1.6 billion		◆		◆	◆	◆
14	New York Presbyterian Hospital	First Consulting group	2000–2005	US$228 million					◆	
15	Sainsbury, UK	Accenture	2000–2005	£2.1 billion			◆		◆	
16	UMass Memorial Health Care	First Consulting Group	2000–2005	US$102 million						◆
17	Gateway	Affiliated Computer Services	2003–2004	US$400 million						◆
18	JPMorgan	IBM	2002–2004	US$5 billion			◆			◆
19	Lehman Brothers	Wipro	2002–2003	US$100 million		◆				
20	Cable & Wireless, UK	IBM	1998–2003	US$2.1 billion			◆			◆
21	Halifax Bank of Scotland	IBM	2000–2002	US$1 billion					◆	

(continued)

TABLE 4.3   Continued

	Client	Supplier	Period	Size of deal	Contract problem/ cost	Change in strategy	Loss of control	Knowledge mismatch	IS role change	New executives
22	Oxford Health Plans	CSC	2000–2002	US$195 million	◆		◆			
23	Bank One	IBM	1998–2002	US$1.4 billon	◆		◆			◆
24	Washington Mutual	IBM Global Services	1996–2002	US$533 million	◆					◆
25	Eckerd	IBM Global Services	1993–2000	US$440 million	◆				◆	◆
26	Farmers Group	Integrated Systems Solution	1992–2000	US$150 million	◆			◆		◆
27	East Midlands Electricity	Perot Systems	1992–1999	US$230 million					◆	◆
28	Xerox	EDS	1994–1998	US$3.2 billion		◆				
29	MONY	CSC	1994–1997	US$210 million		◆	◆			
30	ABB Power	Sungard Services	1988–1991	US$840,000 annually	◆					◆

Note: The period column contains the duration of the outsourcing venture indicating when the service was terminated and brought back in-house. The table includes major cases but not exhaustive.

or which does not fully understand the client or the market it operates in. Either case may drive client firms to disengage and backsource.

Sometimes, both client and provider may see the wisdom of the decision. In 1996, for example, Continental Airlines ended collaboration with its outsourcing partner, EDS, after four years of successful work together. Continental wanted to improve its reservation system to enable more efficient fleet capacity usage and better ticket pricing. Since EDS was neither familiar with the air-travel industry nor with Continental's customers, Continental decided to run the project in-house. In this way, Continental re-evaluated the strategic importance of its outsourced IT functions and built an innovative online business on its own – one that improved user satisfaction and attracted new customers, all without the aid of a third-party supplier.

The management angle

Internal management changes at the client company generally lead to shifts in power. Research finds that when companies bring new executives onboard, the new members are three times more likely to make changes. In particular, new CIOs and CEOs may reconsider the value of an IT outsourcing deal and identify new strategic importance in those outsourced activities. This may persuade them to backsource.

Of course, internal changes are often triggered by external influences and most organisations report structural changes immediately before a backsourcing decision is made. These changes include mergers, divestments and acquisitions – another factor in the JPMorgan Chase case study (in Chapter 6, p. 173) after its takeover of Bank One brought new management onboard. The refreshed leadership team strongly influenced the decision to bring IT back in-house.

The Halifax Building Society's merger with the Bank of Scotland is another example of external structural changes prompting a decision to backsource. In the wake of the merger, the Halifax cancelled a ten-year IT services contract with IBM, worth over £700,000.

So when are client firms most likely to backsource? It might be assumed that it is in the final stages of a failed relationship; but ongoing research at Loughborough Centre for Global Sourcing and Services (CGSS) (e.g., survey by Oshri, 2013; Ejodame and Oshri, 2014) shows that not all clients bring back services at the end of such a deal. In fact, recent examples show that backsourcing often happens in the earlier stages of a project, once sufficient information has been gathered by the client as to whether outsourcing is likely to work.

That said, few outsourcing projects offer instant payback, and the quest for immediate, unrealistic costs savings is often the root cause of outsourcing failure. Firms that consider backsourcing at the end of a project may be able to assess their internal capabilities far more realistically against those of the supplier, in addition to evaluating the contract's true value over its course.

The human angle

There may be other repercussions of backsourcing, tactically and reactively rather than as a carefully planned sourcing strategy. For example, backsourcing is rarely something that happens in isolation; it is likely to involve managing organisational change and knowledge re-integration, rebuilding capabilities and re-coordinating expertise with administrative functions. All of that costs time, money and human resources.

Knowledge re-integration, in particular, is not a process for which most client firms have developed a methodology. This is because 'knowledge re-integration' is really people re-integration and may have negative impacts on morale, productivity and trust.

This was also demonstrated in the JPMorgan Chase case (see Chapter 6). When the bank outsourced IT services to IBM in 2002, some 4,000 staff transferred to the supplier. When the new management team came onboard from Bank One two years later, most of the outsourced IT staff were brought back to their old employers. That sort of upheaval and lack of management continuity will create an uncertain and unstable working environment in any organisation, and the costs of that may be impossible to estimate until it is too late.

Whatever the long-term advantages of backsourcing might have been, JPMorgan Chase incurred significant costs, including its outsourcing fees, the premature contract termination with IBM, its reinvestment in thousands of skilled IT staff and also in the hardware and software needed for the newly backsourced department.

In all, analyst firm Gartner estimates that the total cost of backsourcing is typically around 15% of annual contract cost. In short, the switching costs are high. This is particularly true in knowledge-intensive functions such as R&D, product development and engineering services. Indeed, CGSS research finds that switching suppliers may be preferable to backsourcing if there is an internal human-resources cost or a significant transfer of knowledge.

Based on the business drivers described above, nearly any client firm could be considered a candidate for backsourcing. However, the decision to backsource cannot be based on those drivers alone, especially if it is taken 'in anger'. More than anything, executives should be mindful of the challenges involved and attempt to mitigate them by developing critical capabilities and a clear path forward.

Critical success factors for backsourcing[3]

Bhagwatwar et al. (2011) examined two backsourcing JP Morgan and Sainsbury in their study and developed a framework which stresses the importance of knowledge transfer in such undertaking. The process of knowledge transfer is very complex since it contains both explicit and implicit knowledge and therefore requires frequent communication and inter-personal interactions (Szulanski, 1996). Furthermore, barriers such as distance, language, management differences, beliefs and cultural norms, and lack of incentives, can all hinder a smooth re-transition of knowledge (Bhagwatwar et al., 2011). These barriers can also be equally associated with outsourcing. To overcome them, Bhagwatwar et al. (2011) formulated lessons learned which could be considered to be critical success factors at backsourcing decisions.

First of all, once the decision of backsourcing has been taken, the client firm should immediately inform the supplier in order to prepare for contract termination and any financial and relational implications. Indeed, the decision to backsource must not be connected with an abrupt termination of the relationship. Instead, the collaboration needs to continue to secure knowledge transfer and re-integration from the supplier to the client firm (Warner and Brown, 2005). Another critical success factor is the composition of a capable backsourcing project team with 'executives, managers and technical staff from the client side as well as from the outsourcing service provider side' (Bhagwatwar et al., 2011). The teams should agree on a plan, make stakeholders aware of the activities and timeline and ensure a clear and functional backsourcing governance for this project. The supplier should be committed to provide support and information until the success-ful re-integration of the service. As part of re-integration knowledge and services, the client firm should consider re-transferring employees from the supplier to the client's organisation. Client firms with little capacity for sig-nificant backsourcing should consider piloting the repatriation of part of the service prior to commencing with the re-shoring of the entire service.

Summary

In this chapter, we discussed how to examine the attractiveness of Western countries for outsourcing services and the option of bringing back oper-ations onshore from offshore locations. It is our contention that while offshoring remains a strong proposition, multinationals will consider all options, including setting up delivery centres onshore and, in some cases, will repatriate work under the appropriate conditions.

part II

Building Sourcing Competencies

5

Supplier Configurations and Capabilities

As we have illustrated, the global sourcing market is large, and the services it offers range from relatively simple processes such as data entry to very complex projects such as the transformation of the entire back-office function. The supplier base is equally diverse, ranging from locally based firms that specialise in particular services or industries to offshore or global suppliers that offer high-quality service at a low cost. Tables 5.1–5.3 identify the dominant players in the sourcing market: the top ten outsourcing companies (Table 5.1), the top ten outsourcing advisers (Table 5.2) and the top ten BPO and IT Services companies in India (Table 5.3). These rankings provide important information regarding the expertise of a number of suppliers and thus help clients identify potential partners. Of course, these rankings may change over time as existing, developing and new players increasingly compete across global geographies.

This chapter provides an overview of suppliers, supplier configurations and the role intermediaries play. Supplier landscape will, therefore, be discussed in terms of firm size, areas of specialisation and location. The chapter focuses on a supplier's core capabilities and discusses suppliers' strategies for sustainability and growth.

In this chapter, we focus on:

- Supplier configurations, including multisourcing arrangements
- Bundling services
- The role of intermediaries in sourcing arrangements
- A supplier's core capabilities for sustainability and growth

TABLE 5.1   Top ten outsourcing companies, 2014

Rank	Company	Key strength
1	ISS	Balanced performance
2	Accenture	Balanced performance
3	CBRE	Balanced performance
4	Kelly Outsourcing and Consulting Group	Balanced performance
5	Colliers International	Management capabilities
6	HCL Technologies	Management capabilities
7	NCR Services	Demonstrated competencies
8	Pactera	Demonstrated competencies
9	Capgemini	Demonstrated competencies
10	CGI	Management capabilities

Source: International Association of Outsourcing Professionals.

TABLE 5.2   Top ten outsourcing advisers, 2014

Rank	Company	Key strength
1	Quint Wellington Redwood	Balanced performance
2	Avasant	Management capabilities
3	EY	Balanced performance
4	PwC	Management capabilities
5	Deloitte	Balanced performance
6	Alsbridge	Balanced performance
7	Kirkland & Ellis	Balanced performance
8	Strategy& (formerly Booz & Company)	Balanced performance
9	Baker & McKenzie	Management capabilities
10	Bird & Bird	Management capabilities

Source: International Association of Outsourcing Professionals.

Overview of Supplier Configurations

In addition to choosing a supplier that specialises in a particular line of services, it is of vital importance to choose the right configuration for the outsourcing arrangement. The different high-level configuration options for the client are the sole-supplier model, the best-of-breed model, the panel model and the prime-contractor model.

TABLE 5.3   Top ten BPO and IT services companies in India in 2012–2013

Rank	BPO companies	IT services companies
1	Genpact India Pvt. Ltd	Tata Consultancy Services Ltd
2	Tata Consultancy Services Ltd	Infosys Ltd
3	Serco Global Services	Wipro Ltd
4	Aegis Ltd	HCL Technologies Ltd
5	Wipro BPO	Tech Mahindra Ltd
6	Infosys BPO	iGate
7	Firstsource Solutions Ltd	Mphasis Ltd
8	WNS Global Services (P) Ltd	L&T Infotech Ltd
9	Aditya Birla Minacs Worldwide Ltd	Syntel Ltd
10	EXL	CSC, India

Source: NASSCOM.

Sole supplier: In this model, a single supplier provides the entire service. The main benefit of this model is the sole accountability of the supplier, which makes the governance of the venture easier relative to other configuration models. Its main risk is associated with the high danger of compromising service quality because no supplier is outstanding in all areas. However, over the past five years, the practice of bundled services outsourcing has grown, stimulated by better-integrated supplier capability, and client moves to rationalise and reduce their multiple supplier bases. We discuss bundled services in detail later in this chapter.

Best of breed: In this model, the organisation has a number of suppliers and plays the role of the head contractor. Willcocks et al. (2006) emphasise that this type of configuration constitutes a low-risk outsourcing option and has become a prevalent outsourcing model. According to their research findings, more than 75% of UK and US organisations use the best-of-breed model as an approach to mitigate outsourcing risks. Willcocks et al. (2009) point out the trade-offs on operational and management costs, supplier capabilities, risks and control when comparing best-of-breed versus bundling outsourcing models.

Panel: In this arrangement, a company compiles a list of preferred suppliers that work in continuous competition. Every supplier constantly competes for a project or a contract. This approach is very common in applications development, hardware purchasing and consulting, as the requirements differ from one initiative to another, and thus it makes more sense for client firms to have a list of preferred suppliers and call them for the work they are best at.

Prime contractor: This model consists of a network with several suppliers that operate under the control of the head contractor. The head contractor is accountable for the delivery of the service and liable for this under the terms of the contract. Typically the head contractor chooses as subcontractors firms that have expertise in a specific niche area and/or operate in specific regions. By using subcontractors, this approach offers a combination of superior expertise and geographical coverage.

In every outsourcing venture, there are service-level arrangements (SLAs) that specify the level and quality of service that the supplier is contractually obliged to deliver. If the supplier does not deliver, there is a risk that the supplier will suffer the imposition of service credits (these issues are further discussed in Chapter 9).

Multisourcing configurations and the role of service integrator

By adopting *best-of-breed* or *panel* sourcing configurations a client firm is engaging in managing multiple suppliers. While each supplier is contracted to deliver a specific service, in practice some of the services delivered by different suppliers are interdependent. The five-year outsourcing deal for the total amount of US$2.2 billion that Dutch ABN AMRO bank signed with five suppliers – IBM, Accenture, Tata Consultancy Services (TCS), Infosys and Patni Computer Systems – for applications development, support, enhancement and infrastructure is an example of a large multisourcing arrangement where interdependencies between services provided by multiple suppliers required cooperation and coordination between them to create value for the client. Under this arrangement, IBM was providing infrastructure, Infosys and TCS provided application support and enhancements (Infosys was responsible for ABN AMRO's applications in the North American Business Unit, and TCS was responsible for the Latin American and Private Client Business Units). In this arrangement all five suppliers could bid for new development work.

Multisourcing, which implies buying interdependent IT and IT-enabled business services from a set of internal and external suppliers to achieve optimal outcome, appears to be the long-term dominant trend in global sourcing. Levina and Su (2008) outline the benefits and risks associated with the multisourcing strategy. Benefits of multisourcing include increased competition among suppliers in terms of price, quality and degree of innovation; lower operational risks and dependency (each supplier becomes less critical); and lower strategic risk (sensitive information is split among different suppliers (see Levina and Su, 2008). Among the risks of multisourcing are reduced incentives to make customer- or supplier-specific investments. Along these lines, the two parties are less willing to make investments in relationship building, technology, dedicated staff or physical assets as the basis for enhancing their collaboration. Furthermore, multisourcing arrangements increase management overheads as client firms incur costs associated with contracting, developing relationships with suppliers and coordinating work. Multisourcing also has implications for suppliers, as each supplier needs to be aware of interdependencies and commitments of other suppliers. Operational-level agreements (OLAs) between suppliers are set to ensure that such awareness exists and the responsibilities of all parties are clearly defined.

Multisourcing can be characterised by different breadth and depth of supply relationships that constitute a supply base for a particular multisourcing engagement. Su and Levina (2011) define *supply base* as a set of contractual supplier relationships that are directly managed by the sourcing firm for a given business function at a given time. The breadth of the supply base reflects the number of suppliers the focal firm uses for a given business function, and the depth of a supply relationship is characterised by the client's level of investment in a particular supply relationship for a given function. Figure 5.1 describes different combinations of breadth and depth of supply relationships. Breadth and depth of the supply base also have a number of implications on the outcome of outsourcing arrangements (see Table 5.4).

One of the major challenges in multisourcing is the integration of interdependent services. Oshri and Kotlarsky (2014) mapped four main multisourcing configurations that client firms and suppliers have applied in recent years. In multisourcing there are three main actors: the client, a network of suppliers and a service integrator (SI), which may be the client, one of the service providers or another third party. Our configurations captured in Table 5.5 consider the role of the service integrator as one key

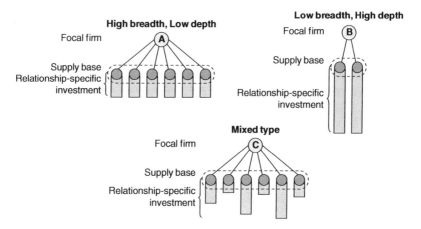

FIGURE 5.1 / **Supply base types**
Source: Su and Levina, 2011.

TABLE 5.4　Benefits and risks of supply base characteristics on outsourcing arrangement outcomes

	Advantages	**Disadvantages**
Increased breadth of supply base	Reduced dependency on individual suppliers and therefore relatively low switching costs	Limited economies of scale and therefore higher production costs
	Access to best-of-breed suppliers reduces operational risk and is likely to yield intangible benefits such as flexibility and innovation	Increased supplier management costs because more suppliers need to be managed
Increased depth of supply base	Supplier is likely to invest in developing client-specific capabilities such as deeper understanding of the client's unique business practices, routines and culture (aiming at long-term benefits from the relationship)	Higher switching costs because the supplier has deeper knowledge about the client and customised solution and cannot be easily replaced
	Reduced supplier management costs due to better communication and collaboration between the parties	
	Deeper relationship may create opportunities for innovation and other synergies	

Source: Based on Su and Levina, 2011.

TABLE 5.5 Multisourcing configurations

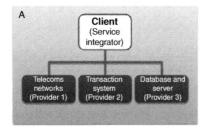

A: SI by the client

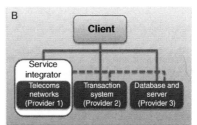

B: SI by a lead provider (1)

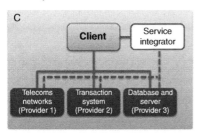

C: SI by a third-party specialist

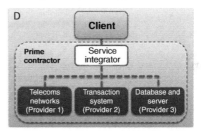

D: SI by the prime contractor

Source: Oshri and Kotlarsky, 2014.

element that affects the effort needed by the three actors. (Note: dotted arrows represent responsibility for the management of interdependencies; smooth lines represent contractual agreements. Multisourcing configurations A, B and C fall under the best-of-breed or panel category, and multisourcing configuration D falls under the prime contractor category.)

In configuration A, the client firm plays the role of a service integrator. The client is, therefore, responsible for the coordination and integration of the work, while suppliers focus on delivering services according to SLAs. Interdependencies between outsourced tasks require suppliers to interact with each other to ensure the smooth delivery of the entire service (as captured in the SLAs).

In configuration B, the service integrator is a supplier, often a lead party of a particular function. In this configuration, also known as the guardian model, the service integrator (one of the suppliers) is playing two roles: first, delivering service as part of its SLA commitment and, second, monitoring and coordinating the delivery from the remaining suppliers to ensure that the SLA for the integrated service is met. The client in configuration B is involved in managing commitments of the individual suppliers against SLAs as part of a network governance approach and also paying particular attention to the service integrator's performance.

In configuration C, the service integration function is outsourced to a third-party specialist. The service integrator is monitoring, coordinating and integrating services delivered by individual suppliers.

In configurations B and C, suppliers that do not perform a service-integrator role tend to focus on delivering the services allocated to them, while ensuring that both OLAs between them and client SLAs are met. The client firm is involved in monitoring the performance of individual suppliers, according to the contractual agreements it holds with them; however, it also relies on the OLAs monitored by the service integrator. The main difference between configuration B and configuration C is that under configuration C the client has an additional supplier to manage (i.e., the service integrator).

In configuration D, a client is contracting one supplier to act as a prime contractor who, in turn, is (sub)contracting interdependent services to other suppliers and then integrating their work to ensure seamless delivery. The prime contractor is responsible for coordinating and integrating work delivered by the multiple suppliers it selects and contracts, while the client firm is only managing the relationship with the prime contractor. There are no direct contractual agreements between the client firm and subcontractors.

Multisourcing configurations present a number of challenges for both clients and suppliers:

- *Challenge number 1:* Client firms are often tempted to pursue either configuration B or configuration D. The reason for that is clear: these configurations offer client firms an easy opportunity to detach themselves from the daily management of the supplier network while assuming responsibility for monitoring the service integrator's performance, rather than the true network performance.[1] The danger in this approach is that the client loses sight of individual supplier performance and contributions and becomes dependent on the service integrator's capability to both integrate service and assess individual supplier performance. One outcome of this is the formation of a two-tier relationship circle in which the client firm gradually drifts to the second tier, weakening its relationship with its suppliers.

- *Challenge number 2:* In configurations B and C, suppliers supervised by the service integrator may abuse information asymmetry between the client and the service integrator in order to spur a 'blame game' when things go wrong. Since the client firm is not involved directly in the management of OLAs, it has little direct exposure to information about individual supplier performance and it relies on information provided by the service integrator. Therefore, the client may not be in the position to objectively assess the source of a problem when something goes wrong. The end result of that is similar to Challenge 1: worsening relationships within the network that often results in reluctance to collaborate and exchange information and knowledge between the suppliers, which is critical for the coordination of interdependencies.

- *Challenge number 3:* Both client and suppliers seek remedies for managing interdependencies between outsourced services through additional control mechanisms in the form of OLAs. The expectation is that the formalisation of such interdependencies will improve awareness among the suppliers. However, the exchange of information and knowledge required to develop awareness around such interdependencies cannot be substituted by a formal clause. OLAs should serve as a guide that encourages information exchanges rather than substitutes them.

How can client firms and suppliers cope with such challenges?

First, the role of service integrator should not be seen as the outsourcing of the multivendor governance to a third party. Instead, the parties should clearly define areas of responsibilities and communicate those to the other suppliers in the network. Furthermore, in order to deal with information asymmetry between the client, service integrator and the rest of the suppliers, it is imperative to establish both procedures for dealing with situations when there is a breakdown in service provision and protocols for investigating which supplier is responsible for the breakdown.

Second, the governance of multisourcing settings needs both individual and network governance approaches to be adopted by the client firm. While an individual governance approach is typically supported by SLAs and individual incentives and penalties, a network governance approach involves setting joint objectives that require suppliers to collaborate and consider team incentives and penalties. Moreover, in addition to the role of the service integrator in managing interdependencies between the services, the client firm has to maintain some degree of control over the supplier network simply because, in the end, the client firm is the prime client, regardless of subcontracting.

Third, as a balancing act to the fairly heavy investment in formal governance on the client side, we suggest that client firms assess their supplier relationship strategy and consider investing in developing strong relationships with suppliers that deliver transformative services, while maintaining workable, well-structured but somehow less intense relationships with suppliers of transactional services.

Bundling services

As we see multisourcing gaining popularity with some clients, we also see an increase in bundling services in order to reduce the number of suppliers. *Bundled services* are defined as 'a mix of business process and/or information technology (IT) services purchased separately or at the same time from the same supplier where synergies and efficiencies are sought in end-to-end processing, governance, relationship management, cost and performance' (Willcocks, Oshri and Hildle, 2009). They found that 75% of the deals were for bundled services across two or more IT towers, with the rest either IT and BPO combined or mixed BPO contracts. Bundled services can help clients reduce transaction costs in a number of ways. They typically include the following:

- Risk reduction
- Lower levels of governance
- Simpler contracting
- Ability to move to standardised practices
- Synergies across services and processes
- Less management time getting to contract
- Lower relationship management costs.

There are two types of bundled services: price bundling and product bundling (Harris and Blair, 2006). Price bundling refers to offering a discount in the sale of two or more products that are not integrated in a package. Product bundling is the integration and sale of products at any price. Studies have shown that the propensity and capability of organisations to buy and manage bundled IT services is much higher than in the case of business process outsourcing and the offshoring of IT services (Willcocks and Lacity, 2006). Three dimensions are reported to affect the customer's propensity to bundle services (Agarwal et al., 2000):

- *The bundle dimension.* This encompasses the bundle choice, that is, the newly formed combinations of products, and the bundle size, or the number of products per bundle.
- *The client dimension.* The following factors affect a client's propensity to buy bundled products: the tendency for single sourcing, the extent of the use, the number of products currently used and certain client-specific characteristics.
- *The supplier dimension.* The key factors are the perceived quality of the service and the lock-in position of the supplier (Willcocks et al., 2009).

Table 5.6 explains these dimensions as situated in the outsourcing context.

One critical element in achieving successful bundled services is to demonstrate that the client benefits from the synergies among the various services provided by the supplier. Our research shows that most clients have not developed capabilities to evaluate their suppliers of bundled services based on the synergies achieved.

The Role of Intermediaries

While competition for cost arbitrage in the global sourcing market is growing, offshore intermediation is gaining momentum as a tactic for managing the complexity of offshoring ventures (e.g., Jarvenpaa and Mao, 2008). Mahnke et al., (2008) explain the value of intermediation in outsourcing and offshoring and provide an overview of services that intermediaries offer to clients and suppliers:

1. *The mitigation of cultural disparities.* Cross-cultural tensions such as differences in language and organisational practices can cause turbulence in offshoring ventures. If an outsourcing firm does not understand and manage these differences and the tensions that arise because of them, substantial conflicts are likely to emerge and reduce the benefits of the venture. Along these lines, an intermediary with experienced staff and managers who are aware of the cultural specifics of both regions can

TABLE 5.6   Factors affecting firms' propensity to buy bundled services

	Factors affecting propensity to bundle services	Dimensions	Relevance for the outsourcing context
Bundle	Bundle choice	New or perceived new services	Clients might be more inclined to consider bundled services if they are perceived as new services (higher value proposition). Needs to be considered from early adopter's viewpoint. Who are the early adopters in this industry?
	Joint functional compatibility	Risk associated with the performance of bundled services	Buyers might tend to add services to the package if they think the bundling will not harm additional services but will present cost advantages that non-bundled services offer
	Bundle size	Number of products per bundle	Flexibility in bundle size may increase propensity of small firms but might have a negative effect on the supplier's cost structure
Client	Single-sourcing tendency	Tendency to purchase from single supplier	Clients with limited resources or weak learning capabilities will tend to contract with a single source
	Extent of use	Heavy consumers of outsourcing versus light consumers of outsourcing	Clients for whom a large portion of their expenditure is on outsourcing will be more inclined to buy bundled services (sensitivity to discount on high-value activity)
	Number of products currently used	High number of services in use	The more the client is familiar with the product, the more likely it is that the client will buy the bundled service
	Firm characteristics	Size, performance	Large, well-performing firms will tend to buy bundled services. High spenders on IT services will tend to consider bundled services
Supplier	Perceived supplier quality	Perceived quality across the various bundled services	Propensity to buy experienced services if quality is high or services with quality perceived as high
	Lock-in position	The dependency between the various services	Propensity to buy or renew bundled services will increase when the dependency between the services is high (regardless of whether performance is enhanced by buying bundled services)

Source: Willcocks, Oshri and Hindle, 2009.

more easily foresee and manage the tensions that arise as a result of different communication styles.

2. *The mitigation of cognitive distance.* Cognitive distance can result from different mind-sets and different ways of thinking, processing information and communicating. More often in the offshoring context, cognitive distance arises when relatively less-skilled clients attempt to exploit the high technological expertise of an offshore supplier at a relatively low cost. This is a major area where an offshore intermediary can add value. In particular, the offshore intermediary may offer services such as specialised translations between perceived client needs and supplier requirements and codified interfaces, so that systems can be connected and contracts can be designed and managed. Furthermore, intermediaries can contribute to the creation of sufficient common ground to facilitate mutual understanding and avoid conflict.

3. *Comprehensive preparation of the client for an offshoring venture.* A number of offshoring ventures have led to disastrous results because the client lacked knowledge, experience and maturity in offshore supplier selection and negotiations. An offshore intermediary can help an organisation be prepared for offshoring ventures in a number of ways, including creating awareness of objectives, establishing common expectations with the supplier and contributing to contract formulation and negotiation.

4. *Facilitating and managing the ongoing relationship between the client and the offshore supplier.* Offshore relationships are not static and, in comparison to domestic ventures, they are more prone to unforeseen situations and contingencies. Especially in offshoring ventures in which project outcomes are hard to identify (and thus the performance of the supplier is more difficult to measure), the role of offshore intermediaries is key. More specifically, the offshore intermediary can contribute significantly to the detection of misunderstandings and the resolution of conflicts. Furthermore, it can create relational awareness by generating mutual understanding, clarifying implicit assumptions and defining a common vocabulary from which joint future action can proceed. Finally, the intermediary may, if necessary, work with the client to make sure that appropriate communication structures are in place so that the inter-firm governance mechanism can be tailored to relational requirements.

A number of consultancies (e.g., Deloitte, TPI, EquaTerra) and law firms (e.g., DLA Piper, Berwin Leighton Paisner) play the role of intermediary in outsourcing ventures and provide services in domestic and offshore operations. Their services range from strategy consulting, programme management and change management to contract design, contract management and dispute resolution.

Supplier Capabilities

While supplier configuration is highly significant for the outcome of the venture and firms must analyse extensively which model best fits their purposes, another critical area for consideration is the actual capabilities and competencies that selected suppliers can demonstrate.

Levina and Ross (2003) studied large IT suppliers and distinguished between three types of operational capabilities (also referred to as 'competences'), that is, capabilities involved in the provision of a service or a product:

(i) *Client relationship management capability* involves routines and resources that align the vendor's supplier's practices and processes to the client's goals. More specifically, this capability is associated with the knowledge that a service provider must have of the client's business model and industry, as well as of the specifics of the client's operations.

(ii) *Methodology development and dissemination capability* concerns task delivery routines and resources that accomplish software design, development and execution. Six Sigma and the capability maturity model (CMM) are some of the better known methodologies that aim to improve software development processes. This capability is important for introducing efficiencies in project delivery and operational improvements (Levina and Ross, 2003), as well as managing dispersed knowledge and expertise in a global supplier organisation (Oshri et al., 2007a).

(iii) *Personnel development capability* is related to recruitment, training and mentoring practices; designing jobs that will expose individuals to a variety of tasks and enable them to broaden their skills; and developing performance appraisal and compensation systems.

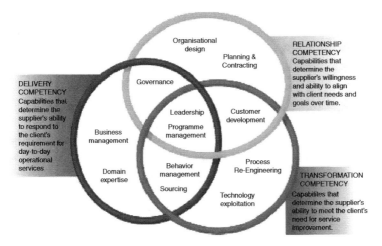

FIGURE 5.2 / **Twelve supplier capabilities**
Source: Willcocks et al., 2006.

Levina and Ross argue that these three operational capabilities are mutually reinforcing and need to be simultaneously present in the supplier organisation. In the offshoring context, Ethiraj et al. (2005) find that higher levels of client relationship management and methodology development capabilities lead to higher levels of firm performance.

Complementary to these works is a more fine-grained view of supplier capabilities developed by Feeny et al. (2005) who identify 12 capabilities (see Figure 5.2) that service providers could leverage into three competences, as seen through the eyes of the clients: delivery competency that reflects the supplier's ability to respond to the client's ongoing needs; transformation competency indicating the supplier's ability to deliver radically improved service in terms of quality and cost; and relationship competency reflecting the supplier's willingness and ability to align its business model to the values, goals and needs of the client. We argue that these broad competences and fine-grained capabilities should be taken into account by client firms when looking for a supplier.

1. *Leadership.* Leadership refers to the capability of delivering the desired result throughout the lifetime of the deal. Feeny et al. find that individuals who occupied supplier leadership roles have a considerable impact

on the success of an outsourcing venture. They identify three patterns that emerge when they examined how these leaders could generate a difference to the outsourcing result. First, in unsuccessful cases, the leader of the supplier team is often too focused on business management issues such as delivery and meeting SLAs while delivering the required profit margin to the supplier. These are important operational aspects of management, but they are distinct from leadership. Second, the quality of the relationship between the leaders of the supplier's and the client's teams exerts an impact on the wider client–supplier relationship. Third, the relationship between the leader of the client's team and the top management of the supplier's organisation can be a critical success factor. Because most suppliers tend to create more of a front-end team, rather than a full-function business unit when serving a client, the local team is extremely dependent on its leader's relationship with headquarters to gain access to key resources and approval for client-aligned business policies.

2. *Business management.* This is the capability of delivering products and services according to the agreement and the business plans of both parties. If either of the two parties is dissatisfied with the sourcing arrangement, the venture will fail. Often clients try to fully exploit their power position at the expense of the supplier, but this tactic erodes the relationship and undermines the sourcing result. As the contract manager of an Australian public sector agency noted, 'Suppliers have to make a reasonable margin to stay in business. You don't want them to lose money because the worse their business gets, the worse your business gets' (Feeny et al., 2005, p.44).

3. *Domain expertise.* This is the capability to retain and apply professional knowledge. The key issue is not only the supplier's technical expertise or know-how but also the ability to understand and manage the customer's business needs. A number of suppliers acquire domain expertise by transferring employees to the client's site. For example, Deutsche Bank moved its procurement people to Accenture, and Barclays transferred cheque-processing staff to Unisys. Such arrangements have two advantages for clients. First, it becomes the supplier's responsibility to adjust capacity and use the best people. Second, both parties are reassured that the operating staff not only have the required expertise but also understand the specifics and particularities of the client's service.

4. *Behaviour management.* Behaviour management refers to the ability to motivate and inspire people to deliver services of high value. It is highly significant for clients to evaluate the extent to which a supplier has acquired this capability – in other words, how competent the supplier is in motivating and managing people to deliver service with a front-office culture. Different suppliers use different methods to acquire this capability. For example, CGI Group of Montreal puts employees who will be transferred to clients' sites through a process that it calls 'harmonisation'. A CGI partner explained that this process is much more than an orientation to the client. The goal is 'to show every employee – not just a subset – this is what we do, how we do it, the timing. We want to set the stage for good behaviour management beforehand, not react to bad behaviour afterwards.'

5. *Sourcing.* This is the ability to access the necessary resources. This ability may take the form of generating economies of scale, using a superior infrastructure or turning to efficient procurement practices. For example, the procurement services deal between BAE Systems, a British defence, security and aerospace company, and Xchanging, a business processing company, was based on two key areas: the superior ability of Xchanging to attract high-level professional skills for certain procurement categories (such as office suppliers, health plans and training) and its ability to generate economies of scale by aggregating BAE's part-time needs with those of other clients.

6. *Process improvement.* This is the capability to change processes in a way that generates a dramatic improvement. Supplier track records can be useful resources in the evaluation of the supplier's capabilities for improvement. Most clients are familiar with Six Sigma methodologies or alternatives such as CMM and are looking for these. However, it is important to look beyond such tools to consider the people and behavioural aspects. Key areas for consideration include: who has the critical skills, who owns the change process, who defines what an 'improvement' is and who benefits. It is important to note that, often, improvements appear on the surface to be targeted to the needs of the client, but in fact are intended for the convenience of the supplier.

7. *Technology exploitation.* This refers to the capability of rapidly deploying new technology, one of the key reasons behind the growing BPO industry (Lacity and Willcocks, 2009). This capability requires careful evaluation from the client's perspective and should go beyond

the supplier's pure technical skills. Significant areas for consideration include the values and behaviours the supplier brings to using technology, the processes that are followed and the infrastructure. The importance of these areas, as well as security, data protection and compliance, is evident when a client organisation is considering exploiting a cloud-based service delivery.

8. *Programme management.* Programme management refers not only to project-level capabilities but also to the capability of delivering a set of interrelated projects. More specifically, it involves prioritising, coordinating, mobilising the organisation and promoting a series of tasks that aim towards change and improvement. Programme management aims to facilitate reuse of knowledge and business and technical components across individual projects, thus contributing to the supplier's ability to better manage dispersed knowledge resources and facilitate innovation in products and services that supplier firms offer to their clients. For example, in our study of the development and implementation of the Quartz banking platform (a collection of architectural and business components that could be integrated with third-party components to provide a solution according to the requirements of a specific customer) developed jointly by TCS and TKS (Teknosoft is a Swiss-based company that specialises in financial services), the Quartz programme manager, who was coordinating all Quartz implementation projects across all dispersed locations, played a central role to ensure the rapid growth of the Quartz offering. As he was aware of new components being developed for a specific customer, he facilitated the reuse of these components across different implementation projects and their inclusion in future product offerings (Kotlarsky et al., 2007). Feeny et al. (2005) highlight the fact that this capability has played a major role in clients' decision to expand the use of a particular supplier for more projects.

9. *Customer development.* This is the capability to enable clients to become customers who can make informed choices about their business needs, service levels and costs. Feeny et al. (2005) suggest three steps that suppliers should take to achieve the reorientation from 'user mindset' to 'customer mindset': (1) establish personal contact with a number of end users to understand what sort of service they want to use and how (this will also lead to trust development); (2) cooperate with client managers to arrive at an agreement on the provisions of

the service; and (3) work towards relationship development by which the end user becomes a customer who feels fully informed of service functionalities, options, potential enhancements and associated costs. For example, in our recent research on innovation through outsourcing (discussed in detail in Chapter 12), we observed a proactive approach that IBM designed to keep their clients informed of areas in which IBM could help them to innovate, and innovations they have implemented for other customers (clients). This approach relies on multiple channels, including newsletters and innovation days where IBM combines case studies, life presentations and panels. Panels include representatives from client firms, academics and intermediaries (e.g., Oshri, 2014).

10. *Planning and contracting.* This is the capability to plan resources and deliver 'win-win' results for the supplier and customer. The planning component involves envisaging potential rewards for both the supplier and client and finding a way to achieve these rewards. For example, in the outsourcing arrangement between Deutsche Bank and Accenture, Accenture committed to fund creating a new platform for procurement, with 200 people assigned to its development. It expected to gain a good revenue from Deutsche Bank, as well as the opportunity to attract other clients to the service. Deutsche Bank estimated that the plan will deliver 15–20% savings through the consolidation, standardisation and restructuring of its 14 procurement units. The contracting component defines how rewards are to be shared during the execution and delivery of the plan. Many possibilities for sharing rewards exist. For example, the Bank of America and Xchanging structured their major deals as profit-sharing arrangements, while the Bank of America chose to take an equity stake in Exult during its HR outsourcing arrangement.

11. *Organisational design.* This is the capability required to design and implement successful organisational arrangements. Feeny et al. (2005) find that a number of major deals took approximately two years to reach an organisational fit between the client and supplier. Often in these deals, clients were experimenting with various organisational arrangements without fully understanding the supplier's design strategy. In this regard, suppliers vary greatly in terms of their organisational approach, the choices they make and their levels of flexibility. For example, some emphasise a thin front-end client team, interfacing

with consolidated service units (silos) that have ownership and the responsibility for profit and ownership of most of the resources. While such arrangements may lead to the generation of significant economies of scale, they can also limit a supplier's ability to deliver the business plan for a specific client. By contrast, other suppliers allocate most of their resources to enterprise partnership units created for each major deal. These units are responsible and accountable for the delivery of the business plan and have their own chief executives, senior executive teams, dedicated staff and resources. Clearly the supplier's organisational design and its fitness with the client's operational mode will affect the success of the outsourcing project (Lacity and Willcocks, 2009).

12. *Governance.* This refers to the governing processes and structures that facilitate the alignment of the client's objectives and strategies with the supplier's delivery system. Key areas for consideration are as follows: the structures need to be in place to ensure that the supplier is delivering according to the contract and that decision-making is visible and accountable; procedures are set out for dealing with problems; and the governance structure addresses powers and authorities.

These 12 core capabilities of the supplier can be leveraged into three key competences (Feeny et al., 2005; Lacity and Willcocks, 2009; see Figure 5.2):

1. *Delivery competency.* This is based on the supplier's ability to respond to the client's ongoing needs. This competency primarily involves the supplier's leadership, business management, domain expertise, behaviour management, sourcing, programme management and governance capabilities.
2. *Transformation competency.* This is based on the supplier's ability to deliver radically improved service in terms of quality and cost. It primarily involves the supplier's leadership, behaviour management, sourcing, process improvement, technology exploitation, programme management and customer development capabilities.
3. *Relationship competency.* This is based on the supplier's willingness and ability to align its business model to the values, goals and needs of the customer. The key capabilities are leadership, customer development, planning and contracting, organisational design, governance and programme management. Among these, the planning and contracting

capability presents the major challenge, because it is not easy to align the goals and incentives of the two sides.

Furthermore, recent work by Oshri and Kotlarsky highlights the importance of developing innovation capabilities that together form a fourth key competency: *innovation competency*. We discuss innovation capabilities in detail in Chapter 12.

The following case illustrates the evolutionary path that TCS followed to develop capabilities imperative to compete successfully in the IT outsourcing industry.

CASE STUDY

Tata Consultancy Services: Building Capabilities

by Shankar Narayanan

Credibility: 1970s–1990s

In 1968, Tata Sons in India established TCS as a division to service its electronic data-processing (EDP) requirements and provide management consulting services. Over the next few years, some young engineers at TCS realised that they were staring at a potential new business opportunity and started offering data-processing services to clients outside the group.

India's first-generation computer experts felt handicapped by an outmoded computing environment in the country. When TCS started, there were only 17 computers in the entire country. The first breakthrough in India came in 1969, when TCS won a contract from the Central Bank of India to automate branch reconciliation processes. But progress was slow, because India's foreign exchange laws made it difficult to import hardware.

As a result, TCS became the exclusive distributor for mainframe computer-maker Burroughs and simultaneously started doing programming for the hardware-maker customers in the USA. Using its export revenues, TCS was able to bring in new computers, enabling the fledgling company to keep pace with the evolving needs of its growing client roster in the USA.

The defining moment for the Indian software industry was in 1974 when TCS won a large export project for the Detroit Police Department. It was followed by some other projects in the USA and UK, and the notion of offshore services or the ability to provide services from remote locations was born. Without an adequate telecommunication infrastructure, programmed tapes were sent on weekly flights to the USA, while software requirements came through the postal services.

In 1977, the Indian government enacted legislation forbidding foreign firms from operating fully owned subsidiaries in India. As a result, IBM chose to leave India, a decision that opened up a new window of opportunity in India: as its core competency, TCS installed hardware and systems software and created and ran data centres.

From the 1980s, TCS expanded aggressively. The average size of its deals grew beyond 25 person/year to over 100 person/year. In 1988, with improvements in telecommunications, TCS began to drive the offshore business by installing a water-cooled IBM 3090 mainframe, an aggressive move for a company that decided to invest heavily in a single machine with substantial export guarantees to the national government. The gamble paid off and eventually led to a complete redefinition of the business model, which, in turn, led to the creation of today's US$60 billion Indian IT industry.

With its business growing steadily in the 1980s, TCS became the hub for new technology knowledge in India. It started creating opportunities for Indian IT professionals with focused academic–industry partnerships beginning with IIT Bombay and IIT Kanpur, followed by new engineering colleges with course design and faculty developmental programmes. By the end of the 1980s, a robust system was in place for the education and research needs of the country's IT professionals.

In 1981, TCS established India's first IT R&D division, the Tata Research Design and Development Centre, at Pune.

Simultaneously, TCS worked closely with the Indian government on regulatory issues.

Because computers were still scarce, the improvement of processes to increase productivity became a focus for TCS. Quality became a cornerstone first for TCS and subsequently for the entire IT industry in India. The relentless pursuit of excellent quality began to draw the attention of customers and competitors alike.

Scale: 1990–2004

With the end of the century approaching and the impending Y2K problem looming, TCS was becoming known for its software factory, a development that helped it leapfrog into the global environment. TCS spread its footprint worldwide by setting up global development and near-shore delivery centres in Hungary, China, Uruguay, Brazil, Japan, the USA and Canada. By the 1990s, the dot-com boom had the IT industry on steroids making it a highly lucrative sector.

It became a period of exponential growth for TCS, which saw its first change of the guard. The visionary Massachusetts Institute of Technology (MIT)-trained electrical engineer F. C. Kohli, who had started TCS, stepped down as he passed the leadership to Subramaniam Ramadorai, who had the drive, rigour and passion to lead TCS through its next phase of growth. Taking over as CEO in 1996, Ramadorai made organisational changes, beginning with a more empowered management style. Having grown from the ranks and having served TCS in different departments, his understanding of the organisation was deep, and his vision was to take TCS into the global top ten leagues of IT services companies. Under his leadership, TCS was restructured into a domain-led organisation, capabilities evolved to deliver end-to-end solutions, and uniform organisation-wide quality processes were introduced and reinforced.

TCS became the world's first organisation to achieve an integrated enterprise-wide maturity level 5 on both the capability maturity model (CMM) and people capability maturity mode (People CMM), frameworks conceptualised by the Software Engineering Institute at Carnegie Mellon University to benchmark and appraise the software process and people-management process of an organisation.

As the offshore model of software development gained currency among global corporations, Ramadorai played an active role in establishing offshore development centres in India to provide high-end quality solutions to major corporations such as HP and GE. Under his leadership, technology excellence centres were set up in India with a vision of remaining abreast with changing technologies at all times.

TCS's internal operational efficiency was given a boost by an enterprise-wide digitisation initiative. One turning point in 1989 was SEGA, a project to design, build and implement on a turnkey basis a new system for the Swiss Corporation for Securities, Clearing and Settlement. The 350 person/year project went live on schedule and established TCS as a global technology partner with unmatched credentials for delivery excellence. This provided a platform for TCS to build India's financial and capital market infrastructure, including the state-of-the-art National Stock Exchange, which is among the biggest exchanges in the world in terms of volume, as well as a national securities depository that made the Indian stock markets paperless.

New horizons emerged for the business, including addressing the Y2K problem before the end of the millennium and developing e-business, BPO and engineering services. TCS's global growth saw an expansion in its client list, its global network and presence, increased interaction with professional groups, and it earned a greater presence in the Indian government on policy matters.

In 2003, TCS became India's first billion-dollar IT services company. The following year, it went public through an initial public offering (IPO) that at that time was the largest ever such offering.

Leadership: 2004–2011

As the Indian economy continued to grow, the need for technology to drive growth became part of the national agenda. TCS, which had been investing in the domestic IT market since its inception, was well positioned to help the government at the central and state levels in its new initiatives. This largest IT company in India was firmly in the spotlight not only as the jewel in the Tata Group's crown but also because of its growing global presence.

Strategic acquisitions were also playing a role to position TCS for future growth. TCS had acquired CMC in 2001, prior to the initial public offering, to expand its presence in the domestic market and joint ventures in the BPO space. In 2005 and 2006, it acquired FNS, an Australian software products firm, and Comicrom, a BPO company in Chile.

Together with other growth initiatives, including expansion into Brazil, Mexico, China and Hungary, and setting up strategic units to pursue new opportunities in the financial services products space or new services like remote infrastructure management and platform-based BPO, TCS set the stage for positioning its brand and its offerings to global customers.

Concurrently, a strong talent localisation initiative was being undertaken: the number of non-Indian employees rapidly increased to over 10,000 at the end of 2008–2009, including 1,200 in China and over 6,000 in Latin America, creating a multinational, multicultural global organisation. The company's greatest asset is its young workforce, whose synergy and vitality extend beyond TCS and into the community. Employee engagement channels like Maitree, for example, offer employees the opportunity to contribute to their communities in a number of ways – education, health care and conservation, among other areas.

Despite its size, TCS has stayed true to its roots of building collaborative models of development, reaching out to work with partners, venture capitalists, academia and government in order to innovate. These reflect the new models of innovation where global teams work virtually to create and build new solutions and ideas. Being at the hub of this system, TCS has been able to leverage its relationships to build a network of innovation labs and create new solutions to address customer challenges.

In 2009, a new leader emerged: N. Chandrasekaran, popularly known as Chandra, assumed charge as the CEO and MD. He had been at the helm of several key strategic transitions at TCS since 2002 when he took over the role as head of global sales. As chief operating officer, he had been the architect of the new organisational structure unveiled in 2008, which created multiple agile business units focusing on domains and markets, as well as built strategic business units in order to pursue new initiatives.

Chandra personifies TCS's commitment to customer satisfaction and high-quality deliverables. Through his experience in a variety of operating roles across TCS, he has built a reputation in the IT services industry for his exceptional ability to build and develop new businesses and nurture long-term relationships. He has also been a champion of software and business quality for the industry.

Under his leadership, TCS pioneered the creation of its unique Global Network Delivery Model across five continents and ventured into new markets, including Europe, China and Latin America, and it added new business lines. At the end of 2009–2010, over 25% of TCS revenues came from new services such as BPO, infrastructure, assurance and asset-leveraged solutions, reflecting the effectiveness of this strategy.

Chandra has also driven domain diversification as TCS has entered new areas like media and information services, as well as high technology. All of these have matured into sizable businesses under his guidance. In 2008, the company went through an internal restructuring exercise designed to bring agility to the organisation. The philosophies of leadership and delivery excellence and the promise of 'experience certainty' are pillars on which the success of TCS is cemented.

Four decades ago, when TCS began to promote the concept of global sourcing in IT and application services, it was a market-defining model. Today it is the mainstream model for the global IT industry. TCS now has the same opportunity to create new business models for the future.

Summary

This chapter explored different supplier configurations and the role of intermediaries in sourcing arrangements. Furthermore, particular attention was given to the core capabilities suppliers should develop to maintain their competitive position and to ensure their ability to provide quality services to their clients.

6

chapter

Supplier Selection, Retained Management Capabilities and Legal Issues

One key factor in achieving success in global sourcing arrangements is the quality of the client–supplier relationship. Selecting the most appropriate service provider is critical to maximising the benefits and minimising the risks associated with the venture. In this chapter, we review the major considerations during the supplier selection:

- Supplier selection: the approach and key considerations
- Which client capabilities need to be developed and retained
- The critical legal and contractual aspects of outsourcing and offshoring.

Supplier Selection: Key Aspects and Considerations

There are two key aspects in a client's decision to outsource: the configuration of the outsourcing arrangement and the market in which the client would like to operate. With regard to the configuration, a client should consider the configuration that will best facilitate the objectives of the firm in this particular sourcing arrangement. Different configuration options (discussed in Chapter 5) are the sole supplier (a single supplier providing the entire service), best of breed (the client organisation plays the role of the head contractor to manage a supplier network), panel (a list of preferred suppliers that work in competition) and the prime contractor model (a supplier network that operates under the control of the head contractor). A firm should examine thoroughly its business needs in comparison to the benefits and risks associated with each configuration model. These are summarised in Table 6.1. If a client firm is engaging in multisourcing, aspects such as interdependencies between services, desired supply base characteristics and service integration responsibility should be carefully assessed (see discussion in Chapter 5).

Market considerations for supplier selection

With regard to the markets in which the client may wish to operate, the client has three main choices to consider about suppliers operating in various settings:

1. *Domestic versus offshore.* When going offshore, most firms tend to use a best-of-breed approach. However, some organisations choose to establish a prime contractor to manage the offshore suppliers. Typical services for which the offshore market has been shown to generate increased cost savings include applications coding, call-centre operations, data entry and transaction processing. Consequently, the offshore market has tended to be rather niche-oriented. However, as the larger offshoring suppliers are expanding the scope of their services as well as the geographical areas they cover, this trend appears to be changing. In doing so, they compete against existing global suppliers. On this issue, in fact, Indian service providers such as Infosys, Wipro and TCS are gaining ground against established global suppliers such as IBM, Accenture and HP. An interesting trend that appears to be emerging in this context is best-shoring – mixing offshore, nearshore and onshore in the same deal. In this way, the supplier locates its resources where they are best deployed, according to the notion of fair quality for a fair price.
2. *Local versus global.* In a majority of the cases where an organisation follows the sole-supplier configuration, global providers are used because of their worldwide reach and the broad scope of services they offer. Such large suppliers have access to more resources and economies of scale and can deal with fluctuations in the demand for services.
3. *Niche versus broad.* Because niche suppliers offer a limited range of services, they are usually deployed in a best-of-breed configuration and are contracted either directly with the customer or indirectly through

TABLE 6.1 Supplier configuration options and associated benefits and risks

Option	Benefits	Risks	Management issues
Sole supplier	Sole accountability Potential for the supplier to create economies of scale, the benefits of which may be passed on to the client Streamlined contracting costs and processes End-to-end key performance metrics	Monopolistic supplier behaviours Compromise quality where the supplier is not best of breed in services, industries or geographical locations	Extensive contract flexibility rights due to dependence on the supplier Independent expertise to avoid solution channelling and ensure value for money
Best of breed	Greater control Flexibility to change suppliers Promotes competition and prevents complacency	Attracting the market for small slices of work Keeping suppliers interested, giving management focus and allocating staff Interdependent services and contracts Integration complexity Tracing accountability	Designing interdependent contracts between independent suppliers Multiparty interface and handover management End-to-end process management is more difficult Multiple life-cycle management

(continued)

TABLE 6.1 Continued

Option	Benefits	Risks	Management issues
Panel	Buy services and assets when required Promotes ongoing competition Prevents complacency	Attracting the market when panel is a pre-qualification and does not guarantee work Adding new panel members or wanting to use suppliers not on the panel	Panel bidding process for work Ongoing ranking of panel members based on performance Managing and evaluating the total programme
Prime contractor	Single point of accountability Allows best-of-breed subcontracting Streamlined, but a bit more complex, contracting costs and processes End-to-end Key Performance Indicators	Prime contractor should be expert at subcontracting (selection, management, disengagement) Client may desire different subcontractors Client is often required to resolve issues between the prime and subcontractors Primes and subcontractors often encroach on each other's 'territories'	Contract ensuring various rights over the subcontracting (access, selection, veto) Compliance auditing ensuring the prime contractor passes obligations to the subcontractors Oversight ensuring all parties are operating as an efficient and unified front

Source: Willcocks et al., 2006.

the prime contractor. The respective advantages of these two types of suppliers are illustrated in Table 6.2.

Supplier-selection process

Most client firms struggle with the supplier-selection process. It is an arduous task that can take months and significant resources. Supplier selection begins with solid preparation: assembling a selection team, defining a detailed process, and acknowledging and scheduling sufficient time to fully evaluate suppliers and supplier responses to the Request for Proposal (RFP) and Scope of Work (SOW). In large deals it might be worth assembling an internal team to bid against external bidders. ABN AMRO applied this tactic in 2005 and was rather successful. While ABN AMRO

TABLE 6.2   Niche versus broad suppliers

Supplier capability	Niche supplier	Broad supplier
Leadership	Supplier leaders will be well known, and there will be easy access to the CEO and straightforward deployment of resources	Harder to contact top management
Planning and contracting	Suppliers have more vested interest in the relationship because they cannot absorb or afford failures	The client should push hard for creative contracts, as suppliers have a greater ability to absorb risk than niche players do
Organisational design	Less formal design is required, and the deal is based more on personal relationships.	Formal organisational design is more important
Process improvement	Niche suppliers may rely less on processes (like Six Sigma, CMM), but make up for this with domain expertise	Broad suppliers may rigidly use CMM
Domain expertise	There will be better domain knowledge because of specialisation, but specific elements of business knowledge will still need to be transferred to the supplier	Clients need to pay special attention to knowledge transfer. Large suppliers can gain domain knowledge through the transfer of relevant employees

Source: Willcocks et al., 2006.

spent quite significantly on the internal team as part of the bidding process, in the end it was the internal team who was able to truly assess the value delivered by the short-listed suppliers and help ABN AMRO executives decide which suppliers were the most promising to meet their expectations.

Assembling the supplier-selection team

This is the first step in the supplier-evaluation process and arguably the most critical. The team should be cross-functional with deep expertise in both core and auxiliary functions that are going to be affected by outsourcing. Typically it would include representatives from IT, production/operations, finance, human resources, legal and quality functions. Each member of the team should be educated and trained in the process of supplier selection and evaluating RFP responses. They should clearly understand their roles and responsibilities within the process, the specifics of the supplier scoring system and the necessity of objectivity and fairness when evaluating suppliers. Overall, the team as a whole should have the same understanding of these principles.

Defining the process

While different companies have different processes and selection criteria, all supplier-evaluation processes should be standardised, fair and well documented. Standardisation is critical for accurate comparisons. Evaluation of suppliers should be based upon the selection criteria and scoring methods, not intuition or personal opinion, or there is a risk of creating bias. While this may seem self-evident, in the real world bias is natural. It is easy for team members to be biased by qualifications or supplier assets beyond the scope of the scoring criteria, especially if these are included in the RFP. Peripheral assets are attractive, but if they are not a part of the evaluation criteria, they are superfluous and should not factor into decision-making. Transparency and documentation in the process also helps to keep it fair and honest. Making accommodations for certain suppliers or erecting barriers will only prevent a client firm from choosing the right supplier(s) for the project. Capturing and distilling information is also critical when it comes to documenting and auditing the selection process. Some organisations – especially government bodies – require documentation of the process for auditing purposes. The information should be readily available whenever needed.

Patience: It is important to give suppliers the opportunity to respond to the RFP. The evaluation process should not be started (beyond a brief look to check for completion) before the deadline for receiving responses has come and gone.

Assessment process

Once all the responses to the RFP have been received, it is time to assess the pool of potential suppliers:

Shortlisting: Depending on the project in question, a company may receive a large number of responses to the RFP. Trying to evaluate each and every proposal in depth can make the process difficult. The initial task is to 'weed out' the good from the bad and reduce the number of potential suppliers to a viable and realistic candidate pool.

Firstly it is advisable to eliminate suppliers that have not submitted their proposals on time or those with proposals that do not, on the face of it, meet the requirements outlined in the RFP. Suppliers who submit incomplete or disorderly responses do not show the standard of care needed for building a solid, long-term business relationship. They can and should be eliminated immediately.

For those that remain, a broad set of criteria should be applied in order to narrow the selection. For instance, if nearshoring is desired, both onshore and offshore suppliers can be eliminated. In another example, the work may call for multiple supplier sources requiring deep, task-specific knowledge. Thus, suppliers with limited to broad knowledge and experience without the specific technical knowledge needed for any single component to the work outlined can be eliminated. At the end of this process, there should be a smaller, more manageable list of suppliers to evaluate more carefully.

Supplier evaluation: This step involves assessing specific supplier capabilities in depth. Here it is important to look at desired attributes, strengths and weaknesses. It is helpful to develop a scorecard, chart, spiderweb chart or other visual means of summarising the desired capabilities. The list of desired attributes varies from business to business, project to project. Some of the core attributes many companies look for in their suppliers are included in Table 6.3.

TABLE 6.3   Weighted scorecard for supplier assessment

Attribute	Score	Weight	Weighted score
Functional capabilities	3	0.2	0.6
Flexibility	4	0.2	0.8
Reputation	4	0.2	0.8
Technical capabilities	5	0.1	0.5
Overall experience	5	0.1	0.5
Stability	3	0.1	0.3
Trust	4	0.1	0.4
Total	28	1.0	3.9

The key attributes for clients to look for in a supplier fall into seven main categories and include the following: reputation, stability, flexibility, trust, functional capabilities, technical capabilities and overall experience. With respect to reputation, it makes sense to look at past personal dealings with the supplier. If the client and supplier firms have any prior business relationship, past experience is a good indicator of what could be expected in the future. A supplier's past track record with similar projects, along with customer satisfaction ratings, can also help determine the potential for success. The supplier could be asked to provide references for clients where projects went well, as well as those where things went less smoothly (see more about supplier capabilities in Chapter 5).

Clients can determine a supplier's stability by looking at staffing practices, attrition rates and company financials. Suppliers should include these measures in their RFP responses as indicators of stability. If company financials are not included in the responses, this should raise a red flag.

Supplier flexibility is indicated by their ability to meet schedule milestones and project deadlines, budgets, and by their change management practices. Suppliers must be flexible enough to adapt to and incorporate changes in the project.

Trust is a soft issue between entities in a business relationship. The client may look at such things as past and pending litigation, disaster-recovery protocols and supplier security to get a feel for the level of trust that is possible. Suppliers with numerous suits and security issues should be avoided.

Functional capabilities are often assessed by looking at project and relationship practices, the amount of resources available for the project, management philosophy and staff expertise. Clients should ask to see the qualifications of staff who would be assigned to handle various aspects of the project. Does the supplier currently have sufficient resources to assign to the project, or would they need to pull in additional resources? What is the state of the labour pool in the supplier's location? Is the supplier's management philosophy one of empowerment or one of constant vigilance by necessity?

Technical capabilities can be measured by looking at the supplier's product development capabilities, quality methodologies and metrics and vertical industry experience. This area should be fully addressed by the supplier's responses to the RFP. Past experience in analogous projects should be looked at, in either scope or detail.

Furthermore, clients should look at the depth and breadth of the supplier's overall experience. Have they served the same or similar industries? How many projects have they handled that are similar in scope?

Depending on the specifics of the outsourcing project, the client firm may consider evaluating all or some of the 12 supplier capabilities (discussed in Chapter 5). It is important to stress that suppliers do not need to demonstrate high levels of performance in all 12 capabilities and all three competencies. For example, if a client contracts with a supplier only to maintain legacy systems, the client is likely to focus on the capabilities related to delivery competency (domain expertise, business management, behaviour management, sourcing, programme management, leadership and governance capabilities) and less on other capabilities. However, if the objective of outsourcing is transformation, then the supplier will need requisite capabilities, including in reengineering and technology exploitation. Along these lines, a firm should identify and focus on the capabilities and competencies that are more relevant to its business when selecting a supplier.

Finally, the assessment team must have a method for keeping score and ranking suppliers. Charting or graphing is an important step. Each team

TABLE 6.4   Supplier attributes and indicators of capabilities

Attribute	Indicator
Reputation	Past dealings Track record Customer satisfaction ratings
Stability	Staffing practices Attrition rates Company financials
Flexibility	Ability to meet schedule and budget Change management practices
Trust	Past and pending litigation Disaster recovery protocols Security
Functional capability	Project and relationship practices and experience Resources available for the project Management philosophy Staff expertise
Technical capability	Product development capabilities Quality methodology/metrics Vertical industry experience
Overall experience	Experience in industry Experience in similar projects scope

member should perform independent assessments of the supplier, and any discrepancies should be worked out through an open exchange of findings and rationale.

In charting, it is important to weight the factors according to importance, based upon assessment of the needs. If the project requires a high degree of technical skill, for example, the technical capabilities attribute should get higher weight than perhaps reputation. Table 6.3 presents a sample scorecard the client can use to assess suppliers on a weighted scale.

It is important to remember that each supplier has unique and distinct advantages and disadvantages that need to be weighed in any evaluation process. Failure to account for these particularities will result in an incomplete analysis of the relationship and its potential for addressing the client's outsourcing needs. Without an idea of the other options available in the market, the client takes a subordinate position in the negotiating process and will be subject to the vagaries of the supplier's needs. For example, if the client has identified a critical need and the particular supplier is only partially capable of fulfilling that need, it would be important to know whether other suppliers are capable of fully satisfying the requirement and what would be the trade-offs.

Proposal evaluation

Evaluating the proposal involves addressing the pricing issue and the quality of the proposal itself. As stated earlier, clients should not choose suppliers with price as the primary focus. Clients who select suppliers based primarily on price need not bother with a detailed assessment process. The old saying, 'You get what you pay for,' applies to those who focus on obtaining the lowest price for products and service. If a detailed assessment is conducted and all other variables point to the supplier with the lowest price, then due diligence has been served.

Take note: clients should be cautious of suppliers whose pricing is significantly lower than the average, or below client expectations. There are three possibilities:

- The supplier is trying to call attention to itself to get an interview
- The supplier has not taken into account all aspects of the project requirements
- There may be financial stability issues, and the supplier is seeking short-term cash flow to correct the issue.

The proposal should also be assessed for completeness, clarity, detail and rigour. Here it is a good practice to use different scorers than those who performed the supplier assessment, in order to eliminate bias. It is also good practice to 'blind' each proposal for the same reason, redacting identifying details. Scorers should assess whether each proposal is complete: that it addresses each element of the RFP in detail. The proposal should also be written with clarity, showing whether each element of the proposal is clearly understood, or whether there is room for misunderstanding and ambiguity.

Due diligence and site visit

While the weighting and scoring technique is helpful to compare suppliers and their proposals and to narrow the list of candidates, due diligence focuses on validating the suppliers' claims. This due-diligence process involves calling references and setting up meetings and a visit with the potential suppliers to get more insight. Due diligence requires the client to validate references, not merely accept them on face value. Clients should ask references about their experience with the supplier, with respect to unforeseen costs, quality of output and adherence to milestones. Clients should also ask the supplier to provide contact information for clients where projects did not run altogether smoothly and find out from those clients how they made the relationship work and how the supplier responded to problems.

Whenever practicable, a visit to a potential supplier's offshore facilities is encouraged. It is the best way to assess the potential of the business relationship. Meetings should revolve around a confirmed agenda and involve a review of company business and project objectives. The visit should be conducted by the assessment team in order for them to get a complete picture for the purpose of making recommendations. Pay attention to the soft elements of the potential relationship: cultural compatibility, values, trust and the feeling of personal fit.

Assessing supplier vulnerabilities

The final stage of the evaluation process consists of an assessment of supplier vulnerabilities. The client must perform a full and documented formal risk assessment at this stage. The assessment team should run through various possible scenarios to seek out the main vulnerabilities for each supplier. A few things to look for include:

- Dependency on one client
- Political instability in the home country
- Adequacy of the supplier financial portfolio
- Debt collection success
- Propensity for innovation in the industry.

The risk assessment should mirror the process used for the supplier evaluation, including a scorecard/chart and weighting. Once the supplier and proposal assessments are complete, the pool of candidates can be reduced to the top scorers. It is a good idea to define beforehand what will constitute an adequate candidate pool, either by number or minimum score.

It is important to remember that between making a final decision about the supplier and signing the contract, the client firm needs to invest significant efforts in negotiations with the selected supplier (or suppliers in the case of multisourcing). We discuss the negotiation process in detail in Chapter 8.

Common mistakes when selecting suppliers

There are six common errors clients often make when engaging in a supplier analysis:

- Being tempted by the 'glamorous' supplier
- Basing the evaluation on cost savings
- Not completing, or poorly completing the risk assessment
- Rushing the process
- Failing to assess cultural fit between suppliers (in multisourcing engagements)
- Failing to balance current and new suppliers.

It can be tempting to go with a high-profile supplier, regardless of their fit with respect to the needs analysis. Many times, the glamour involved with announcing a new partnership with a high-profile supplier is stimulated by the desire for a positive shareholder response with a resultant increase in stock prices. However, this response is temporary and fleeting and should not be a basis for supplier selection. Instead, a client should consider the extent to which the supplier would be willing to exert extra effort for its success. In other words, the willingness of suppliers to deliver to client expectations and above depends also on their desire to work with a particular client.

Again, it is important to emphasise that cost savings should not be used as a decisive factor in the selection or evaluation of a supplier. An outsourcing relationship needs to add value to the organisation and align with the business' strategic goals and advantages, not simply reduce costs.

Without a complete and rigorous risk assessment, the organisation may be exposed to the supplier's vulnerabilities. All relationships bear risk; it is the nature of business and business relationships. However, the client must weigh the individual risks and consciously decide which risks it is willing to accept.

Rushing through the supplier-selection process will result in the incomplete assessment of strengths, capabilities and vulnerabilities, and ultimately lead to poor choices that expose the organisation to risk. Looked at another way, poor supplier choices can significantly impact the bottom line, not only in financial terms but also with respect to reputation and customer satisfaction. In the rush to select a supplier and launch the project, evaluators often fail to 'dig deeper' and simply accept information on face value. For instance, a supplier well known for 'IT development' may not possess the correct IT development capabilities for the project in question. Does the project call for technical capabilities in customised application development or packaged software implementation? Does it involve system or service integration? Without digging deeper, it is difficult to know whether actual supplier capabilities fulfil the needs analysis for the project. As one CIO put it simply: 'Never set up Christmas as the deadline to complete the selection process.'

One area that is often neglected is the consideration of the cultural fit between suppliers, if multisourcing. Naturally, clients focus on assessing whether there is a cultural fit between the client organisation and the supplier. However, the client must also look at how the potential supplier will work with current suppliers with whom it already has developed relationships. This is even more important if collaboration is expected between them. Suppliers that are expected to work together need to have an adequate degree of cultural fit to foster cooperation and meet critical milestones. Ideally, there should be a degree of balance between cooperation and healthy competition. Healthy competition will promote a sense of urgency in getting the work done and enhance the quality of the work performed. However, too much competition will only hinder cooperation, so a solid assessment and management of supplier interactions is required.

Finally, many client organisations fail to maintain a balance between using current and new suppliers. Whenever a new project arises, organisations must decide whether to solicit proposals from current suppliers or new suppliers. There is a trade-off involved. Current suppliers offer a level of trust, comfort and predictability not available with new suppliers. On the other hand, new suppliers can offer innovative, bespoke solutions, may work harder to build a long-term relationship, and inject renewed enthusiasm into current supplier relationships by promoting an atmosphere of competition. However, it must be said that the risks are significantly greater when choosing a new supplier.

When making the choice between the two, we suggest clients avoid unnecessary risks. It is costly to bring in new suppliers: they must be trained, acclimated and brought into the fold, which requires significantly more client resources than needed when selecting from the current supplier pool. A new supplier is more appropriate under the following circumstances:

- When terminating a current supplier relationship
- When a current supplier has become lax or lackadaisical
- To inject vigour or a sense of renewed competition among current suppliers.

Client attractiveness, through the supplier's eyes

However, the matter at hand is not only about a client who is choosing a supplier. Suppliers also assess the attractiveness of potential clients before deciding whether to engage in an outsourcing relationship. Several factors can make a client more attractive than others for a supplier: the prestige of the customer; the degree to which the client CEO is involved in the venture; the size of the project; the potential for additional supplier revenues; the opportunity to enter new markets or business; or the opportunity to acquire new knowledge. Furthermore, the supplier's desire to obtain business from a particular customer may depend on the sales targets of the supplier's headquarters. By this, we mean that a supplier may take business from a client even when the terms and conditions of this contract are not in the supplier's favour but are mainly to meet its sales figures. In the case where the supplier is satisfied with its current revenue stream, it is likely that the supplier will be cautious in attracting business when the terms of the contract are not in its favour. The following case illustrates the importance of long-term decision-making in outsourcing and the consequences for the parties when circumstances change.

JPMorgan Chase: To Outsource or Not Outsource?

In 2002, JPMorgan Chase (JPMorgan) and IBM Global Services (IBM) signed a contract. The deal, to extend over seven years, was worth US$5 billion, which made it the largest outsourcing contract at the time. In August 2004, one month after JPMorgan merged with Bank One, JPMorgan cancelled the contract with IBM. Austin A. Adams, chief information officer for JPMorgan, said, 'After a rigorous review, the merged firm concluded it has significant scale, enhanced capabilities, tools and processes to build its own global infrastructure and services organisation.'

JPMorgan was not new to outsourcing. The bank had previously contracted with IBM in 1995, and in 1996 it contracted with a group of suppliers including Computer Sciences Operations (CSC), Anderson Consulting, AT&T Solutions and Bell Atlantic to manage its data centres, desktops, networks and some corporate applications in the USA and Europe. Clearly JPMorgan had developed strong client capabilities that allowed it to manage its suppliers as well as ensure that suppliers delivered value in line with the bank's business strategic road map.

Two years after the start of the contract, JPMorgan had merged with Bank One, the largest player in the consumer banking business, in order to reduce its dependence on investment banking. Bank One, however, had a history of contract termination with IT suppliers. Indeed, in 2001, it had terminated a service contract with IBM and AT&T and, following this, successfully centralised its IT systems. Clearly, Bank One's management believed that the bank needed to keep its IT capability in-house. Outsourcing IT was not part of its sourcing philosophy.

While Bank One was restructuring its IT function in-house, JPMorgan decided to outsource its IT infrastructure to IBM with the aim of cutting costs and centralising the IT function. JPMorgan shortlisted three suppliers in the search for an IT services provider – IBM, EDS and CSC – and finally chose IBM as a sole supplier. On 30 December 2002, JPMorgan and IBM signed the outsourcing contract. The contract specified that a large part of JPMorgan's IT services infrastructure, which included data centres, help desks and data and voice networks, would be transferred to IBM. JPMorgan would retain application delivery and development, desktop support and other functions in-house. It was also expected that IBM would help and host mission-critical functions such as trading applications for the securities side of the banking giant's operations. Under the contract, IBM would deliver a somewhat new service: on-demand computing services. This meant that JPMorgan could buy and pay for only the IT services they used instead of buying fixed IT services and paying fixed prices. The contract also included the transfer of approximately 4,000 IT employees to IBM. This transfer of employees was planned to take place during the first half of 2003. Indeed, the transfer of employees and IT assets began in April 2003 and was completed by January 2004. By then, work had begun on consolidating data centres, upgrading hardware and setting up a common networking infrastructure. This was scheduled to take two years to complete.

A year after the 4,000 IT staff had been transferred to IBM and two years into the contract, JPMorgan decided to backsource the IT functions that it had outsourced and bring the entire IT staff back home.

In retrospect, should JPMorgan have outsourced its IT infrastructure at all?

Client Sourcing Capabilities: The Retained IT Function

In Chapter 5, we examined the supplier capabilities that client firms should assess carefully when deciding on their sourcing strategy. In this section, we focus on the capabilities that a client firm should retain (in their IT function) to ensure that it can exploit the business advantages of technology over time. Willcocks and Feeny (2006), in revisiting their earlier research (Feeny and Willcocks, 1998), identify nine such capabilities:

1. *IT leadership*. This capability is related to the challenge of integrating IT efforts with business goals and practices. A major activity for

leadership is to devise organisational arrangements in terms of governance, structures, processes and staffing, with the aim of managing their interdependencies in a way that does not constrain or inhibit the value delivered by the IT function. Leaders can also influence perceptions with regard to the role of IT and its contribution to organisational processes and practices. Furthermore, they can establish strong business and IT relationships at the executive level and exploit them for the creation of a shared IT vision.

2. *Business systems thinking.* This capability is related to the challenge of envisioning the business process in terms of its functions, efficacy and utility as a result of technology. A business systems thinker is capable of building and communicating holistic views of current organisational activities as a basis to identify new patterns that will generate the optimal integration of strategy, process, technology, systems and people.

3. *Relationship building.* This capability is related to the challenge of getting the business engaged in IT issues in a constructive way. It is important to note that while the business systems thinker is concerned with the integrated business or IT thinking, relationship building is concerned with the wider communication between business and IT communities. More specifically, relationship building involves helping users understand the potential of IT for the creation of value, helping users and IT experts collaborate, and ensuring users' ownership and satisfaction. For most organisations, this is a major challenge resulting from the difference in culture between 'techies' and 'users'. Role holders with this capability have to facilitate a shared purpose and constructive communication among people engaged in the business and IT function.

4. *Architectural planning and design.* This capability is related to the challenge of creating a coherent design of a technical platform that will be able to support current and future business needs. People holding this role are involved in shaping the IT architecture and infrastructure by envisioning the type of technical platform that will best serve the firm's business and by formulating policies and processes that will ensure integration, flexibility and efficiency in IT services. The principal challenge for the architect planner is to ensure that the organisation is up-to-date with technology trends and is consistently able to operate from an efficient IT platform.

5. *Making technology work.* This capability is associated with the challenge of achieving rapid technical progress. The capability of making technology work lies in the overlap between the challenges of IT architecture design and the delivery of IT services. The role of technology 'fixers' is to manage problems associated with IT and figure out how to address business needs that cannot be sufficiently facilitated by standard technical approaches. Even organisations that are engaged in total outsourcing acknowledge the need to retain this sort of capability.

6. *Informed buying.* This capability is related to the challenge of managing the IT outsourcing strategy in a way that meets the interests, priorities and goals of the business. People involved in this role are concerned with different tasks, including analysis and benchmarking of the external market for IT providers; the design of a five- to ten-year sourcing strategy; and tender leadership, contracting, and management processes of the sourcing venture.

7. *Contract facilitation.* This capability is associated with the need to manage and govern the relationship between suppliers and business users. Along these lines, the contract facilitator aims to ensure the success of existing contracts for IT services and to provide a major point of reference through which problems and conflicts are resolved promptly and efficiently. From our experience, the need for this role is rarely identified at the beginning of the outsourcing relationship. It tends to emerge as a response to ongoing issues such as users' requesting more services or changes, the need to coordinate multiple suppliers or the need to monitor service delivery.

8. *Contract monitoring.* This capability concerns the protection of the current and future contractual position of the firm. It involves the development and maintenance of a robust contract as a fundamental element in the governance of the outsourcing relationship. It is important to note that while the contract facilitator is mainly involved in the day-to-day operations, the contract monitor ensures that the business position is contractually protected at all times. The supplier is assessed against both the standards in the contract and external benchmarks.

9. *Supplier development.* This capability is about ensuring value-adding activities within the outsourcing relationship. The person concerned with the growth of this capability seeks to cultivate and enhance the long-term potential of suppliers to add value to the firm's operations. One major goal in supplier development is to create a win-win situation

where the client receives increased value-adding services and the supplier generates better revenues and learning opportunities. One of the hidden risks of outsourcing is the costs incurred in changing suppliers. When taking into account such a risk, it would be in the client's interest to maximise the value-adding activities from its suppliers while guarding against 'midcontract sag', where the supplier meets the delivery criteria of the contract but only to the minimum required.

Figure 6.1 illustrates these nine capabilities, as well as the way in which their combination contributes to the delivery of the four fundamental tasks of the IT function:

1. *Governance.* This task refers to the dynamic alignment of the activities of the IT function with those of the overall organisation.
2. *Business and function vision.* This is a demand-driven task associated with defining the systems, information and processes needed. This task is also geared towards exploiting such business components to improve business efficiency.

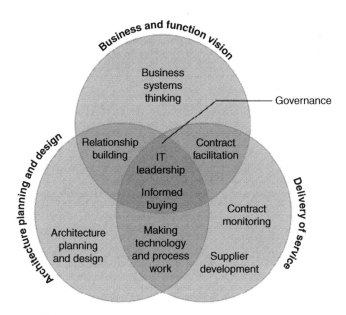

FIGURE **6.1** Nine core management capabilities for retained IT function
Source: Willcocks and Feeny, 2006.

3. *Architecture planning and design.* This task is supply driven and associated with defining the architecture of the evolving technical platform and dealing with the risks related to non-routine technical issues.
4. *Delivery of service.* This task is concerned with managing the sourcing strategy. It seeks to investigate and understand the external market and involves the ability to select, engage and manage third-party IT resources and service delivery.

Client organisations use primarily three mechanisms to identify and develop capabilities: certain organisational processes, the firm's culture and the firm's structure. Table 6.5 illustrates how capabilities emerge as a result of an organisation's processes, culture and structure and presents some examples.

Retaining these management capabilities in-house is critical for the client because these capabilities offer more control over the firm's IT operations. However, developing a high-performing (retained) IT function is not free of challenges. Growing popularity of cloud services and the

TABLE 6.5   Organisational mechanisms for building capabilities

Mechanism	Definition	Examples
Processes	Capabilities emerge from problem-defining and problem-solving routines interwoven with individual skills. At a higher level, these are formally combined into organisational processes	IT governance Strategic IT planning Contract reviews and market testing IT investment reviews Process models (e.g., ITIL) Compliance
Culture	Capabilities emerge from links across a mosaic of organisational elements, such as incentive plans, operating systems, corporate culture or behaviour-shaping practices	Career models Reward and recognition Competencies Service orientation
Structure	Capabilities emerge as a key product of the organisation as an entire system. In other words, capabilities are embedded in organisational processes and are bounded by the structure of the organisation	IT organisational model Group CIO reporting line Business-unit IS function reporting lines Roles and responsibilities

Source: Willcocks et al., 2007.

future projections for expansion in cloud adoption and deployment require client firms to think about building retained capabilities with cloud considerations in mind. Below we discuss five major challenges for building management capabilities to retain in-house and highlight the impact of the projected cloud-based future that client organisations should prepare for.

1. *The human resource challenge.* The nine roles that have already been illustrated and associated with each of the nine retained management capabilities demand high performers. Each role requires a mix of business, technical and interpersonal skills (these are summarised in Table 6.6). In practice, recruitment and retention of the small high-quality group described in Table 6.6 has always been a challenge. Cloud has just made it that much harder – cloud skills were running at a 20–40% premium throughout 2011–2014 and the skills shortages have indeed slowed client organisations in their ability to adopt cloud technologies, especially where they also have to compete with suppliers.

2. *The supplier challenge.* In specific projects and services, suppliers need complementary rather than competing or duplicating skills. Furthermore, it is important to create a climate of cooperation between the in-house management team and the supplier groups. Taking into account the multisourcing trend, a supplier's ability to cooperate with other suppliers is of great significance for the performance of the venture.

3. *The perennial challenge: relationships.* The way the relationship between the supplier and the client evolves is a critical element that can affect the success of the project. For example, one element that affects the way the relationship evolves is the power balance between the two partners. Maintaining good relationships throughout the outsourcing project is extremely challenging because power is likely to shift from the client to the supplier over time. While it is expected that both clients and suppliers will exploit this power position, there should be a tipping point in which the goodwill and future development of the relationship is not diminished.

4. *The project management challenge.* In dynamic business environments, there is an increased need for appropriate project management skills. Project management must be an organisational core capability and not an asset of a particular division or department. In the retained management capabilities framework (see Figure 6.1 and Table 6.6), candidates for the project manager role are most

TABLE 6.6 Skills for retained management capabilities in traditional and cloud-based IT function

Core retained capability	New cloud challenge	Description	Business (B), technical (T) and interpersonal (I) skills	Time horizons
IT leadership	Integrates the technology – cloud effort with business purpose and activity	Cloud staffing Cloud business strategy Technology function redesign Cloud project oversight Innovation through cloud	B: High T: Medium I: High	Future and Present
Business systems thinking	Ensures that technology – cloud capabilities are envisioned in every business process	Cloud fit and timing Cloud projects to support business objectives Relationships with business executives	B: High T: Medium I: Medium	Future
Relationship building	Gets the business constructively engaged in operational cloud technology issues	Cloud operational business leverage Business education	B: Medium T: High I: High	Present
Architecture planning and design	Creates the coherent blueprint for a technical platform that responds to present and future needs	Cloud strategy Cloud technology and business alignment Systems integration Cloud project planning New security/data issues	B: Low to Medium T: High I: Medium	Future
Making technology and processes work	Rapidly troubleshoot problems which are being disowned by others across the technical supply chain	Apposite IaaS, SaaS, PaaS skills Broader technical skills base 'Fixing' role in cloud projects	B: Low to Medium T: High I: Low to Medium	Present

(continued)

TABLE 6.6 Continued

Core retained capability	New cloud challenge	Description	Business (B), technical (T) and interpersonal (I) skills	Time horizons
Informed buying	Manages the cloud technology sourcing strategy to meet the needs of the business	Cloud market knowledge Matching business demand with cloud supply Cloud supplier contracting and management	B: High T: Medium I: High	Present and Future
Contract facilitation	Ensures the success of existing contracts for external cloud technology services	Cloud service development and integration Cloud product manager Fast service delivery	B: Medium T: Medium I: High	Present
Contract monitoring	Protects the business's contractual position present and future	Cloud SLA assurance Regulatory implications Cloud security issues	B: Medium T: Medium I: Low to Medium	Present and Future
Supplier development	Identifies the potential added value from cloud technology service suppliers	Expanding cloud supplier service capabilities Maturing strategic cloud relationships Securing future innovation and value added from cloud deployment	B: High T: Medium I: Medium to High	Future

Source: Based on Willcocks, Venters and Whitley, 2014.

likely to be found among relationship builders and technology fixers; but clearly business systems thinkers, leaders, architects and
informed buyers must have very active roles in projects with a
strong technology/cloud component. In practice, project management capability is often rebuilt in the face of large-scale outsourcing,
especially where IT-enabled business transformation is on the
agenda.

5. *Rising challenges.* IT security has moved up the organisational agenda
   not only because of the increased security risks arising from increased
   offshoring but also because of the growing concern of hacking and
   potential terrorism. Along these lines, there is a need to retain internal capability around security. On this issue, the senior IT executive of
   a multinational company suggested, 'Clearly we don't want to do security administration. We are happy for that to be outsourced. But all the
   monitoring and compliance, all that sort of thing, we believe we need
   to keep a pretty tight control over.'

Legal Issues

The legal issues that arise in sourcing arrangements are numerous. Some of
the most common ones are related to confidentiality, security, intellectual
property (IP) and compliance.

Confidentiality

Both the customer and the supplier will want to protect their confidential
information during their sourcing partnership. For this reason, each party
should examine what information it regards as confidential and what safeguards it should implement. These issues should be carefully considered by
both parties and resolved before the agreement is signed. In practice, both
clients and suppliers appear to underestimate these issues and can run into
serious problems.

It is important to note that issues with regard to the confidentiality of data
are more likely to arise on termination. Often in such situations, the client
will attempt to ensure access to information required for continuation of
uninterrupted service by either the retained organisation or a subsequent

supplier. Similarly, the supplier will attempt to protect its proprietary procedures and information, which can be seen as distinctive competences critical for its competitive position.

Security

The security requirements of the sourcing partners will vary significantly from one arrangement to another depending on the nature of the customer's business, the personal data being processed and the services being sourced. For example, it may be compulsory to include a commitment to comply with specific security standards.

The following lists present examples of common security issues and the means to address them (based on Lewis, 2006):

Data security
- Securing access to data to validated and authorised employees
- Taking all reasonable steps to ensure that outsourcing employees cannot and do not copy data
- Ensuring appropriate levels of authorised access with audit trails of all access being provided
- Providing access rights standards
- Holding data in a manner compliant with all legislation and best practice guidance
- Having detailed written procedures for data handling
- Keeping data separate from other companies' data
- Ensuring that data is not corrupted by other companies' data
- Ensuring that data is held in secure storage on appropriately licensed software
- Ensuring that data is held on appropriate hardware that is physically and technically secured.

Staff security
- Appropriate security checking of all authorised personnel
- Using only validated contract staff to maintain physical or technical security and access
- Periodically checking that authorised personnel are following designated procedures
- Ensuring that new staff sign protocol and procedural documentation.

Backups and disaster recovery
- Keeping all data appropriately backed up
- Having appropriate disaster-recovery plans and recovery procedures in place
- Periodically testing all disaster-recovery plans
- Documenting disaster-recovery procedures and ensuring that valid recovery contracts are in place.

Hardware
- Ensuring that all hardware is maintained in an appropriate secure location
- Ensuring that correct power, air-conditioning and fire prevention are available with hardware
- Providing a validated hardware list to the customer
- Allowing the client to inspect and query the hardware used
- Conforming to any legislative or procedural requirements for physical equipment maintenance
- Ensuring that data is removed in a secure manner from redundant, broken or otherwise damaged equipment
- Providing a log of the procedures for removing data from equipment
- Ensuring that equipment is swept before it leaves the supplier's premises.

Security documentation
- Providing physical and technical access logs to the client
- Providing procedures for ensuring that no physical or technical breach of security occurs
- Providing reports on any security breach together with remedial action taken
- Documenting all security procedures including reporting procedures for breach of security.

Intellectual property

IP rights are also of major concern to the client and supplier. These refer to the rights that have been given to people over the creations of their minds: literary, musical or artistic works; inventions; symbols; names; images, and so on. The key forms of IP are patents, copyrights, trademarks and trade secrets. IP shares many of the characteristics of physical property, and thus is treated as an asset that can become the object of different forms of transactions (buying, selling, licensing, etc.).

IP protection and enforcement mechanisms differ by country. For this reason, offshoring arrangements can become particularly complicated in managing IP issues. In addition, courts in different parts of the world operate under different laws and regulations and often give conflicting judgements. In these judgements there is regularly evidence of bias that is associated with the country in which each company domiciles (courts tend to favour companies residing in their respective countries). Along these lines, companies (from both the client's and the supplier's side) should be particularly careful, because the absence of suitable contractual safeguards can put at risk the firm's rights to its own IP.

Baldia (2007) suggests that IP concerns are particularly important in the case of knowledge process outsourcing (KPO), and that IP ownership, IP violation and issues related to confidentiality and privacy must be carefully addressed in every KPO venture. According to Baldia, in any KPO venture, a client must:

- Perform careful legal due diligence on national and local IP regulations
- Examine the legal issues that arise in relation to the specific KPO arrangement
- Take appropriate action (measures and safeguards) to protect the firm from losing its IP rights.

Compliance

Both the customer and the supplier need to ensure that they operate in compliance with the wider legal framework. For example, with regard to data protection, the sourcing partners will need to ensure that they comply with their respective obligations under the Data Protection Act (DPA) 1998 and that they follow its principles (based on Lewis, 2006):

1. Personal data shall be processed fairly and lawfully
2. Personal data shall be obtained only for one or more specified and lawful purposes and shall not be further processed in any manner incompatible with that purpose or those purposes
3. Personal data shall be adequate, relevant and not excessive in relation to the purpose or purposes for which they are processed
4. Personal data shall be accurate and, where necessary, kept up-to-date

5. Personal data processed for any purpose or purposes shall not be kept for longer than is necessary for that purpose or those purposes
6. Personal data shall be processed in accordance with the rights of data subjects under the DPA
7. Appropriate technical and organisational measures shall be taken against unauthorised or unlawful processing of personal data and against accidental loss or destruction of, or damage to, personal data
8. Personal data shall not be transferred to a country or territory outside the European Economic Area unless that country or territory ensures an adequate level of protection for the rights and freedoms of data subjects in relation to the processing of the personal data.

Another example of a wider regulation with significant legal implications for sourcing arrangements (more specifically outsourcing arrangements in the financial sector) is the Markets in Financial Instruments Directive (MIFID), an EU directive that came into force in November 2007. The principal objective of MIFID has been to harmonise the operations of the financial sector throughout the European Community. MIFID was intended to replace the Investment Service Directive and, unlike its predecessor, has been explicit in addressing outsourcing governance within the financial industry. More specifically, MFID outlines the obligations of each party in relation to the outsourcing relationship and identifies detailed rules on the steps that firms need to take to comply with these rules.

On this basis, MIFID has significant governance implications for existing and future IT outsourcing relationships. Firms currently in IT outsourcing relationships need to address the MFID regulatory requirements and take appropriate action for renewal, renegotiation or change of existing contracts. Firms intending to enter into new IT outsourcing relationships need to focus on issues of governance.

The Contract

A key mechanism for dealing with legal issues that arise in the supplier–client relationship is the contract. In essence, the contract sets a framework for the sourcing relationship by defining objectives and responsibilities, as well as the processes and procedures to be followed by the partners. In terms of contractual agreements between client and supplier companies, most popular ones are *time-and-materials, fees-for-service, fixed-price*[1] and *partnership-based* (e.g., *joint-venture*) contracts. These contract types support different pricing models of services delivered by the supplier and rely on different measurement instruments to indicate whether contract conditions have been met.

Time-and-materials contracts. These rely on a fixed hourly or daily fee and the costs of the materials that the supplier needs to purchase to accomplish the work. Under this contract, the supplier typically provides services that complement the customer's capabilities and the service delivery is managed in-house. This is the most common sourcing model and poses the least risk to the client. A common example is consulting projects, such as the implementation of an ERP system.

Fixed-price contracts. These specify a fixed fee for large work packages (e.g., a fixed monthly or annual fee for the maintenance of a portfolio of applications or systems) to agreed SLAs, regardless of how much time the supplier will spend on this work package in a given period of time. Such contracts are also popular for the one-off implementation and integration of IT projects, where clients prefer a fixed fee for project completion. Such contracts often lead to win-lose situations. For example, the supplier 'wins' if the amount of time it eventually spends on the maintenance of the client's systems is lower than the estimated workload when the fixed fee was calculated. However, the supplier might 'lose' if the actual amount of work is, in the end, higher than the estimate.

Fee-for-service contracts. These specify fixed fees for small well-defined work packages, often referred to as *tickets*, which rely on actual rather than estimated volumes of work. *Tickets* are associated with instances in which the supplier needs to provide help (i.e., to resolve a problem). Per-ticket service contracts are measured by SLAs that specify the time for resolving a problem. Such contracts usually have a breakdown of fees per ticket, specifying a different fixed fee per ticket for different volumes of tickets. For example, for the first 50 tickets, a client will pay US$1 per ticket and if the number of tickets exceeds 50, the client will pay 80 cents per ticket. The breakdown of fees and ticket volumes captured in the contract provides the supplier with incentives to invest in various improvement initiatives that may reduce ticket volumes. This may result in savings for the client and better margins for the supplier.

Joint-venture (JV) contracts. These are one of the most popular partnership-based contracts. In this partnership model the contract defines how client and supplier firms contribute resources to the new venture and states how profits will be shared. The partners define the mission and objectives for the joint venture, provide funding, initial physical assets, intellectual capital, staff members and management capabilities. In most cases, the strategic objectives behind the formation of a joint venture include overcoming entry barriers into new markets, faster access to new markets and new technologies, economies of scale, risk sharing and getting access to complementary assets (tangible and intangible) located outside its boundaries (Koh and Venkatraman, 1991; Hennart, 1988), as well as pursuing an offshoring strategy at lower risks and costs associated with setting up an offshore captive centre. When the client and service provider form a joint venture, they are usually pursuing one of the following goals:

- Setting us a *new business venture* aiming at developing new and innovative solutions and services for the clients' vertical markets, Such JV often take the form of an offshore development centre that has a similar mission as a captive offshore R&D centre for the purpose of developing new products or services. Profit sharing incorporated in the contractual agreement keeps both parties engaged and motivated to maximise the profits. The joint venture between Indian supplier Tata Consultancy Services and Teknosoft Swiss-based financial services firm that focused on development and implementation of the Quartz banking platform is an example of a JV that pursue new business opportunity.
- *The transformation of large-scale complex business functions and processes of the client firm.* Risk sharing helps clients to deal with the uncertainty and complexity of the changes and for the supplier it provides motivation to perform well to materialise the profit-sharing option. The agreement between the Commonwealth Bank of Australia and Electronic Data Systems formed in 1997 to manage the bank's IT and processing activities is one example of such a joint venture.

Although the contract plays a fundamental role in the management and governance of the sourcing relationship, it cannot encapsulate all the contingencies that may occur. For this reason, although the role of the contract is critical in the creation of legal boundaries between the partners, the management of the venture goes beyond the legal reach of the contract to rely on the actual relationship between the sourcing partners.

An illustrative landmark case of contract, relationship and performance issues is provided by the BSkyB versus EDS judgement in early 2010, as introduced in the 'BskyB: The bumpy road of outsourcing' case study included in Chapter 1. We elaborate here on the contractual aspects of this trial: In February 2000, Sky announced its £50 million project to create a world-class customer relationship management system at its contact centres in Scotland. EDS was selected as the software supplier and systems integrator in July 2000. A contract worth £48 was signed in November 2000 setting out EDS's obligations as the systems integrator. Early delays and problems led to the parties amending their original contract in July 2001 to give EDS more favourable terms. However, poor performance continued. Sky eventually removed EDS and assumed the role of systems integrator in March 2002. The system was finally completed by Sky in March 2006 at an estimated cost of £265 million.

Sky sought compensation from EDS, ultimately leading to Sky issuing court proceedings against EDS in August 2004 for multiple claims, including fraudulent and negligent misrepresentation and breach of contract. Sky alleged that, as a result of EDS's wrongful conduct, it was fraudulently induced to award the contract to EDS. But for the misrepresentations by EDS, Sky argued that it would have contracted with one of the other bidders who would have successfully implemented the project earlier and at a lower cost overall.

The court held that EDS did not carry out a 'proper exercise of planning, sequencing and resourcing' to determine whether it could comply with the time frame. The court also found EDS liable in the tort of deceit, because misrepresentation as to the time it would take to deliver the system had been made by the managing director of the relevant division of EDS, who knew it was false. For EDS, one of the consequences of being found liable for fraudulent misrepresentation was that the contractual cap of £30 million on its liabilities in relation to the project was no longer effective. As a result, EDS was likely to have to pay damages in excess of £200 million. As an additional claim, Sky alleged that EDS made further misrepresentations prior to the parties agreeing to amend the contract in mid-2001. Sky claimed that EDS falsely represented that it 'had a programme plan that was achievable and the product of proper analysis and re-planning'. Sky argued that the plan was unrealistic and was not based on proper investigation and planning. The court accepted Sky's argument and held

EDS liable for negligent misstatement. The court also found that, having amended the original contract, EDS 'failed properly to resource the project', did not adhere to contractual deadlines and ultimately made minimal progress. At the end, EDS was ordered to pay BskyB £200 million of damages.

For clients, the case is a highly useful reminder of the need to vet suppliers' claims carefully, assess risks comprehensively and pursue contract breaches more vigorously (Moreover, adoption of a thorough life-cycle approach to outsourcing which we discuss in detail in Chapter 8 would mean that cases such as BSkyB versus EDS would rarely get to court due to the application of effective management processes). The case reminds suppliers of their duty of care in bid preparation and submission and suggests the importance of such practices as internal peer review and capability checks and motivating and incentivising sales teams appropriately. In this case, the role of systems integrator also needed more careful delineation. A key point from this example is the need to take extra care when drafting limitation clauses in ITO and BPO contracts and settlement agreements, both of which were found to be partially ineffective in this case.

Summary

This chapter has reviewed various aspects that a client firm needs to consider when selecting a supplier and rebuilding management capabilities of their retained IT function. Although the selection process of a partner is critical for the long-term success of the outsourcing venture, understanding which capabilities the IT function should retain will need to eliminate, develop or acquire has proven to be no less challenging. As in marriage, understanding the legal implications, in case things go wrong, remains an abiding necessity.

7

Leveraging Knowledge and Expertise

What happens to knowledge when an organisation outsources or off-shores? Despite the rapid growth of ITO and BPO, there is still a considerable time lapse on grasping the implications for knowledge and expertise management in these processes. Organisations often have a limited understanding of how new knowledge can be created and exploited, especially when outsourced activities are considered non-core services. In the current outsourcing market, as client companies become evermore demanding, suppliers are increasingly competing on leveraging knowledge-related value.

In this chapter, we discuss what happens to knowledge and expertise in outsourcing arrangements, and how to realise benefits of knowledge creation and exploitation to achieve better performance and innovation. We focus mainly on the following topics:

- How organisations leverage knowledge in outsourcing relationships
- How supplier firms integrate diverse domains of expertise to facilitate knowledge transfer between on-site and offshore teams and across projects
- Managing expertise within and between projects.

Integrating Knowledge and Outsourcing Strategy

Researchers find that client organisations that engage in ITO often make inadequate investments in retaining core knowledge capabilities, which sometimes lead them to lose control over the destiny of their IT function and can result in belated re-insourcing of these capabilities. In BPO, which is often conducted on a fee-for-service basis, knowledge implications are just as often neglected, although they may well be disguised by improvements in real cost and service (Willcocks et al., 2004; Willcocks, Oshri and Hindle, 2009).

Quinn (1999) advises companies to develop an integrated knowledge and outsourcing strategy to mitigate these risks. The key is to identify and build up selected areas of a company's competitive strength to a best-in-world level. The most effective core competency strategies focus on a few cross-functional, intellectually based service activities, or knowledge and skill sets critical to customers. Such strategies allow the company to build selective specialised capabilities and provide a flexible platform for future innovations. Quinn points out that at least one of these competencies should be related to the notion of customer and market knowledge. On such a basis, integrating knowledge and outsourcing strategy into organisational core competency strategies will enable companies to:

- Focus and flatten their organisations by concentrating their limited resources on a relatively few knowledge-based core competencies through which they can develop best-in-world capabilities
- Leverage their internal innovation capabilities through effective personnel, IT and motivational links to outside knowledge sources
- Eliminate the inflexibilities of fixed overheads, bureaucracy and physical plant by conscientiously tapping the more nimble resources of both their customer chain downstream and their technology and supply chain upstream
- Expand their own knowledge and physical investment capabilities by several orders of magnitude through exploiting the facilities and programme investments of outside sources.

Leveraging knowledge through intellectual and social capital

How do companies effectively tap into knowledge sources from outsourcing suppliers? Willcocks et al. (2004, 2009) argue that outsourcers should have knowledge management strategies that enable the creation and exploitation of intellectual capital. Creating intellectual capital is more than simply hiring bright people or buying knowledge management software. Stewart (2001) suggests that three essential elements or assets contribute to the development of intellectual capital:

- Structural capital, which refers to the codified bodies of semi-permanent knowledge that can be transferred and the tools that augment the body of knowledge by bringing relevant data or expertise to people
- Human capital, which represents the capabilities of the individuals to provide solutions to customers
- Customer capital, which is linked to shared knowledge, or the value of an organisation's relationships with the people with whom it does business.

The mere possession of these assets is not enough. Intellectual capital can be generated only through the interplay between these essential elements. Therefore, as Willcocks et al. (2009) suggest, there should be a fourth kind of capital, *social capital,* which helps to bring these elements together and encourages interplay among them. Examples of social capital are trust, loyalty and reciprocity within a community, that is, the values created from social networks. There is a reciprocal relationship between social capital and intellectual capital: the former facilitates the development of the latter, which in turn strengthens the former.

Social capital has three dimensions: structural, cognitive and relational. Since social capital to a great extent involves social connections, mutual respect, shared identity and culture, trust, and common motivation, organisations are in a better position to generate these qualities than markets are. However, outsourcing often disrupts and reduces social capital by dis-embedding people, systems and institutional knowledge from the client organisation. Therefore, attention should be paid to cultivating social capital.

Rottman (2008) conducted a case study with a US manufacturer and its offshore outsourcing partner in India. Using the three dimensions of social capital, he derived eight practices from the case study that facilitate effective knowledge transfer:

Structural (network ties and configuration)

1. Use multiple suppliers to strengthen network ties and increase social networks
2. Increase network use and frequency, and maintain multiple connections by breaking projects into small segments
3. Ensure knowledge retention and transfer by requiring suppliers to have shadows for key supplier roles

Cognitive (shared goals and culture)

4. Strengthen cultural understanding by visiting the offshore suppliers and meeting project teams
5. Clarify goals by communicating the offshore strategy to all parties
6. Integrate the suppliers' employees into the client's development team
7. Co-train internal employees and supplier employees to communicate goals and increase cultural awareness

Relational (trust)

8. Increase internal trust by understanding and managing the talent pipeline.

Rottman shows in the case study that managing the structural, cognitive and relational dimensions of the relationship allowed the partners in the strategy alliance to increase network stability, reduce cultural barriers, share and understand common goals, and strengthen network ties.

Knowledge Transfer between On-Site and Offshore Teams

To leverage the value of knowledge and expertise of both sides in an offshore partnership, a crucial element is to ensure effective knowledge transfer between on-site and offshore teams. Knowledge that is not transferred gets lost. This is relevant to both *captive offshoring* or *offshore outsourcing* settings. In captive offshoring, on-site and offshore teams belong to the client organisation, and knowledge transfer is typically from the on-site team to the offshore team. In offshore outsourcing, there are client and supplier organisations involved, which makes knowledge transfer more complicated, as it is typically the on-site supplier team who works closely with client personnel to acquire relevant client knowledge and then engage with the offshore supplier team to refine and codify this knowledge. In different outsourcing engagements, the offshore supplier team may be more or less actively engaged in direct communications with client personnel during the knowledge transfer.

Despite advances in information and communication technologies, breakdowns in the transfer of knowledge across distributed sites still constitute a major challenge. Oshri and associates identified that the following factors contribute to the difficulty of transferring knowledge between remote sites, especially across national boundaries:

- The diversity of local contexts, which exacerbates the 'stickiness' of information, a notion developed by von Hippel (1994), which refers to tacit knowledge rooted in action, commitment and involvement in a specific context
- Different local routines for working, training and learning that obstruct the development of shared understanding of practices and knowledge
- Differences in skills, expertise, technical infrastructure, development tools and methodologies
- Changes in membership
- The lack of prior experience of working together between the distributed teams.

Dealing with knowledge asymmetry in offshore sourcing

In captive offshoring settings, one way to achieve successful knowledge transfer from the onshore to the offshore organisation is by carefully selecting learning processes that suit the types of knowledge that need to be transferred. For example, Chua and Pan (2008) conducted a case study of a global Information Systems department in a multinational bank that was transferring its business application support and development experience to an offshore location. They examined how different types of knowledge were transferred and identified the following types of knowledge (Iivari et al., 2004): technical knowledge, application domain knowledge, Information Systems (IS) application knowledge, organisational knowledge and IS development process knowledge. They showed in their case study that, depending on the type of knowledge required, different learning sub-processes are needed (see Table 7.1). While some areas of the IS knowledge can be easily grafted, some require intense, vicarious and

TABLE 7.1   Organisational learning sub-processes in different IS knowledge areas

IS knowledge areas	Learning sub-processes
Technical knowledge Application domain knowledge	Grafting of staff with as much of these two knowledge areas as possible will form the basis to which new knowledge will be added
Organisational knowledge	Experiential learning and vicarious learning were carried out through presentations, support simulations, on-the-job training, and playback. Self-appraisal techniques, such as quizzes and individual and team appraisals, were used to check if learning was effective
IS development process knowledge	A separate training programme for analysis design, using the same knowledge transfer mechanisms as above, was created for the more experienced members of the offshore team. Offshore staff have to be retained to enable continued offshore learning

Source: Based on Chua and Pan, 2008.

experiential learning using rich data. Certain types of knowledge which are 'sticky' and difficult to codify are also difficult to transfer.

In offshore outsourcing settings, one of the major issues raised by scholars is related to concerns that the client firms have regarding the service provider's domain-related expertise (Oshri et al., 2007a) and cognitive alignment (Levina and Vaast, 2008; Vlaar et al., 2008), where the efforts in addressing such concerns have typically been on enhancing the task-related expertise of the delivery team. Such enhancements entail the supplier's ability to understand the client's business context, business processes and the socio-cultural environment in which they operate (Dibbern et al., 2008). Task-expertise correspondence supports effective knowledge sharing between the client firm and the supplier, which is assumed to eventually contribute to outsourcing success (ibid). For instance, Levina and Vaast (2008) propose that client–supplier competence differences with regard to understanding the client's industry, computer science, business software development, the client's information systems and language proficiency give rise to boundaries and status differences. In turn, such boundaries and differences may inhibit collaboration in offshore outsourcing. Knowledge transfer is supposed to bridge such differences in expertise and competences. Such bridging may involve building the conditions for knowledge acquisition through processes of sense-giving and sense-making in the relationship between onshore and offshore teams (Vlaar et al., 2008); team-level cognitive processes through transactive memory systems (TMSs) (Oshri, van Fenema and Kotlarsky, 2008); and developing the supplier's expertise offshore through codification practices (Kotlarsky et al., 2014).

A transactive memory system between on-site and offshore teams

So what can we do about sticky knowledge that is embodied in experts and is thus difficult to transfer between distributed teams? While co-located teams may develop various memory systems that support knowledge transfer, globally distributed teams face various barriers in developing such systems that may facilitate the transfer of contextual and embedded knowledge. A TMS is the combination of individual memory systems and communications (also referred to as 'transactions') between individuals that enable the shared division of cognitive labour used to encode, store and retrieve knowledge from different but complementary domains of expertise while being engaged in collective tasks (Wegner, 1986). A team-level TMS consists of individuals using each other as a memory source.

Individuals encode information for storing and retrieving in a similar way that a librarian enters details of a new book in a particular library system before putting it on the shelf. Three core TMS processes – directory updating, information allocation and retrieval coordination – enable the formation and further operation of a TMS.

Directory updating is associated with learning about areas of expertise of team members and creating awareness about 'who knows what' in the team or organisation. Through this process knowledge is categorised (i.e., assigned labels that reflect the subjects of the knowledge) for systematically storing the location of the knowledge but not the knowledge itself.

Information allocation is about communicating information to the relevant experts for processing and storage. Individuals store this information internally (building their own memory) or externally (storing it in artefacts or indirectly in other people's memories).

Retrieval coordination implies knowing whom to contact for which information and in what sequence so that the retrieval process is effective and efficient (Wegner, 1995).

Through this process, information about the location of the knowledge or expertise is retrieved when someone else asks for it. Retrieval thus consists of two interconnected sub-processes: person A communicates the need for information with person B; person B retrieves the information (Oshri, van Fenema and Kotlarsky, 2008).

In practice, the development and activation of the core TMS processes (directory updating, information allocation and retrieval coordination) is supported by knowledge directories that point to where knowledge and expertise reside. Two types of directories can be differentiated (Oshri, van Fenema and Kotlasky, 2008): *codified* (e.g., information systems and technologies) and *personalised* (e.g., personal memory or other people's memories). Table 7.2 details how codified and personalised knowledge directories support TMS processes in globally distributed teams.

Oshri van Fenema and Kotlarsky (2008) suggest that in order to overcome differences derived from the local contexts of the on-site and offshore teams (e.g., different work routines, methodologies and skills), organisations should invest in developing a TMS. In particular, they recommend specific mechanisms supporting the development of codified and personalised TMS directories to help develop a TMS between on-site and offshore teams and keep it updated. These include the standardisation of templates and methodologies across remote sites as well as frequent teleconferencing sessions and occasional short visits (see Table 7.3). These mechanisms contribute to the development of the notion of 'who knows what' across on-site and offshore teams, despite the challenges associated with globally distributed teams, and support the transfer of knowledge.

In order to enable the transfer of knowledge between remote sites, organisations should consider the mechanisms we have noted that support the development, management and coordination of collective expertise and enable the transfer of knowledge between on-site and offshore teams. In doing so, organisations should consider two key aspects with respect to work division. First, they should attempt to select project members based on their shared histories of collaboration in their respective area of expertise. In this way, remote counterparts who already know each

TABLE 7.2   Transactive memory system processes and codified and personalised directories in globally distributed teams

TMS processes	How knowledge directories support TMS processes	
	Codified directories	Personalised directories
Directory Updating Having a shared 'cataloguing' system	Creating a shared system to categorise information Developing a set of rules of how to label the subject and location of the expertise	Creating a shared understanding of context and work-related processes, terminology and language
Information Allocation The way in which the information is organised in physical locations and in the memories of dispersed team members	Storing information about the subject and location of the knowledge. This can be achieved by creating pointers to the location of knowledge in an expertise directory Storing up-to-date records of available documents and expertise	Storing information about 'who knows what' and 'who is doing what' in individuals' memories
Retrieval Coordination 1) Knowing where and in what form information is stored in the dispersed team 2) Being able to find required information through determining the location of information, and, sometimes, the combination or interplay of items coming from multiple locations	Developing search capabilities (e.g., keyword-based) for effective and efficient search and retrieval processes	Developing interpersonal channels through which individuals can search for information about who has expertise and in which areas, and where this expertise resides

Source: Based on Oshri, van Fenema and Kotlarsky, 2008.

other have developed a meta-knowledge relating to their counterparts and have established procedures for working together. Such a staffing approach is likely to speed the development of the TMS because procedures, codified routines and social ties have already been established. Second, an expertise-based division of work should be considered when members of the team have worked with each other previously and have developed shared histories. Teams that do not have shared histories, however, may

TABLE 7.3   Organisational mechanisms and processes supporting the development of a TMS in globally distributed teams

TMS processes	Codified directories	Personalised directories
Directory updating	• Standard document templates (for product deliverables and process phases) • Glossary of terms to include unique (e.g., product-specific) terminology	• Rotation of on-site and offshore team members • Joint training programmes • Team-building exercises • Social activities
Information allocation	• Central project repository • Standardisation of tools and methods across locations • Centralisation of tools on the central server; Web access	• Expertise-based division of work • Creating complementary documentation for software applications and components (to include the name of the developer)
Retrieval coordination	• Standard processes and procedures (that include pointers to the location of information) • Keywords-based search capabilities • Tools that enable automated notification of changes and requests (e.g., software configuration management and change management tools)	• Systematic and frequent communications using instant messaging, email and tele- and videoconferencing • Technologies that enable reachability when on the move and out of working hours (e.g., mobile and smartphones, pagers)

Source: Based on Oshri, van Fenema and Kotlarsky, 2008.

benefit from a division of work that is based on geographical location for a period of time, which enables them to establish procedures, standards and templates from the development of codified directories before changing to an expertise-based division of work approach.

The case study that follows illustrates how one IT supplier, TCS, dealt with challenges faced during the transition phase in an offshore outsourcing project.

CASE STUDY

The Key Knowledge Management Challenges in the Outsourcing Project Between ABN AMRO and TCS

When the IT industry started it was more like a cottage industry, very much people dependent. It is now changing from people dependent to process dependent. When this happens, knowledge management becomes part of the process itself.

TCS, part of the Tata Group, was founded in 1968 as a consulting service firm for the emerging IT industry. Since then, it has expanded to become a global player with revenues of US$13.4 billion in 2014. With over 300,000 associates and 58 subsidiaries and service delivery centres, TCS has established a presence in 46 countries. It provides various services, including BPO and IT maintenance and development, to clients around the globe (The evolutionary path of TCS is illustrated in detail in the 'Tata Consultancy Services: Building Capabilities' case study included in Chapter 5.).

TCS has developed a global delivery model in which projects are handled mainly by teams located remotely from clients but often with a small team at the client site. Generally TCS's on-site and offshore teams transfer work packages back and forth to each other until the task is completed. TCS's project teams, which are based on-site, onshore and nearshore, depend on the expertise and knowledge that reside within TCS at various locations. Thus, TCS has developed knowledge management practices to acquire and retain knowledge globally, regardless of the physical location of the expert or the knowledge seeker.

In late 2005, Netherlands-based ABN AMRO Bank announced a US$2.2 billion outsourcing contract with five providers, including TCS, to provide support and application enhancement services. The outsourcing project organisation of ABN AMRO's contract with TCS consisted of three arrangements across three continents. Each arrangement type had an on-site component at the client site and a remote component somewhere else:

1. In the Netherlands, on-site TCS teams at ABN AMRO's Amsterdam locations worked with corresponding offshore TCS teams in Mumbai, India.
2. In Brazil, on-site TCS teams at ABN AMRO São Paulo locations worked with corresponding onshore teams at TCS's delivery centre in Campinas, 100 kilometres away.
3. In several countries (e.g., Switzerland, Germany and Monaco), on-site TCS teams communicated with an onshore TCS delivery centre in Luxembourg and a nearshore TCS delivery centre in Hungary.

Typically TCS team members resided in one location throughout a project – either on-site, onshore, nearshore or offshore. Only a small number of TCS staff travelled between locations for short visits. An on-site TCS team included project members, project leaders, portfolio managers, programme managers, a transition head, a relationship manager and those with other functions – mainly quality assurance, human resources and organisation development personnel.

The ABN AMRO–TCS offshore outsourcing project was divided into two phases: transition and steady state. In the transition phase, the on-site TCS team learned about ABN AMRO's systems and transferred this knowledge to its corresponding offshore TCS team. In the steady-state phase, the offshore TCS teams provided the main support for the bank's systems and services as well as developed new applications. This multisite mode of working required the on-site, onshore, nearshore and offshore teams to overcome two expertise management challenges: the relationship and organisational challenges.

The relationship challenge deals with the client–supplier relationship. With respect to managing knowledge, the supplier needs to answer the question: How can a client's knowledge be captured and retained at both on-site and remote locations to ensure uninterrupted service to the client and to develop further services for the client? This challenge requires the supplier to quickly and effectively assimilate the client's knowledge. TCS viewed success in meeting this challenge as having no knowledge gaps between its corresponding teams; that is, the pairs of on-site/onshore, on-site/nearshore and on-site/offshore teams. TCS addressed this challenge by requiring the remote TCS team to develop the same level of knowledge as its corresponding on-site TCS team.

Eliminating knowledge gaps between on-site and remote teams is particularly important for offshore service companies like TCS, because they need to demonstrate to clients that offshoring application maintenance and development will not reduce service or application quality. As one TCS delivery manager on the offshore team in Mumbai noted:

> When I had my initial discussion with the bank's portfolio managers, they asked, 'How are you going to take care of the knowledge base? We have ten, 15, 30 years of experience at the bank, yet you are going to join afresh. You are just going to have a knowledge transfer for a short time.' They asked, 'So how do you ensure that you have this knowledge with you? And how are you going to retain this knowledge?'

The organisational challenge concerns the provider's mechanisms for managing knowledge within its own organisation. It answers the question: How do we turn local learning and knowledge into global assets? The challenge is to capture knowledge from an on-site TCS team and then refine and reuse it globally on other teams that may need it. TCS addressed this challenge by developing knowledge-coordination competencies to ensure that knowledge is reapplied across the company.

TCS and other outsourcing providers are exposed to vast amounts of knowledge through their numerous outsourcing relationships. However, this knowledge often becomes the asset of just a single project. It is rarely shared with other projects that will likely confront similar challenges. The head of the learning and development department at TCS explains this challenge by saying:

> How do we create a kind of customer-focused experience?
> How do we share this knowledge? How can we enhance our
> learning about banking and insurance so that we can say
> that we know technology and we also know about the bank-
> ing industry? Basically, I need to develop specific domain
> knowledge and link it to other value activities, share it with
> the entire workforce so our employees can talk to the cus-
> tomer in their own language and in their own domain of
> expertise as an expert. That is a challenge for me to create
> this kind of expertise.
>
> Kamal Joshi, the TCS transition head in Amsterdam who was
> responsible for ensuring that the client's knowledge possessed
> by ABN AMRO experts would be transferred to TCS offshore
> teams in Mumbai, was confident that TCS would meet the
> client's expectations; however, he was also wondering: 'Have
> I considered all the risks involved in my knowledge manage-
> ment strategy? What can go wrong?'

Managing Expertise Within and Between Projects

While knowledge transfer is an important step in offshore outsourcing,
the question remaining for the client's executives is where they should
draw the line on outsourcing their knowledge and expertise. How can the
selected supplier develop the knowledge and expertise of their domain,
systems and practices to maintain continuity of service and achieve the
sought-for innovation and transformation? The IT outsourcing supplier
executives also have to ask themselves how they can quickly develop
expertise in new areas, particularly where their teams are remote and dispersed, and how they can retain knowledge when people equipped with
key knowledge and expertise move on.

Coordination mechanisms to facilitate knowledge processes in global teams

In offshore outsourcing, some suppliers adopt a multisite mode of work,
often referred to as a global delivery model (GDM), which consists of
various types of arrangements that involve an on-site component at the

client site and one or several remote components somewhere else, typically in the supplier's home country or other locations (offshore, nearshore or onshore) where the supplier has development or customer support facilities. The idea behind the GDM is to complete the work where it can be done best, makes the most economic sense, with the least amount of acceptable risk. Large suppliers like IBM, Accenture, TCS and Infosys set up global delivery centres in locations where they have cost, flexibility and time-to-market advantages and access to large pools of talent and specialised expertise. For the same reasons, many client companies, in particular large multinationals, set up captive facilities around the world.

The multisite or GDM mode of work requires significant coordination. Otherwise organisational performance may encounter problems like asymmetries, knowledge that is 'stuck' at a particular site, and lost opportunities in knowledge creation. Coordination mechanisms become knowledge management instruments and contribute to the coherence of knowledge processes (Kotlarsky, van Fenema and Willcocks, 2008). Kotlarsky and associates (2008) developed a model of how each category of coordination mechanism has an impact on knowledge processes and thus ultimately on coordinated outcomes as shown in Figure 7.1. There are four types of coordination mechanisms:

Organisation design mechanisms, which encompass formal structures such as hierarchies, linking pins, teams and direct contacts. They facilitate knowledge flows by providing a structure through which knowledge workers can channel their expertise. Organisation design clarifies who is supposed to know what and who is supposed to communicate with whom. It therefore simplifies knowledge flows.

Work-based mechanisms, which involve the specific structuring of tasks to be accomplished. They include plans, specifications, standards, categorisation systems, and representations of work in progress such as prototypes and design documents. Work-based mechanisms that capture knowledge are important for making knowledge explicit, as they enable activity replication and commonality. The use of such mechanisms implies that knowledge and expectations are made explicit and thus are known and useful to other people working at different sites or times. In such dispersed organisations, knowledge must be rapidly disseminated by means of technology.

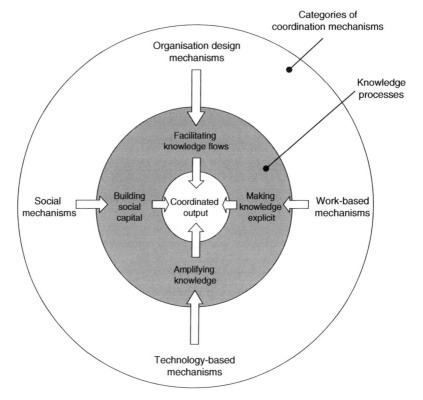

FIGURE 7.1 / **How coordination mechanisms facilitate knowledge processes to achieve coordination**
Source: Kotlarsky, van Fenema and Willcocks, 2008.

Technology-based mechanisms, which amplify knowledge management processes by enabling information capturing, processing, storage and exchange (e.g., electronic calendaring and scheduling, groupware, shared databases). These technologies not only process data and information but also trigger new ideas and enable coordinated actions.

Social (interpersonal) mechanisms, which involve communication activities, working relationships and social cognition. They help to establish social capital and facilitate the development of a TMS (knowledge about who knows and does what). Individuals are thus knowledge workers who negotiate points of view and transform their understanding to generate innovative outputs; they have relational needs that are relevant for coordinating their work.

Practices for managing dispersed expertise

Firms engaged in offshore outsourcing face a relationship challenge and an organisational challenge (Oshri et al., 2007a). The former refers to the client–supplier relationship: how a client's knowledge can be captured and retained at both on-site and remote locations to ensure uninterrupted service to the client and to further develop services for the client. This is the knowledge transfer challenge we discussed above. The organisational challenge concerns the supplier's ability to manage expertise within its own organisation. In other words, the challenge is to capture expertise from an on-site team and refine and reuse it within other distributed teams. Based on a case study at TCS and its globally distributed service delivery centre, we observed that TCS employed the following practices to address these challenges (shown in Figure 7.2). We discuss these practices in detail after the figure.

1. *Implement an organisational structure that is a mirror image of the client's structure ('organise').* TCS used an organisational structure that ensured that client personnel and offshore TCS personnel could easily identify their counterpart. Oshri and associates identified three types of organisational structures found in offshore outsourcing arrangements: the funnel (a single point of contact and control between client and supplier), the network (multiple points of contacts and control) and the mirror (replicating client's organisational structure). The mirror structure has been proven as the most effective of the three in terms of organising knowledge assimilation and transfer.

2. *Implement a knowledge transfer methodology ('transfer').* Codifying knowledge is the key practice here. TCS's on-site team provided documentation based on standard templates and passed these templates to the offshore team. But this was only the first step. The offshore team then had to 'play back' what they learned from the documentation by giving presentations to the on-site team. Again, while codified knowledge is useful, the transferring of tacit knowledge, which can be obtained only through learning by doing, is more difficult.

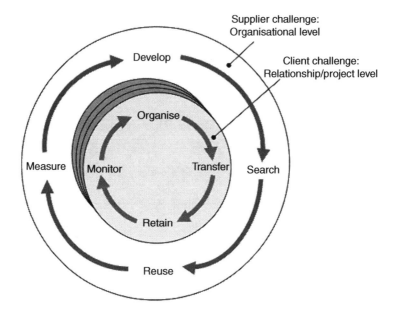

FIGURE 7.2 **Expertise management processes at the relationship and organisational levels**
Source: Oshri, Kotlarsky and Willcocks, 2007a.

3. *Implement a knowledge retention methodology ('retain').* To avoid loss of knowledge due to personnel turnover, TCS adopted a succession plan. TCS managers identified individuals who could replace them in case they left the project or company. These potential successors were trained and backed up the manager's knowledge in their area of expertise. This greatly reduced the disruption and delay resulting from turnover of key players in outsourcing projects.

4. *Monitor expertise development and retention at project and organisational levels ('monitor').* To enable local teams to take advantage of centralised resources, TCS set up centres of excellence (CoEs) to link project and organisational levels of expertise monitoring. The CoEs were networks of experts who had advanced know-how and experience in a particular market or technological domain. They were responsible for acquiring know-how from internal and external sources and then sharing that with project teams. CoEs served as repositories of knowledge as well as directories that pointed to an expert's location.

5. *Make expertise development a key organisational value ('develop').* In TCS, every project was supported by the CoEs – quality assurance, digitisation and codification groups. These groups provided support for the continuous development of know-how and skills. Moreover, employees received various types of training during different phases of their career, especially in terms of where to access knowledge and expertise across team boundaries.

6. *Provide mechanisms to search for expertise at project and organisational levels ('search').* At the project level, the on-site and remote teams kept a regularly updated expertise directory that identified who knows what and who does what. A project portal (or knowledge base) was also built that included information about experts in the project, system and project documents. Using TCS's knowledge transfer and knowledge retention methodologies, the pointers were created and constantly updated during the transition and steady-state phases of each outsourcing project, as on-site and remote counterparts interacted with each other to transfer knowledge and develop their expertise. (This is an example of the development and update of a TMS system discussed earlier in this chapter.) At the company level, a broad memory system brought external expertise into a project in a timely manner. Members of CoEs in a project also served as connection points with experts in other projects or CoEs. Finally, TCS also organised knowledge exchange events and seminars at different locations to facilitate communication and learning between remote counterparts.

7. *Implement a reuse methodology at the global level ('reuse').* TCS adopted a component-based methodology of developing software components and building software systems by integrating components. Components were supposed to be self-contained and could be removed or replaced without affecting other parts of the system. They could therefore also be modified and reused. TCS made its reusable components available on its intranet. Also made available with the components was expertise in that particular technology. It should be noted that fundamental to a reuse methodology is systematic and accurate collection of components from projects. Such practices should be cultivated and routinised so that they become part of the organisational culture.

8. *Continually measure the contribution of reusable assets ('measure').* To reap the benefit of reusable components, firms also have to reach a certain maturity level in terms of systems development standards – for

example, in design, testing and documentation. On top of this, TCS's quality assurance group also regularly tracked how often and how well components were reused. They also optimised the process of reusing components by centralising the process and by carefully managing the pool of reusable solutions.

Summary

This chapter reviewed the challenges that both suppliers and clients face in terms of managing knowledge and expertise. We opened this chapter with a simple question: What happens to knowledge when you outsource or offshore? We illustrated how knowledge can be effectively used by both suppliers and clients and how the management of knowledge and expertise can be perceived as a value-adding activity that can benefit suppliers and clients alike. However, most clients have not fully captured the potential of advancing learning from such opportunities and in most cases have trusted the management of knowledge and expertise to their supplier.

part III

Managing Sourcing Relationships

chapter 8

The Outsourcing Life Cycle and the Transition Phase

Although the multibillion-dollar outsourcing industry is flourishing, a number of outsourcing arrangements have been underperforming, and some have even been terminated. Poor management and governance of the outsourcing relationship have often been cited as two main reasons for less successful outsourcing contracts. Before we investigate the management and the governance of outsourcing relationships, which will be further discussed in Chapter 9, it is important to understand the key stages of the outsourcing process, as well as the key practices that can be applied at each stage.

This chapter discusses the outsourcing life cycle. In doing so, it provides a checklist of key activities that a client organisation needs to fulfil to prepare and properly execute an outsourcing relationship. The chapter also elaborates on the key requirements for designing and executing the transition phase. We therefore focus on the following aspects:

- The key stages of the outsourcing life cycle
- The most effective practices available for clients to cope with challenges throughout the entire outsourcing life cycle
- The key requirements for executing the transition phase.

Key Stages of the Outsourcing Life Cycle

One of the most comprehensive models of the outsourcing life cycle has been provided by Cullen et al. (2005). The model, shown in Table 8.1, consists of four phases: architect, engage, operate and regenerate. These phases are composed of nine building blocks. In the outsourcing life cycle, each phase and its constituent building blocks pave the way for the next phase. Thus, the effectiveness of each building block depends on the preceding ones, with the last phase initiating the next-generation outsourcing strategy and life cycle. In this section, we introduce this model and expand it based on our recent research and other academic sources.

Architect phase

The architect phase comprises the first four building blocks – investigate, target, strategise and design – and thus lays the foundations for the outsourcing venture.

The primary goal of the first building block, the *investigation*, is to identify the goals. The key activities for the client organisation are to gather insights from experts and other experienced groups, determine and test goals and expectations, collect information on market conditions and potential suppliers and investigate similar decisions and peer organisations. Key questions that clients should consider for this building block are:

1. Who are their competitors and what are they paying for similar services?
2. Who are the other service suppliers in their market and what are their offerings, capabilities and weaknesses?
3. What are the market costs like, and what are the trade-offs between suppliers?
4. What are the considerations for the geographical location of their target market?

For example, a state government agency might investigate the sourcing decisions and strategies of two similar state government agencies, a federal agency and two companies from the private sector. The state government agency might also try to gather market insights and understand the implications of different sourcing tactics for its operations. This approach would enable it to develop its thinking on its outsourcing strategy.

TABLE 8.1   The outsourcing life cycle model

Outsourcing phase	Building block	Goal	Key outputs
Architect	1. Investigation	Veracity, not ideology	Gather insights Test expectations Collect market intelligence Peer assessment
	2. Target	Appropriate services identified	Outsourcing model or mode Target services identification Profiles
	3. Strategy	Informed, not speculative, strategies	Rollout Strategic 'rules' Programme Skills Communications strategy Business case rules and base case Feasibility and impact analysis
	4. Design	Well-designed future state	Blueprint Scorecard Draft SLAs Draft price model Draft contract Relationship Retained organisation Contract management function
Engage	5. Selection	Best value for money	Competitive stages Evaluation team Selection strategy and criteria Bid package Bid facilitation Evaluation Due diligence
	6. Negotiation	Complete, efficient contract	Negotiation strategy Negotiation team Effective negotiations
Operate	7. Transition	Efficient mobilisation	Final plans Transition team Managed staff

(continued)

TABLE 8.1　Continued

Outsourcing phase	Building block	Goal	Key outputs
	8. Management	Results	Knowledge retention and transfer Transfers Governance structures set up Engineering Acceptance
			Relationship Reporting Meetings Administration and records Risk management Issues, variations and disputes Continuous improvement Evaluations
Regenerate	9. Refresh	Refreshed strategy	Next-generation options Outcomes and lessons Options: business case and strategy

Source: Cullen, Seddon and Willcocks, 2005.

The second building block is *target*. Its primary purpose is for organisations to identify the areas in which outsourcing can be beneficial to their operations. The key activities for the client organisation in this second building block are to match goals to an appropriate outsourcing model, identify objective criteria suitable for service providers and define the scope of outsourcing.[1] For example, during the initial discussions concerning which activities to outsource, all of the executives of an international airline company supported the argument that the part of the business that was within their control was absolutely core and thus should remain in-house. Later, when consultants came in, the company created a set of objective criteria relating to the long- and short-term benefits to be pursued through outsourcing, as well as relating to the barriers to outsourcing a specific activity. Based on these criteria, they identified the processes that were the best candidates for outsourcing.

The third building block is *strategy*. Its primary goal is to conduct the planning that will enable effective decision-making during the rest of the life cycle. The key activities for the organisation are to decide on the rollout approach (e.g., big bang or phased), determine the key rules guiding the outsourcing relationship, design the detailed life-cycle programme, identify and source the life-cycle skills, prepare the life-cycle communications strategy, prepare the business case rules and the base case, and assess the feasibility, risk and impact of the outsourcing on the organisation. A poorly prepared outsourcing strategy can result in a number of time-consuming and costly mistakes. As an example, the handover period for the outsourcing team of a telecommunications company was delayed by three months because the company did not have a clear plan concerning employee transfer to the supplier. As a result, neither the client organisation nor its chosen supplier had the necessary staff to conduct normal service delivery during this period.

The fourth building block is *design*. Its primary goal is to wrap up the architect phase and define the planned configuration of the deal. The key activities for the organisation are to prepare the commercial and operating blueprint, develop balanced score metrics, draft the service agreement and the price and contract framework, and design the interparty relationship (structure, roles, authorities, etc.), the retained organisation and the governance function. The lack of an appropriate design of the outsourcing relationship may result in poor performance for both supplier and client. As an example, an international airline had created a handshake agreement with a call centre supplier because the two organisations had effectively cooperated in the past. Their cooperation was considered a strategic partnership, and for this reason, both parties believed that they needed only a high-level memorandum of understanding (MOU) for this agreement. Years later, the airline company found that it was being overcharged and that the overbilling resulted from the fact that there were no detailed descriptions of service delivery and pricing.

The foundations for the outsourcing venture laid at the architect phase ensure that the client organisation is making fully informed decisions regarding their sourcing strategy and configuration. Table 8.2 lists the key practices associated with this phase.

TABLE 8.2   Key practices for determining the sourcing strategy and configuration

Identify the business reasons for outsourcing IT, business processes or services. Consider how outsourcing could improve the organisation's ability to use and manage technology
Consider starting with a representative service or selective set of services to outsource; balance against economies of scale
Consider using third-party assistance with experience in a variety of sourcing arrangements when formulating a sourcing strategy
Incorporate lessons learnt from peer organisations that have engaged in similar sourcing decisions
Estimate the impact of the sourcing decision on the internal organisation as well as on enterprise alliances and relationships
Consider optimising IT/business processes/services before deciding on a sourcing strategy
Benchmark and baseline the productivity of internal services prior to making the final sourcing decision

Source: Based on the General Accounting Office, 2001.

Engage phase

During the engage phase, the client chooses one or more suppliers to carry out the work and negotiates the contract. The fifth and the sixth building blocks are central to the activities carried out during this phase.

The fifth building block is *selection*. Its primary purpose is to choose the most appropriate supplier. The key activities for the organisation are to plan in detail the content of the outsourced work, identify the most appropriate evaluation team, determine the most appropriate evaluating criteria, request information from bidders for each bid, apply interactive evaluation techniques, select the supplier based on value for money, and conduct the five due-diligence processes on the final list of potential suppliers (company, price, solution, contract and customer reference).[2] Consider an example of a bank that generated an extensive call for expression of interest (EOI) in an open-tender process but did not develop a clear approach to evaluate the bids it would receive. The company received 14 bids and realised that it would need a structured evaluation methodology to select its supplier. After developing its methodology of evaluation, the company discovered that its EOI had elicited only 30% of the information it needed to choose a supplier. To avoid such disappointments, it is important to be prepared to invest a substantial amount of time and effort in the supplier-selection process.

The sixth building block is *negotiation*. Its goal is to discuss and agree on the terms upon which the service will be provided, contingencies and rewards. It is important that the client organisation is well prepared for the negotiations, demonstrating both technical and business knowledge regarding the current state of the services to be outsourced and expectations regarding how they could transform over time. One outcome of ABN AMRO's investment in setting up an internal team to bid for the 2005 multisourcing deal was the extensive knowledge ABN AMRO developed in understanding what could and could not be done, which was then used as part of the negotiations with the five suppliers.

Preparation: A critical component in preparing for an effective negotiation is to prioritise needs and requirements. In this, self-knowledge plays an important role. The organisation and negotiating team must have a clear sense of which items can be negotiated and which cannot. Here, a four-tier prioritisation system is helpful: critical, important, required and desired but not required (Power et al., 2006). Critical requirements are items that cannot be negotiated under any circumstances; in other words, these are the deal breakers. If a supplier cannot accommodate these requirements, there is no potential for a successful negotiation. Important requirements are items that are also non-negotiable; however, what *may* be negotiable is the method or terms for their delivery. This might include, for example, how information is communicated or at what frequency. Required items are assessed as neither important nor critical but are items that an organisation deems necessary to a fruitful relationship. Here, however, there is room to compromise and negotiate through modification and alteration from the original iteration of the need. Finally, desired items are the 'bells and whistles' of the agreement, the nice add-ons that may be thrown into the mix in the final stages of negotiation – perhaps as a concession with respect to the alteration of a required item.

One point to be made about prioritising needs is that keeping it a secret from the supplier is rarely wise, especially if there is already a good relationship. Disclosing the information can help the parties focus on top-tier items, making the process more straightforward and productive.

Another key component for preparing for negotiation is putting together the right negotiating team. One erroneous assumption is that the right team is composed of either high-level executives or subject-matter experts. Both approaches often result in poor outcomes. A good team mix is comprised of staff who have broad strategic knowledge, not deep domain knowledge. The team must be able to see and focus on the bigger picture, and not get bogged down in the detail. A good team mix might be, for example, a senior-level executive supervising members from different key functional areas within the organisation, such as financial, IT, financial and legal.

While legal counsel is important to the team mix, it is best added as a consultative component rather than a negotiating vehicle in and of itself. Negotiating through lawyers signals lack of trust and excessive formality. While lawyers offer important knowledge with respect to contracts, drafting legal documents and pointing out potential legal issues, they are often less skilled at actual negotiation. Legal opinions should be shared with the team members during private meetings.

Finally, preparation requires an organisation to determine a starting point in the negotiation – their entry position for the negotiation process. Most often this is considered in terms of price, that is, the client is interested in the lowest price for obtaining the services requirements, while the supplier wants the highest return. Every negotiation involves both parties moving to some middle point; therefore, identifying both a starting position and a desired end position is important, in order to know whether negotiation has been successful. Knowledge of the supplier and knowledge of the market are critical in determining both.

Process: Once negotiations are in progress, there are three main aspects to consider: culture, relationship and documentation. Culture can be corporate (internal business practice norms) or national, or both. Negotiation is about exchanging ideas and developing agreements in an atmosphere of mutual respect. This necessitates an understanding of cultural issues, including norms, taboos and expectations unique to the country or companies involved.

It is also imperative for organisations to realise that they are negotiating a business relationship, not necessarily a single contract. Executives must approach the contract-negotiating process with a view beyond cost issues in order to see to the true goal – improved business performance and innovation, which today is becoming an important business proposition by service providers (as we discuss in detail in Chapter 12). This may mean that the organisation will ultimately pay more than they originally envisioned, but these costs will usually be recouped as the business relationship matures through future contracts and even in renegotiating contracts as issues come to light after the relationship goes into effect.

Finally, in order to move successfully into the contract management stage, it is important that the negotiation process is accurately documented. To put it simply, results are only as good as the notes taken. There are several checks client organisations can use to ensure the final contract correctly mirrors the negotiated terms:

- Have a designated note-taker on the team
- Recap the day during a closing meeting
- Recap items to include the following: summary of discussions, key items resolved and action items for the next meeting.

Time frame: Having a suitable time frame – for both the client organisation and the supplier – can prove critical to negotiating success. Unfortunately, this is an aspect often overlooked in negotiating. Negotiations take time and there is a cost involved in negotiating that many companies fail to recognise. Recognition of a supplier's time frame can mean the difference between success and complete failure. As stated by Powers et al. (2006, p. 118), 'A deal offered by the vendor today may not be available tomorrow.'

At the same time, it is imperative not to link the conclusion of the negotiations with an artificial deadline, such as Christmas or Good Friday. Such artificial deadlines might serve the cause of 'having a reason to celebrate', but might also mean missing out on the thoroughness needed when negotiating such a deal.

A negotiation does not happen in isolation – a supplier has multiple other negotiations happening in the background with different clients. What may appear to be a good business pursuit today may not appear so tomorrow if the supplier is able to secure a contract with what it deems a more important player.

A common misperception in negotiation is that the last offer on the board remains valid and that if a supplier does not acquiesce to the client's current counter-offer, the supplier's last offer is still on the table. This is an erroneous and often devastating assumption to the negotiating process. Every time an offer is turned down by either side, it is technically no longer available for consideration. Careful consideration must be given each time an offer is rejected, not only because of the potential for the process to stall and die but because there are marginal costs involved in trying to obtain a better outcome. For example, it may well be worthwhile rejecting an offer because of unacceptable terms on a critical issue for the organisation and even to spend another day or week trying to attain a more favourable outcome. However, the organisation must also consider the marginal costs involved in obtaining less critical terms. For example, spending another day or half-day (or longer) trying to obtain a US$10,000 price concession from the supplier may not make sense in terms of the salaries of the negotiating team or the risk associated with further delay in sealing the deal.

Furthermore, in addition to the specific aspects related to the preparation and the process of negotiations, some good tactics for effective negotiations include the preparation of service-level agreements (SLAs), the pricing framework and the contract before choosing a supplier; requiring the bidders to give exact wording changes and specifications they wish to negotiate; and clarification and a detailed explanation of the issues to be negotiated. Results of our research indicate that companies that followed these tactics were able to complete the negotiations in a couple of weeks, in contrast to companies that lacked a thorough plan of negotiations and took months to complete the negotiations.

Last but not the least, since many outsourcing engagements today involve multisourcing, client organisations should be careful to include a discussion of the interfaces between interdependent services in their negotiations with suppliers expected to deliver these services. Naturally, suppliers tend to focus on their particular scope of responsibility, and to be very specific about what they are and are not responsible for. Bringing to the negotiation table the need to clearly identify and discuss interdependencies between the suppliers is the responsibility of the client and may require all parties to sit around the negotiation table. It may seem to contradict the way that outsourcing contracts are traditionally negotiated; however, clarifying interdependency issues with all affected parties at this stage helps to ensure effective multisourcing governance.

Operate phase

During the operate phase, the outsourcing deal is executed. The seventh and the eighth building blocks are key to this phase.

The seventh building block is *transition*. Its goal is to effectively and smoothly go through the change process in which the client hands over the services to the supplier. The key activities for the client organisation are to complete the project plans, including resourcing the transition process (e.g., the required number of employees, nature of expertise, type of equipment and infrastructure); manage the impact on staff (whose jobs will be affected); manage the staff transfers; manage knowledge retention and transfer; implement the contract (service delivery on behalf of the supplier according to what has been agreed, knowledge input and payment on behalf of the client, etc.); engineer work flows; establish communication channels; conduct acceptance and close-out (making sure that both parties are satisfied with the terms of the venture and that the agreement is operational); and perform a post-implementation review of issues that cropped up during the transition.

Some of the tactics that have proved to be beneficial for the transition of employees include: offering financial and career advice to the affected staff, including staff in the development of the supplier evaluation criteria, and involving staff in the supplier-selection process. As an example of the successful transition of IT staff, an insurance company worked very closely with its supplier on how most of its 70 IT staff would willingly transfer to the supplier. The contract verified that the employment conditions at the supplier's organisation would be the same as in the insurance company. Furthermore, the transferred staff would be employed by the supplier organisation for at least two years. The two parties also tried to agree on a plan that would win the hearts and minds of the transferred employees. The supplier would make presentations to familiarise the employees with its operations. The staff would receive branded material such as hats, mouse pads and T-shirts. There would be training sessions, as well as an opportunity to have individual conversations with the insurance company chief information officers.

TABLE 8.3   Key practices for managing the supplier's performance

Ensure that the supplier measures and reports on performance
Sample performance data frequently enough to perform trend analysis and permit extrapolation based on historical data
Schedule periodic working-level meetings with both the end-user groups and the supplier to review the supplier's performance
Conduct executive-level oversight meetings with the supplier's senior management to review the supplier's performance
Distribute performance data to stakeholders
Reserve audit rights on performance data provided by the supplier
Work with the supplier to redefine service levels as appropriate
Allow employees, and possibly stakeholders, to rate supplier on a regular basis using, for example, scorecards and quarterly report cards
Consider incentives to motivate the supplier to exceed performance requirements
Consider penalties to motivate the supplier to meet performance requirements
Periodically undertake studies to assess how the supplier's performance compares with the value being delivered to similar clients and the extent to which the supplier's performance is improving over time (e.g., validate cost assumptions for multiyear contracts)

Source: Based on the General Accounting Office, 2001.

Key issues during the phase of transition are discussed later in this chapter.

The eighth building block is *management*. Its primary goal is to manage the outsourcing relationship. During this stage, the client organisation makes sure that the supplier has met performance requirements. Table 8.3 identifies key practices for managing a supplier's performance. As an example, General Motors (GM) closely monitored the performance of its suppliers through frequent meetings. During these meetings, GM and its suppliers discussed issues regarding quality and level of service as well as any problems that have surfaced. The aim of these meetings was to ensure that both companies had a common understanding of the required service. In addition, at a steering committee meeting every week, programme managers discussed any problems and performed strategic planning. Frequent interactions with end users also deepened the relationship between end-user needs and service delivery.

Beyond the immediate performance evaluation, the key activities for the organisation are investing in the relationship, monitoring the relationship, using diligent documentation and administration, engaging in risk-management exercises, addressing disputes, developing continuous improvement procedures and evaluating the relationship between the supplier and client.

Regenerate phase

Finally, in the regenerate phase, the options for the next-generation outsourcing contract and the relationship are assessed. The ninth building block, *refresh,* provides a set of activities that assist the client in deciding whether to engage in additional contracts with this particular supplier. The key activities for the client organisation are to assess contract outcomes and the lessons learnt and consider future requirements.

As an example, a university tried to evaluate whether the benefits pursued through its five-year outsourcing deal had been achieved. Towards the end of this deal, the university chancellor conducted an assessment in order to decide on its future outsourcing plans. Several issues had arisen over the course of this period: there were no monitoring reports, and the people who had been involved in the original outsourcing negotiations were not longer at the university. In addition, the current stakeholders had different views on the objectives of the outsourcing venture than had those who were originally involved. Consequently, it was difficult to determine the intended benefits of the outsourcing initiative as well as the extent to which they had been achieved. The contract manager, therefore, had to identify the actual achievements, that is, the extent to which the supplier had performed in a satisfactory way. This was because the supplier had responsibility for a process or a function rather than a task, so it was more efficient to measure business outcomes through key performance indicators. The contract manager also had to establish how the achievements had been accomplished, which were through rewards and through a reduction of incidents.

The next life cycle round

Following this final phase, the life cycle begins a new round. If the decision is to retender, renegotiate or backsource the work, the outsourcing life cycle will be repeated. If the outsourcing configuration differs significantly from the previous engagement, all stages of the cycle may need to be repeated. If the work is retendered with only minor changes, the client organisation may begin with supplier selection. If the client decides to backsource the work, beginning with the transition phase would be appropriate. And if the client wishes to renegotiate the same scope of work but look for an improved deal, it should start from the design stage and then move to the negotiation stage.

Managing the Transition Stage: Key Issues and Best Practices

The transition stage in outsourcing is a time of intense change during which the client and supplier are setting up the governance structure of the relationship and the client is gradually handing over the service to the supplier. For a large-scale outsourcing contract the transfer of services to an (offshore) location is usually organised in several 'waves'.[3] For example, in our study of ABN AMRO's outsourcing relationship with TCS, where TCS was contracted to provide support and application enhancement services to ABN AMRO bank summary of which we included as a case study in Chapter 7 (see also Kotlarsky et al., 2014), we witnessed the transition of more than 100 banking applications. These applications were divided into three groups, so that the transition of each group could be managed separately, as a 'wave', with the aim of completing the transition of all three 'waves' within three months. Each 'wave' was divided into three stages: knowledge transfer, shadowing and primary support (as depicted in Figure 8.1). The 'knowledge transfer' stage involved the transfer of applications to TCS. By the end of this stage, TCS was expected to have developed sufficient expertise of the client systems and applications to be able to support them in the future. During the 'shadowing' stage, TCS staff observed how bank personnel solved incidents. Then, during the 'primary support' stage the roles changed and the TCS staff solved incidents and provided support under the observation of the bank experts. After the transition was completed, the project shifted to a steady state which implied that the bank was running 'business as usual' with TCS providing maintenance and enhancements on the bank's systems.

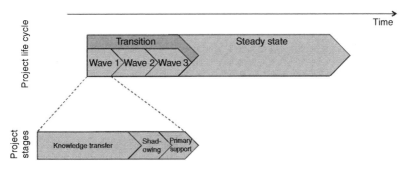

FIGURE **8.1** / **Stages of the outsourcing project (schematic)**
Source: Modified from Kotlarsky, Scarbrough and Oshri, 2014.

Clearly transition is one of the riskier times in the relationship and, therefore, needs close examination.

The transition process often officially begins when the contract goes into effect and ends on a specified date or at the signing of a transition acceptance form (confirming that all aspects of the arrangement are fully operational). Regardless of the official start and end dates, the transition actually begins much earlier and ends much later, and if it is not managed properly, it may not end at all. We have witnessed all too many deals where 'transition' becomes a permanent state.

Cullen and Willcocks (2003) identify the key objectives of the transition as being that:

• Both parties are in a position to fulfil their obligations and complete specific transition actions as laid out in the contract and SLA
• There is a smooth transfer of the staff to the supplier (if applicable) and their integration into the supplier's organisation, systems and culture
• There is a smooth transfer of the assets and obligations to the supplier (if applicable), including licences and warranties
• There is a smooth transfer of the third-party contracts to the supplier (if applicable), including maintenance and service subcontracts
• There is a continuity of services during the transition
• All service levels defined in the SLA will be measured and reported as required
• There is the integration of essential business processes between the supplier's and the organisation's systems.

Prior to embarking on the transition, the following should already be in place:

- *Transition plan*. The customer's needs were outlined in the market package, and the supplier prepared a detailed response in the bid
- *Disruption-minimisation strategy*. The customer's needs were outlined in the market package, and the supplier prepared a detailed response in the bid
- *Communication strategy*. The strategy was developed in the very early days of the IT outsourcing life cycle
- *Staffing arrangements*. Transfer conditions, redundancy and redeployment processes were in place
- *Management function*. The retained organisation and contract management function has been designed
- *Mobilised resources*. Training has been conducted and responsibilities have been reallocated to get the transition teams and operational teams prepared.

The old ways of working will no longer be appropriate under an outsourcing arrangement. A piece of the organisation has effectively been removed. New work flows, communications, paper flows and sign-offs are required within the organisation to ensure a united and efficient interaction with the supplier. New relationships will need to be quickly formed, and people accustomed to a certain way of operating will now need to operate in a completely different manner. Accordingly, a number of tasks need to be performed to set up the ongoing operations, including these major ones:

- Transfer of assets, people, contracts, information and projects that the supplier will be responsible for in the future. In many cases, these transfers require dedicated teams made up of individuals from both parties because these areas of the former business were not designed to be easily transported to another organisation.
- Staff transition. It is a common misconception that in ITO arrangements, the majority of the organisation's IT staff are transferred to the supplier. Although this may be true for the very large deals that receive a great deal of media attention and can involve the transfer of hundreds, if not thousands, of employees, this is not the usual case.

- Understanding the emotional impact on staff. Regardless of the transition option the organisation adopts, all IT personnel will be affected by the ITO arrangement: those who stay, those who transfer and those who are laid off. Many organisations fail to realise that outsourcing can be a tumultuous change and always has an emotional impact on employees. This 'people side' may be difficult to hear or see at first, but it can progress into the loudest problem that the outsourcing project may face if it is not managed well. Sometimes employees (occasionally in conjunction with their union) not only refuse to work but deliberately sabotage the outsourcing process. It is not surprising, then, that some of the larger suppliers have invested quite a lot of time and effort in getting their transition policies and practices well honed. In organisational change management terms, staff who will be affected are known as *change targets*. Organisations need to know the different behaviours that change targets may demonstrate so it can effectively manage any negative behaviours, such as anger and depression, that can be quite destructive. The model in Figure 8.2 shows the behavioural stages that employees are likely to pass through before they accept the reality of any major change. Most people pass through each of these emotions, though not necessarily in this order, and they may pass through some emotions more than once. To help staff come to terms with the impact – career impact or

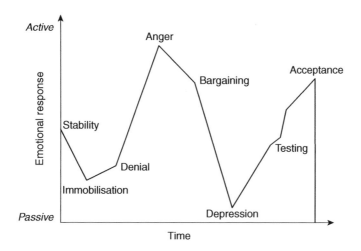

FIGURE 8.2   **The emotional response to organisational change**

even self-esteem impact – organisations have offered career counselling, outplacement, financial planning and personal counselling.

Managing the transition project

The steps outlined in this section document an approach for a large-scale transition. For smaller or less complex transitions, not all the steps may be needed. For example, a small transition may not need a full team to be responsible for the project, but there will be a need to ensure that someone is accountable. We discuss below major areas to focus on in transition projects.

Roles and responsibilities for transition methodology

While for a client organisation transition presents a unique challenge, service providers are typically very experienced in transitions and typically will have their own 'transition methodology' to facilitate knowledge transfer from the client to the supplier organisation and organise the handover of processes in an effective and efficient manner. For example, in ABN AMRO's outsourcing engagement with TCS that we mentioned earlier, the transition was guided by the TCS Transition Methodology. This methodology established as an organising principle that the organisational structure of the on-site-offshore team should 'mirror' the client firm's structure at both on-site and offshore locations (see Kotlarsky et al., 2014). In accordance with this principle, TCS mirrored the bank's three portfolios of applications by allocating separate sub-teams for each. Within this organisational structure, explicit correspondences were established between the roles of bank employees, on-site, and offshore personnel.

Furthermore, a client organisation should consider defining roles and responsibilities dedicated to the transition project. The types of roles to consider for transition are shown in Table 8.4. Depending on the size of transition, it may be that one person has more than one role, or that more than one person undertakes the same role. The transition team typically will use existing client personnel who will be allocated to the transition project until transition is completed. Depending on the nature of the outsourcing contract, it may be appropriate to break down the transition team to sub-teams by division, function or process, in particular when transition is planned to take place in 'waves' that are concerned with different functions, processes or services. Transition role descriptions are rarely

TABLE 8.4   Transition roles

Role	Description
Steering committee or a joint reference panel	Guide the project and provide strategic input to the implementation process Facilitate timely decision-making and resolve issues that the transition team has identified Monitor the quality of key deliverables Provide a forum for communicating progress and achievement of project milestones
Transition programme leader	Manage all the transition activities across all the divisions to ensure consistency Report to the steering committee
Transition project team leaders	Manage the transition for a specific service, geography or customer group
Human resources (HR) representatives	Provide HR-specific advice Coordinate the HR initiatives and services to staff Assist in setting up the retained organisation
Business representatives	Provide specific advice for business units Coordinate business unit transition activities Liaise with business unit line management Test and accept business unit data migration and proper operational functioning
Technical representatives	Provide technical advice Coordinate technical transition activities Liaise with the supplier's technicians Test and accept technical migration, configuration and proper operational functioning
Communications representatives	Provide communication about the advice of the change leadership Develop communications messages and media Liaise with the supplier's communications representative Manage the feedback loop
Administration resource	Coordinate logistical support Create and manage control files

sufficient for understanding and preparing thoroughly for the transition, particularly because at least two parties will be working together. For this reason, Cullen and Willcocks (2003) recommend developing a responsibility matrix for transition deliverables that are tracked until completion. The size and extent of the change will largely determine how long a transition will take. When determining the time frame, the organisation will need to take into account its own unique factors: for example, the amount of consultation required, the speed of decision-making, and the availability and competence of line management. However, most transition projects can be accomplished with one or two months designing the transition and then about three to six months to carry out and close out the project.

Intellectual property and security

During an outsourcing engagement, the client must allow the supplier to access certain critical information and assets that risk loss of intellectual property and security breaches. Suppliers should have access to only required material and systems and nothing more. In implementing proper security protocols, it is essential to tag assets (both physical and intangible), decide which assets the supplier needs to access and then make a dedicated effort to isolate those assets in order to minimise risk.

However, security does not end there. The client must assign responsibility, authority and accountability to people who can monitor access and usage. Without a monitoring protocol in place, loss can go unnoticed until it is too late. If security protocols are breached, the staff responsible must have the authority to act and have accountability for failure.

Risk assessment and contingency plan

By their very nature, transitions are fraught with a variety of risks – for example:

- *Project risks*: Resources skills and availability, lack of commitment from management, disparate levels of concern and priority between the parties, insufficient time and resources allocated, other organisational initiatives that may have a timing impact or require resources that are taken away from the transition project, conflict in coordinating between parties
- *Communication risks*: Mixed or conflicting messages put out by the parties, rumours that drive perceptions, adverse media
- *Employee risks*: Employee-union action, low morale, loss of motivation, loss of key personnel, disgruntled personnel
- *Operations risks*: Disruptions to normal operations and service continuity, data- or systems-conversion failure, missing documentation
- *Assets risks*: Wrong assets moved, assets go missing, assets not in the condition specified in the market package, missing documentation including third-party contracts and licensing agreements

• *Retained organisation risks*: Impact of organisational change that was not adequately identified and addressed, required skills unavailable in the organisation or in the recruitment market.

Accordingly, it is important that the areas of potential hazard are identified, the consequences estimated and strategies developed to mitigate risk.

Moreover, clients should have contingency plans in place if the transition goes poorly. Any number of issues can go wrong: system crashes, failure to integrate and delays. While a client cannot plan for every conceivable scenario, it can make action plans based on the probability of occurrence. High-risk items need a framework in place to guide behaviour should they occur.

Knowledge transfer and training

In order for a supplier to successfully engage in work and ensure uninterrupted service delivery, the client organisation must achieve knowledge transfer with respect to its systems, practices, standards and protocols. The key is to obtain the right balance of knowledge: not too little and not too much. Too little knowledge will impede the supplier's ability to deliver services, as they will lack the contextual details for making the proper assumptions and decisions. And too little knowledge often results in communication errors between the client and supplier, especially when common frames of reference have not been established initially. Too much knowledge opens the client organisation up to security and intellectual property issues and can undermine a client's competitive edge in the industry. The more people have access to privileged information, the greater the risk of losing it to the competition. The client must be clear in elucidating what kinds of knowledge need to be shared and which types must remain private.

Training is another element necessary for successful knowledge transfer. Both client staff and supplier staff will need training in various areas concerning the content of the project (e.g., applications, methodologies and processes). Such training should be conducted jointly with both client and supplier personnel. The joint effort makes it possible for the training team to answer questions more effectively and to ensure both sides are on the same ground. For instance, the supplier may not have the answer with respect to certain client-side information but having an integrated training team allows all necessary information to be imparted to the right people.

Having informal knowledge transfer mechanisms in place also promotes the exchange of information and ideas. Online spaces and portals provide a place where employees can share ideas, ask/answer questions, create focus groups, make document repositories and post Frequently Asked Questions. Such online platforms are well suited for helping client and supplier personnel to connect and for stimulating the free flow of ideas and information.

Communications

Communications within the client organisation: It is important for the transition team to communicate in an accurate and timely manner. Transition is a time of considerable anxiety for staff, and communication is one of the most important ways to minimise uncertainty and anxiety. The transition team needs to identify their key stakeholders and develop a plan to keep them informed. The objective is to provide consistent messages across the organisation, so this includes keeping line management informed as well. The amount of effort that will be required should not be underestimated. Staff under stress need to hear the message several times and through different media (e.g., group, face-to-face, written). Another key part of the communications strategy is to set the expectations of the customers or users of the service. It is important for the organisation to work with the supplier on the communications rollout so that the supplier has the full opportunity to 'sell' themselves and the arrangement to the users and understand any expectation gaps.

Given the importance of the communications strategy and messaging during transition, it is worth looking at these areas in more detail. Neo Group (2005) suggest the following practices for dealing with communication challenges during the transition phase of global sourcing initiatives:

- *Select the right communication vehicles*: Examples include company newsletters, individual meetings, company-wide meetings and meetings with the press and other media
- *Develop key internal messages*: Often it is relatively difficult to communicate precise information with regard to the venture and its outcomes. However, even the communication of alternative scenarios, possible

ranges, estimates and probabilities can be useful. Communication should be iterative and evolving, beginning with relatively uncertain information and progressing towards more solid content.

- *Resist communication that says nothing*: Communicating without saying anything concrete creates rumours and uncertainty. Empty communication decreases levels of trust and confidence in the leading team and creates resistance to implementation efforts. The content of communication efforts should aim to address the concerns of all stakeholders, internal and external, and keep them well informed.

- *It is better not to persuade*: The more an organisation tries to persuade people at the lower levels of the hierarchy with regard to the credibility and reliability of its decisions, the more untrustworthy it seems. Opinion leaders can play a mediating role between the business leaders of an organisation and these employees. The challenge for the organisation is to ensure that opinion leaders have some recommendations to make, that they can communicate alternative scenarios and outcomes and that they can advise their colleagues on how to deal with the subsequent changes. For example, in an insurance company, the CIO played the role of opinion leader and advised staff members who would be transferred to the supplier's site on their professional and financial concerns.

- *Painting a positive story does not always help*: If a positive story raises employee expectations that are not met, employee morale falls and the implementation faces serious challenges. As an example, an organisation may communicate to its staff that some of them will be transferred to the supplier's site with very favourable employment conditions. If this does not happen, employees will lose their trust, will resist implementation efforts and, most important, will develop feelings of anxiety and uncertainty that will inhibit their productivity.

- *Engage in frequent communication*: Successful organisations typically communicate on employees' issues related to the initiative after the completion of each critical phase in the process. The frequency of communication should be related to the level of uncertainty associated with the global sourcing venture.

- *Identify the senders and receivers*: Organisations need to ensure effective message delivery. For this reason, they should clearly identify the senders and receivers of messages. Senders of internal communications may include the CEO, human resource (HR) managers, line managers and business unit heads. Senders of external communications may include the CEO, the corporate communications department or the public relations department. With regard to receivers, internal receivers are mainly the organisation's employees at different levels of the organisation, and external receivers are customers, suppliers, financial analysts, the media and the overall community. Mapping each set of senders to the appropriate receivers along with the right message is critical for the successful communication of information.

• *Develop an effective external communications plan*: In the minds of many people, offshoring is associated with taking work out of a country. Along these lines, people tend to believe that companies engaged in offshoring initiatives are trying to achieve financial benefits at the expense of their national workforce. Therefore, major global sourcing initiatives are highly likely to be faced with negative publicity. To mitigate this image-tarnishing effect, organisations need to develop a communication strategy that will send the sort of message that maintains a positive image of the organisation.

• E-Loan was very effective in managing its external communications strategy regarding its offshore venture in India. The chief privacy officer of the company explained the rationale behind their offshore initiative: 'Essentially, as we close our business day in the US, India begins theirs. This 24-hour processing capability enables us to fund loans one to two days faster – in ten days versus 11 to 12 days – than if they were processed entirely in the US.' He noted further that customers were given the opportunity to decide if they wanted the entire transaction to be processed domestically or overseas. The effort of the company to communicate its philosophy with regard to its offshore venture was particularly effective in convincing its customers about its intentions. The chief privacy officer explained,

> Currently 87% of our customers are selecting the overseas option... While we believed that disclosing the programme, providing a choice and explaining a time benefit would be appreciated by consumers, we didn't think the numbers would be as high as they have been from the start. However, the results of our programme support the idea that when you make the effort to explain the 'what', 'where' and 'why' to consumers, they are comfortable with it.

- An effective communication strategy can help a firm avoid negative publicity and criticism, while maintaining its positive corporate image.

Communications between client and supplier personnel: Furthermore, it is also important to dedicate efforts for establishing communication protocols between client and supplier personnel who need to interact during the transition. It is the most critical aspect for a smooth transition phase and beyond. Miscommunication and a low level of understanding create havoc in an outsourcing project. The use of local jargon, faulty assumptions and poor documentation are key components of miscommunication. Setting forth and defining communication protocols from the outset will help reduce communication errors. For example, in offshore outsourcing ventures, time zone is often a critical issue. When scheduling meetings, whose time zone serves as the reference point? If a task or communication is marked 'urgent', what exactly does that mean? Establish communication protocols that address such issues from the start will help everyone to be on the same page.

Another aspect to communication within an outsourcing relationship regards cultural norms. In some areas of the world, employees are taught that 'no' is not an acceptable response which it is rude. If something is not possible, it is simply not possible, and miscommunication of this fact will only lead to flawed expectations. Therefore, staff on both sides must be trained in the particularities of cultural communication.

Close-out and acceptance

It is quite common to have some form of acceptance criteria that allows an evaluation and approval process to ensure that the transition has been successfully completed; it may even be in the form of a formal acceptance certificate. This is particularly important where there is a separate transition fee payable to the supplier.

Even without this formality around the completion of the transition, most organisations find it useful to conduct a post-implementation review, if only to comply with best-practice project management principles. A more important reason is that the organisation will undoubtedly go through similar events in the future. Therefore, learning from the experience and communicating that learning is very important to future outsourcing engagements.

Summary

The outsourcing life-cycle framework provides a step-by-step guide to integrating the strategic and the operational levels of outsourcing objectives and results. The transition phase, the starting point of most outsourcing relationships, requires special attention. Failing to properly design and execute this phase will likely result in additional challenges for the client and supplier as the relationship matures. In this regard, this chapter provides the most effective practices for transition and the entire outsourcing life cycle.

9

Governance of Outsourcing Relationships

Although the outsourcing industry has demonstrated impressive growth during the past few years, some outsourcing relationships have yielded poor results, and some have even been terminated early. Both the professional press and academic publications have identified poor governance as a primary factor leading to these results. In this chapter, we therefore focus on understanding governance issues related to outsourcing and the practices that could support formal structures. In particular, we review the following issues:

- The governing structures for outsourcing ventures
- The roles involved in governing outsourcing relationships
- The most effective governance practices for outsourcing relationships.

The Basics of Governance in Outsourcing

Governance refers to the processes and structures that ensure the alignment of the strategies and objectives of the parties involved. In most cases, these processes and structures will facilitate the alignment of the client's objectives and strategies with the supplier's delivery system. However, governing structures and processes may also include aligning the goals and strategies of the client, intermediaries and suppliers in multisourcing settings. Clearly, as outsourcing projects become complex, with multiple suppliers, multiple sourcing arrangements and multiple geographical locations, the governing structures also need to be designed so that they offer a wide range of opportunities to govern the relationships under various contexts and settings.

The set of tasks involved in governance structures is managerial in nature. Most books and consultants identify the following elements as critical for a healthy governing structure: the outsourcing organisational structure, the communication channels, the control and monitoring frameworks, and the performance metrics. Both the supplier and the client should agree on the mechanisms put in place as governing structures. More importantly, both parties should also devise problem-solving mechanisms in case of breakdowns in these governing structures and processes.

The literature highlights some aspects of governing structures that require special attention regardless of the settings or geographical location of the outsourcing project. First, communication channels between the client and the supplier should be smooth and effective at all times. Second, trust and building rapport between the supplier and the client are essential for achieving healthy and effective collaborations. And an effective and reliable reporting system should be maintained throughout the life cycle of the outsourcing project.

Service Level Agreement

A key element in governing the outsourcing project is the service-level agreement (SLA), a legal document that details the services contracted to a supplier. It also defines aspects regarding the delivery of these services, such as at what quality the services will be delivered and through what channels, using what methods. The SLA also provides a detailed account of the conditions under which service can be disrupted. Effective SLAs accommodate changes in the method and mode of delivery subject to changes in market conditions or the client's strategic intent. However, such changes may put a heavy burden on the supplier when attempting to meet the client's needs. Therefore, we advise suppliers and clients to build some flexibility into SLAs, along with assessing the impact on the supplier should client needs change.

SLAs are monitored on a dashboard – not as a simplistic indication of whether the supplier has met the basic requirements but as a representation of achieving the business goals behind each SLA. For this reason, the dashboard is a balanced scorecard regarding business-oriented objectives. A simple example is an SLA of a hosting service in which the supplier is required to provide support at all times. This SLA will provide a detailed account of the specific elements relating to this service, the expected service quality and the downtime allowed for each region. The dashboard will provide a general indication of whether these conditions have been met. A green light on the dashboard means that the hosting service is provided without interruption. A red light signifies that one or more of the conditions has not been met, and therefore the service has been interrupted. In this situation, the client and the supplier must resolve this problem.

Governing Structures

Governing the outsourcing project can be an expensive activity. For this reason, clients consider the size of the project as one assessment criterion in their decision regarding the scope and complexity of the governing structure. Evidence suggests that outsourcing projects with a budget of US$50,000 or less are rarely supported with a governing structure. Nevertheless, most outsourcing projects have some elements of the governing structures – for example, an account manager – to ensure the coordination of activities and monitoring of results from the client side.

Mani et al. (2006) argue that insufficient attention to governance is the main reason that some BPO projects fail to deliver value. They identify three key dimensions that shape the nature of governance structures required for BPO:

1. The interdependence of a process with other processes, which refers to the extent that a business process works independently or affects, or is affected by, other processes
2. Process complexity, which refers to how difficult it is to understand the specifics of a process and to measure its output
3. The strategic importance of a process to an enterprise, which refers to the extent that a process has an impact upon its competitiveness.

Mani et al. explain that these three key dimensions of the outsourced process should determine the type of an outsourcing contract to use, the management of the relationship and the technical capabilities, which they refer to as key BPO governance capabilities. Table 9.1 summarises guidelines for determining the necessary BPO governance capabilities.

TABLE 9.1   Guidelines for determining BPO governance capabilities

Governance capabilities	Governance guideline
Outsourcing contract	The BPO contract should take into account uncertainties regarding the outsourced process. If uncertainties regarding the process are high, it can be difficult to build comprehensive contingencies into the contract. Therefore, as uncertainty increases, the client must shift emphasis from controlling uncertainty through performance contracts to managing it through relational contracts.
	Independent processes whose requirements can easily be described can easily be disaggregated from other client processes. They should be owned and managed by the suppliers with the relevant process expertise. However, if the outsourced process shares interdependencies with other client processes, the requirements are more difficult to define. Furthermore, there are fewer opportunities for the supplier to benefit from economies of scale. Thus, the outsourced process needs to be jointly owned.
Relationship management	Effective relationship management helps bridge cultural gaps between companies and fosters a collaborative working approach in BPO. The more strategic the outsourced process is, the greater is the need for more collaboration and the more comprehensive the approach to relationship management needs to be.
	The BPO relationship must strike a balance between coordination and control. The higher the process complexity and strategic importance, the more the emphasis needs to be on coordination and less on control.
Technical capabilities	Technical capabilities are measured by the scope and intensity of the use of IT and the sophistication of the coordination systems. These capabilities must be aligned with the contract type and the depth of relationship management. BPO relationships that need high technical support are those that require collaboration and transparency, have a strategic agenda and aim to improve enterprise competitiveness.

Source: Based on Mani et al., 2006.

For example, Merrill Lynch outsourced the restructuring of its wealth management work station platform – a case of transformational BPO that involved high levels of process interdependence, complexity and strategic importance. More specifically, there was a high process interdependence because the new platform would have links among client management systems, call centres and online service management. Furthermore, the new platform would be particularly complex because it would accommodate 130 applications. Its importance to the organisation was highly strategic as the new platform would facilitate the prioritisation of work, something that was expected to benefit the company significantly. In particular, the new platform would enable the company's financial advisers to focus on the major clients while diverting the rest to the company's call centres or website.

In alignment with the high levels of process interdependence, complexity and strategic importance, Merrill Lynch tried to develop a relational contract emphasising the joint ownership of the outsourced process as well as the partnering nature of the venture that would enable the BPO initiative to be adapted to changing business needs. Furthermore, it developed a partnering model of operations that involved frequent communication and information exchanges from lower to top management levels. In terms of technical capabilities the BPO venture was highly challenging and demanded intense client–supplier collaboration.

As an example of transactional BPO, Qatar Airways outsourced its revenue accounting and recovery processes to Kale Consultants in India. The outsourced system was low in terms of process interdependence, complexity and strategic importance. More specifically, the revenue accounting and recovery process could be disaggregated from the firm's value network, which made it independent. Furthermore, it was a straightforward process with a low level of complexity. In terms of its significance to the competitiveness of the firm, it was considered a strategically peripheral corporate function.

The low levels of independence, complexity and strategic significance of the outsourced process were combined with low BPO governance capabilities. In other words, the company signed a clearly defined performance-based contract with its supplier. The management of the relationship relied on SLAs. Furthermore, Qatar Airways did not need to make any

TABLE 9.2   Characteristics of transformational BPO and transactional BPO governance models

Governance model	Process requirements	Governance capabilities
Transformational BPO	High interdependence	Contract: Relational contract emphasises joint ownership of the outsourced business process
	High complexity	Relationship management: Partnering model marked by relational emphasis on coordination and high levels of information exchange, joint action and commitment between the client and supplier
	High strategic importance	Technological capabilities: High technological capabilities
Transactional BPO	Low interdependence	Contract: Arm's-length performance contract emphasises transfer of ownership of the outsourced process to the supplier
	Low complexity	Relationship management: Relationship marked by emphasis on control and low levels of information exchange, joint action and commitment between the client and supplier
	Low strategic importance	Technological capabilities: Low technological capabilities

Source: Based on Mani et al., 2006.

technological investments. The new system interfaces required only the exchange of transactional data such as manual tickets, coupons and billing data.

Table 9.2 summarises the BPO governance models of transformational BPO (Merrill Lynch) and transactional BPO (Qatar Airways), as well as their attributes.

On this basis, according to the findings by Mani et al. (2006), BPO processes characterised by high interdependence, complexity and of high strategic significance should be combined with high governance capabilities (transformational BPO). Processes that are of low interdependence, complexity and strategic significance should be combined with low governance capabilities (transactional BPO). The misalignment of governance capabilities relative to these process dimensions would yield poor results.

Roles Involved in Governing Outsourcing

Setting up roles for the governing structures is often the responsibility of the supplier, and most large suppliers have developed robust methodologies to govern complex outsourcing projects. The main governing body is the global office, which often consists of numerous units that deal with project management (also known as project management office), quality assurance (quality assurance office) and infrastructure (the infrastructure office). The global office also consists of the business unit officers who are responsible for each relationship based on their functional or geographical area. For example, TCS set up a global office for its contract with ABN AMRO Bank that accommodated business unit officers for the Netherlands business unit (a geographical area) as well as for the private client unit (a functional area). The client should set up a project management office at the global level to coordinate activities and liaise with the supplier's global office. In global outsourcing projects, these roles are replicated at each geographical location. It is also common for the supplier to establish local offices near the client's site.

Figure 9.1 illustrates a governing structure typical of what most large suppliers propose to clients for offshore outsourcing projects. This structure shows parallel roles between client personnel, on-site supplier personnel and offshore supplier personnel. It also emphasises the need to have corresponding roles at various levels. For the application maintenance and development, there is a need for corresponding roles that can liaise and coordinate work regardless of their physical location. At the portfolio level, there is a need for middle managers to align business objectives regarding ongoing maintenance and possible future development. A general manager from the client side is usually responsible for managing and coordinating such efforts. At the strategic level, both clients and suppliers should assign senior managers to strategic roles. The client chief

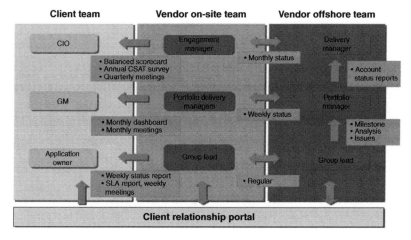

FIGURE 9.1 / Governing structure for a large supplier

information officer should ensure that the client's objectives are met by the supplier and that the client is providing the support needed to meet these objectives by the supplier. The supplier on-site engagement manager and the offshore delivery manager should assume equivalent responsibility on behalf of the supplier to meet the client's expectations.

Effective Governance Practices for Offshore Outsourcing

Companies can devise governing plans and set up governing structures designed to provide ideal conditions for successful offshore outsourcing projects. However, this does not guarantee the success of such projects. Therefore, sensing what might not work and applying effective practices that are suitable for these particular settings could improve the impact that the governing structures we have described would have on offshore outsourcing projects. According to their empirical work, Rottman and Lacity (2006) identify the most effective governing practices for offshore outsourcing projects:

1. *Develop the infrastructure*. Clients tend to underestimate the difficulty of integrating supplier employees based offshore into the work processes of their organisations. Although various sorts of security

concerns, human resource issues and management matters must be addressed before the launch of a project, a special focus should be directed towards infrastructural issues. With regard to these issues, the project manager of one client organisation noted,

> It really took us a long time to figure out how to make it [the onboarding process] run smoothly... Since the suppliers needed access to systems from various business units and IT sectors, we had to cross organisational boundaries and create new protocols and rights profiles. However, without these processes, the suppliers sit idle waiting for us to build a tunnel in the VPN [virtual private network]. We should have had all these processes in place much earlier than we did.
>
> (Rottman and Lacity, 2006)

Consequently, it is important for the client company to facilitate the integration of offshore supplier employees by anticipating and managing infrastructural challenges before the initiation of the cooperation.

2. *Elevate your own organisation's capability maturity model certification to close the process gap between you and your supplier.* Capability maturity model (CMM) certification aims to foster the use of processes that standardise, predict and improve IT software development. More specifically, it defines five levels of software development maturity (level 1 is the lowest) and identifies the sets of processes that need to be in place to achieve each level. A number of clients suggest that the best way to extract value from the supplier's CMM processes is for the client to become CMM certified. The director of application development of a transportation company noted,

> A real problem we had was our CMM level 1.5 guys talking to the supplier's level 5 guys. So together, we have worked out a plan with our supplier to help bring our CMM levels up. When we do, it will be a benefit to both of us; our specifications will be better and so the supplier can use them more efficiently.
>
> (Rottman and Lacity, 2006)

Along these lines, bringing the client's CMM levels up contributes to the process of communication between the two parties, improves requirements specification and facilitates efficiency in software development.

3. *Bring in a CMM expert with no domain expertise to flush out ambiguities in requirements.* In many instances, the specification of the client's requirements is a long and costly process. A major issue is that the clients and suppliers may interpret the requirements differently. To reduce the iterations during the requirements specification stage, an Indian supplier pursued a unique solution. The supplier brought in a CMM level 5 expert to the client's site. Intentionally, the chosen expert had no expertise on the client's business. This forced him to get into the process of clarifying ambiguities in the client's requirements and thus reducing the number of iterations for specification issues.

4. *Negotiate a flexible CMM.* Clients want to use only the CMM processes that will add value to their operations. As the project manager of one financial firm noted: 'You ask for one button to be moved and the supplier has to first do a 20-page impact analysis – we are paying for all this documentation we do not need' (Rottman and Lacity, 2006). Suppliers recognise that their clients are not satisfied with the idea of following CMM patterns to their very last detail; however, this is necessary for the supplier to maintain the reliability of its CMM processes. The managing director of an Indian supplier noted,

> My clients are telling me: you do what you have to do to pass your audits, but I can't afford all of this documentation. So we have developed a 'flexible CMM' model that maintains the processes necessary for high quality but keeps the customer-facing documentation and overheads to a minimum. Our customers have reacted favourably and our internal processes are still CMM 5.
>
> (Rottman and Lacity, 2006)

Consequently, sourcing partners have to find a balance between the client's desire for flexibility and minimum hassle and the supplier's need to maintain the integrity of its operations.

5. *Use an on-site engagement manager.* Studies suggest that on-site engagement managers contribute to the success of offshoring relationships. People in this role are familiar with the offshore supplier's culture, working style and internal processes and thus are able to smooth the transition phase and contribute to the quality of the service provided. However, it is important for on-site engagement managers to be included in the staffing and cost structure model. For example, Biotech, a major biotechnology firm that was working with an Indian supplier,

realised that it had to staff the project differently. A technical leader noted:

> If this project were to be staffed by domestic contractors, we would have added just two new contractors. However, since we were new to offshoring, we priced in an on-site engagement manager (OEM) to interface between the business sponsors and the two offshore developers. We realised that all project cost savings were lost, but the OEM helped us improve our processes, interviewed and managed the developers, and was responsible for status updates.
>
> (Rottman and Lacity, 2006)

Although OEMs carry a significant cost, they can benefit the venture in many ways and lead to cost savings in the long run.

6. *Give offshore suppliers domain-specific training to protect quality and lower development costs.* Although domain-specific training may dramatically increase transaction costs, clients need to understand that these costs protect quality and lower development costs in the long run. The reason is that the supplier becomes more knowledgeable about the client's business and processes and consequently more productive. The client has to make sure that trained employees remain on the account for a certain period of time, or the supplier should reimburse training costs.

7. *Develop governance metrics.* The need for governance tools and measures that consider costs, quality, time, risks and rewards has been widely recognised by clients as a fundamental way to ensure outsourcing value. The metrics used as governance tools as well as their specifications should be determined by the strategy and vision of the organisation. Examples of metrics are 'percentage of supplier business', which measures how much of the supplier's revenues come from the client organisation; the 'comparative efficiency metric', which assesses the relative productivity of in-house staff relative to offshore employees; and the 'bottom-line metric', which assesses the impact of the outsourcing relationship on the client's business. A particular metric may have different meanings for different organisations depending on their business strategy and philosophy. For example, for some clients, the expectation is that the metric 'percentage of supplier business' will be high, providing a strong motivation for the supplier to deliver better service, while other organisations may want this metric to be low

because they do not want their suppliers to be overly dependent on their business for revenue generation.

Another view on how to strengthen the foundation provided by the governing structures described suggests that clients and suppliers should focus on developing their relationship (Liker and Choi, 2004). Among the most effective practices to improve governance of outsourcing projects are the following:

Conduct joint improvement activities

- Exchange best practices with suppliers
- Initiate continuous improvement projects at the suppliers' facilities
- Set up supplier study groups.

Share information intensively but selectively

- Set times, places and agendas for meetings
- Use rigid formats for sharing information
- Insist on accurate data collection
- Share information in a structured fashion.

Develop the suppliers' technical capabilities

- Build the suppliers' problem-solving skills
- Develop a common lexicon
- Hone core suppliers' innovation capabilities.

Supervise the suppliers

- Send monthly report cards to core suppliers
- Provide immediate and constant feedback
- Involve senior managers in solving problems.

Turn supplier rivalry into opportunity

- Source each component from two or three suppliers
- Create compatible production philosophies and systems
- Set up joint ventures with existing suppliers to transfer knowledge and maintain control.

Understand how the suppliers work

- Learn about the suppliers' businesses
- Go to the suppliers' locations to see how they work

'• Respect the suppliers' capabilities
'• Commit to prosperity for both parties.

Ross and Beath (2005) support this view and argue that in developing relationships as part of the governing processes, clients and suppliers should work out the difference between their expectations and the actual offering. They call finding a middle way between a client's expectations and the supplier's offering 'the sweet spot'. Table 9.3 summarises the sources of the differences between clients and suppliers and offers some sweet spots for both parties to build and renew their relationship.

TABLE 9.3　Client expectations, supplier offerings and the sweet spot

	Client expectations	Sweet spot	Supplier offerings
Transaction relationship	• Best practice • Variable capacity • Management focus on core competencies	• Low-maintenance relationship • Reasonable margins • Innovation to ensure process improvements	• Standard best-practice process components • Economics of scale • Distinctive assets
Co-sourcing alliance	• Cost savings • Access to expertise on demand	• Variable project staffing • Leverage offshore • Disciplined project management	• Labour arbitrage • Project management expertise • Expertise on specialised technologies
Strategic partnerships	• Cost savings • Variable capacity • Management focus on core competencies	• Second-choice supplier moving up value chain	• Capability to deliver a broad range of specialised series • Integration expertise • Disciplined practices • Economies of scale

Source: Based on Ross and Beath, 2005.

Summary

This chapter focused on the governing structures, roles and practices for effective management of outsourcing relationships. It emphasised the formal approach of governing structures and the traditional way of setting up roles and communication channels and examined the relational aspects of governing outsourcing. Clearly, investing in both formal governing structures and informal relational mechanisms improves the results expected from governing outsourcing.

chapter 10

Managing Globally Distributed Teams

Globally distributed work is an integral part of offshore outsourcing and offshoring. Offshore outsourcing often implies that the client and supplier teams need to work together in a globally distributed fashion. In such cases, some teams will be based onshore, at either the client's site or the supplier's onshore site, and others will be based offshore. In a similar vein, when a client firm sets up offshore facilities, it divides work between onshore and offshore locations, and often such distributed work requires close collaboration between members of globally distributed teams. *Globally distributed teams* consist of two or more (sub-)teams working together from different geographical locations to accomplish joint goals. These teams face major challenges on various fronts, including cultural differences, language barriers, national traditions, values, norms of behaviour and time-zone differences. Therefore, this chapter focuses on the following topics:

- The challenges faced by distributed teams such as offshore outsourcing teams
- The methodologies available for managing globally distributed teams
- The tools and technologies available to support distributed collaboration
- The role of face-to-face (F2F) meetings in facilitating collaboration and other social aspects that matter for distributed collaboration
- Cultural aspects that emerge in outsourcing and offshoring engagements
- What client firms can do to help build truly collaborative teams.

Challenges Faced by Globally Distributed Teams

Research on the management of globally distributed teams has tended to focus on issues related to the geographical dispersal of work. Because of the constraints associated with globally distributed work, such as distance, time zones and cultural differences, traditional coordination and control mechanisms tend to be less effective in globally distributed projects. Distance reduces the intensity of communications – in particular, when people experience problems with media that cannot substitute for F2F communications. Cultural differences expressed in different languages, values, working and communication habits and implicit assumptions are believed to be embedded in the collective knowledge of a specific culture and thus may cause misunderstandings and conflicts (see the case study included at the end of this chapter). Time-zone differences reduce opportunities for real-time collaboration, as response time increases considerably when working hours at remote locations do not overlap. Therefore, receiving an answer to a simple question may take far longer than in co-located projects.

Globally distributed teams, including offshore – onshore teams, have reported problems and breakdowns in various areas – for example:

- The breakdown of traditional coordination and control mechanisms
- Loss of communication richness (e.g., Cramton and Webber, 2005), limited opportunities for interactions and leaner communication media (e.g., Espinosa et al., 2007)
- Lack of understanding of the counterpart's context and lack of communication norms in coordinating distributed teams. In particular, the risk factors in offshore outsourcing scenarios are client–supplier communication (e.g., the miscommunication of the original set of requirements, language barriers and poor change management controls), the client's internal management issues (e.g., lack of top management commitment, inadequate user involvement, lack of offshore project management know-how, poor management of end-user expectations and failure to consider all costs) and supplier capabilities (e.g., lack of business and technical know-how by the offshore team)
- Language barriers (e.g., Sarker and Sahay, 2004)
- Misunderstandings caused by cultural differences, such as different conversational styles and different subjective interpretations (e.g., Lee-Kelley and Sankey, 2008)

- Dissonance or conflict, such as task or interpersonal conflict (e.g., Lee-Kelley and Sankey, 2008)
- Loss of team cohesion and motivation to collaborate, such as decreased morale and lack of trust
- Asymmetry in distribution of information among sites (e.g., Carmel, 1999)
- Difficulty collaborating because of different skills sets and training methods, various tools, technologies and IT infrastructures (e.g., Sarker and Sahay, 2004)
- Lack of informal interpersonal communications (e.g., Cramton and Webber, 2005)
- Difficulties working across time zones (e.g., Lee-Kelley and Sankey, 2008)
- Delays in distributed collaborative work processes. This is often described in terms of unproductive waits for the other side to respond with clarifications or feedback, which can be the result of time-zone differences but may also be because of different interpretations of priorities, especially when local and global priorities are not the same.

Studies report some of these challenges in depth. For example, Oshri et al. (2007b) describes how Baan, a software development firm based in the Netherlands that offshored software development to India in the late 1990s, struggled to develop successful collaboration between the Dutch and the Indian teams. One problem area that the Indian counterparts described was the lack of ownership of the product, which affected the Indian team in their perception of themselves as part of the Baan global team. The Indian engineers kept referring to their Dutch counterparts as 'them' and portrayed the relationships as if these were between a client and a supplier.

In another study, Kotlarsky et al. (2007) describe the challenges regarding knowledge sharing between onshore and offshore teams involved in component-based development. It was shown that, while the common wisdom regarding distributed component-based development suggests that each site should take responsibility for a particular component, in reality, as illustrated by TCS, the Indian IT service provider, success stories are based on a development methodology that encourages the joint development of a component by more than one site. As a result of such methodology, remote sites, such as TCS's on-site team in Zurich and their offshore team in Mumbai, developed collaborative methodologies that quickened the development process and produced highly reusable components.

Another study (Kotlarsky, van Fenema and Willcocks, 2008) illustrates the challenges in co-developing software across remote sites. Here, the emphasis is on the transfer of work packages between on-site and offshore teams. Although generally there has been a growing dependency on the codification of knowledge and, therefore, the transfer of documentation back and forth between on-site and offshore teams during the various software development stages, it was shown that the codification of knowledge is not sufficient for successful collaboration (see also Kotlarsky, Scarbrough and Oshri, 2014). Successful teams, such as at SAP, the German software warehouse, combined informal and formal mechanisms to support collaborative software development.

Clearly globally distributed teams face a number of challenges. In particular, offshore and on-site teams may experience these challenges to a greater extent because of the cultural and time-zone differences and the effects of the local context in relation to global priorities. In a globally distributed environment, work is divided between teams and individuals at multiple geographically dispersed places, thus the coordination and integration of work need to be done across these remote locations. This can cause a delay in work completion, because distributed tasks appear to take longer to finish compared to similar tasks that are co-located. Solutions have been developed for software development that is carried out in a distributed manner in three key areas: (1) the division of work, by which the coordination and integration of work conducted at remote locations can be made easier; (2) coordination solutions for distributed environments; and (3) communication patterns aiming to make inter-site co-ordination more efficient through planning systematic communication between remote counterparts and establishing rules of communications. We now describe these three areas in depth.

Division of work

Typically, strategies to divide work between remote locations are such that their main objective is to reduce the need for inter-site coordination and communications. These are, therefore, the most commonly mentioned strategies for the division of work in globally distributed teams in the specific context of engineering, digitally enabled products and software development:

• *Phase/process step,* when globally dispersed sites engage in different phases of a project in a sequential manner. This means that work is handed over to a remote site after completing certain process steps. For example, requirement analysis may take place in a front office located in New York, after which specifications are transferred to Dublin for the conceptual design and then coding will be carried out in Mumbai. Figure 10.1, which we refer to as scenario A, illustrates this strategy.

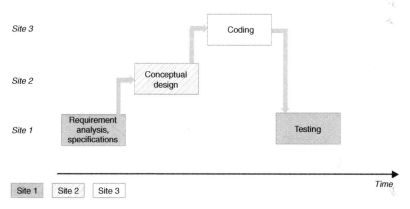

FIGURE 10.1 / Scenario A: globally distributed work based on phase/process step

• *Product structure (product module),* when each product module or feature is developed at a single site. This approach allows different sites to work on different modules in parallel. Figure 10.2 illustrates such a scenario (scenario B), when a system is divided into modules (typically different product functions) and each module is allocated to a different site. For example, while the requirement analysis is carried out in London, the specifications, design, coding and testing of the three key modules of a complex system are carried out in Ireland, India and Russia, respectively. We wish to emphasise that structured, well-defined tasks are more suitable to be allocated by phase/process step, while unstructured, loosely defined tasks are more appropriate to be allocated by product structure (product module).

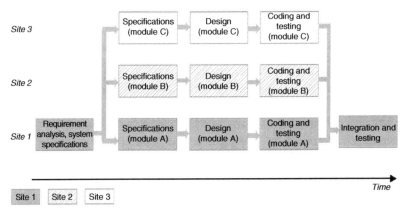

FIGURE **10.2** Scenario B: globally distributed work based on product structure

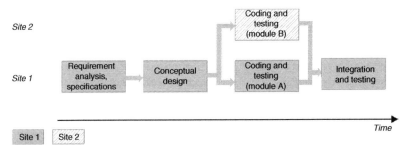

FIGURE **10.3** Scenario C: globally distributed work based on minimising requirements for cross-site communication and synchronisation

- *Minimising requirements for cross-site communication and synchronisation;* however, this works only for particular types of product architectures. The philosophy behind this practice is that 'tightly coupled work items that require frequent coordination and synchronisation should be performed within one site' (Mockus and Weiss, 2001). Figure 10.3 illustrates such a scenario (scenario C) in which some tasks require frequent coordination. In this example, requirements analysis and specification, conceptual design and integration and testing are conducted at one site, and only well-defined tasks (coding and testing of different modules) are conducted at two locations in parallel.

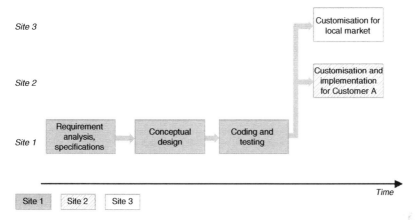

Site 3

Site 2

Site 1

FIGURE 10.4 Scenario D: globally distributed work based on product customisation

- *Product customisation*, so that one site develops the product and other sites perform customisation, that is, changes such as adding features and enhancements for specific customers. In this case, the sites that customise the product are geographically near the customer. Figure 10.4 illustrates this scenario (scenario D), in which a system is developed in one location (site 1) and other globally dispersed sites customise the system for specific customers (site 2) or for local markets (site 3).
- *Division of work across time zones,* where a task is passed from one person to the next person, located in a different time zone, at the end of a workday to reduce project completion time and improve resource utilisation through 24-hour development.

Clearly, offshoring projects that work with onshore teams have a range of work division practices to rely on in making a decision regarding where to place activity X and how such a decision will affect the mode of collaboration between onshore and offshore teams.

Inter-site coordination mechanisms

While work division in offshoring and offshore outsourcing projects typically aims to reduce/simplify interdependencies between sites, when it comes to integrating distributed work such projects often face serious coordination challenges (Srikanth and Puranam, 2011). Past experience tells us that there are a number of strategies that can help such teams cope with these challenges – for example:

- Having an explicit, documented and formalised project process: Standardising and documenting the development methodology, distributing it across sites, and storing it in a shared repository; educating all team members about the chosen methodologies. A recent study we conducted at Capgemini showed that front-office teams based in the Netherlands were facing major challenges collaborating with back-office teams, which were based in India, because approaches to development methodologies were not standardised.
- Promoting task-related interaction by encouraging interdependence and reliance on one another among the members of distributed teams. Our study at TCS has shown that this practice is particularly successful between on-site and offshore teams.
- Providing approaches that can coordinate distributed software development tasks, such as integration-centric engineering processes, which aim at managing crucial dependencies in distributed software development projects (e.g., Taxén, 2006).
- Adopting a more structured project-management approach. Ghosh and Varghese (2004) propose a project management framework based on process restructuring that can be used efficiently for managing and tracking the distributed development of large-scale projects.
- Encouraging visits to remote sites and F2F meetings (e.g., Malhotra and Majchrzak, 2005). In a study we conducted at SAP, TCS and LeCroy, we noticed that while F2F meetings were important, it was far more important to build a socialising system within which remote teams renew social ties and re-socialise after a kick-off meeting and after each project meeting. In this regard, remote teams need to re-norm and re-establish a shared team identity (Oshri et al., 2007b).
- Establishing liaisons between remote locations.
- Creating transparency in project goals and the company vision.
- Identifying different modes of task assignment mechanisms: self-assignment, assigning to others and consulting with others (e.g., Crowston et al., 2007).

- Building awareness of the work conducted at remote sites by making project plans accessible over the Web and awareness of who is doing what by creating an online profile for each team member with personal information.
- Sharing the local context with the global team by providing information about local working hours and holidays.
- Creating opportunities for extensive communication among interdependent team members so that they achieve reciprocal predictability of action (e.g., Srikanth and Puranam, 2011).

These coordination practices will help remote teams avoid the pitfalls often associated with distributed work. Agreeing on communication styles and setting up communication protocols is another important area in the management of globally distributed teams.

Communication practices

Extensive research has been conducted on communication patterns that could have a positive or negative effect on collaboration between remote counterparts. In particular, these practices can lead to successful collaboration among globally distributed teams:

- Scheduling phone and video-conference meetings between remote counterparts, including managers and team members.
- Establishing communication protocols that cover the ground rules and expectations concerning communications. In our research, we observed that SAP held team-building meetings between German and Indian counterparts during which some of the discussions were dedicated to the remote teams' agreeing and accepting certain communication protocols.
- Providing appropriate training and access to collaborative tools and communication technologies.
- Being clear and patient in communications because not all counterparts can comprehend and communicate in English.
- Investing in language and cultural training. For example, New York-based LeCroy has invested in the language training of Geneva-based engineers (Kotlarsky and Oshri, 2005).

Carmel and Tjia (2005) recommend set of formal and informal flow structures to support communications between client and supplier personnel. They define these terms as follows:

> *Formalisms* are the conventions, structures and social agreements that standardise communication. By formalising, we mean that you inspect your informal work behaviours, and formalize them ... The other side of the coin is to intentionally create *informalisms* (a truly informal word!). Creating an informalism across distance means deliberately creating social relationships between distant individuals.

In creating these structures, Carmel and Tjia (2005) develop eight practical principles, as follows (Table 10.1):

TABLE 10.1   Formal and informal flow structures

Formalisms	Informalisms
Create a rhythm of interaction, such as weekly meetings in real-time	Create a cohesive team culture by fostering relationships across distance
Iterate for synchronisation, with frequent deliverables across distance	Foster interaction via real-time interaction
Standardise communication protocols	Put warmth into cold email by taking the time to create e-touch
Build an awareness infrastructure	
Create protocols for acknowledgements and urgency	

Source: Carmel and Tjia, 2005.

Creating a rhythm: Managers can create a rhythm of interaction via routine, regular meetings that take place in real time. The purpose of meetings in outsourcing relationships is to synchronise and coordinate the project. Despite the almost universal distaste for corporate meetings, they are a critical element to managing a long-distance relationship. Whether a weekly hour-long meeting or a daily 15-minute meeting, projects stay synchronised and on track when monitored in this manner.

Scheduling frequent deliverables: In an outsourcing relationship, informal structures for communicating are not available: spontaneous conversations, a quick F2F meeting with managers or even a brief inspection of the process by the coordinator. One way to combat this problem is to iterate numerous small deliverables into the timeline. Important deliverables to consider can include documents, reviews, test results, product prototypes, process development implementations and so on. In creating these schedules, it is important to remember that there is a balance between creating a frequency that catches potential problems before they arise (or at a very early stage) and a frequency that causes information overload. In practice, a frequency of every one to two weeks works well.

Standardising communication protocols: In the age of instant communication, individuals in outsourcing collaboration groups tend to be overwhelmed with email, instant messages and chat. The overload ultimately leads to the loss of information about the project, as these items are stored in local hardware or lost altogether through deletion. Collaborative information is best stored in central repositories and databases where team members can pull or review the information as needed. Here, cloud technology (discussed in Chapter 2) and persistent instant messaging (all messages are stored) become viable solutions to the problem. Here, it is also important to standardise the terminology used between the parties from the beginning, so as to prevent confusion inherent in different company or geographic cultures.

Building an awareness infrastructure: There is significant potential for coordination in distant collaborations to break down as a result of lack of awareness as to who does what. Awareness of different types of information includes being cognizant of processes, environments, activities, tasks, availability and presence of personnel. Organisations are combating this problem more and more by creating 'White Pages', especially those in distributed software collaborations. White Pages are a relatively new tool that includes basic information about each member of a team. These tools can be transformed into 'Yellow Pages' that give more detailed information about a team member, such as expertise, history and task assignment.

Introducing acknowledgement and urgency protocols: Silence is the enemy of successful communication. In distributed work groups, communication often occurs across multiple time zones and diverse email platforms. Acknowledgement, therefore, becomes key in building trust between the parties. Similarly, urgency must also have an escalation protocol in order for both sides to have an accurate understanding of the message. For example, if an urgent matter is communicated via email in the first instance, the originator should give some indication of the urgency of the matter by iterating a time frame for completion or response, such as, 'I need this by Friday, the 12th by noon my time.' Here, the expectations and urgency are clearly set forth in the first instance. Escalation protocols should incorporate email, telephone, mobile phone and even home telephone for very urgent matters.

Creating a cohesive team culture: Creating cohesive team cultures in disparate groups working across distances is seldom an easy task. The problem centres around creating a high level of trust in a very short period of time. One way to combat this is by making the qualifications and reputation of the team members known to other team members in the project. This can establish a foundation of respect among the team members necessary for forming trusting relationships. A more effective means of establishing trust is through F2F meetings. Many companies find in-person kick-off events to accomplish this task work quite well, as human beings build trust quickly when they interact and share common experiences. This, however, is expensive. A virtual experience can have similar effects at less expense.

Interacting in real time: Most individuals are more effective when communicating and interacting in real time. Email can create significant delays in receiving information and clarification and can create its own confusion. Real-time communication platforms, such as IM, telephone and video conferencing, can cut waste out of the communication and collaboration process. Company liaisons should make frequent (or as frequent as the budget allows) visits between project sites to create F2F interactions, as well.

Putting warmth in e-communications: There is no doubt that email can be a very impersonal communication tool that works to depersonalise relationships. Email etiquette between distributed teams should encourage personality, warmth and sociability. Small things like 'thank you' and 'please' and simple social chatting help bond team members and increase cooperation and a sense of belonging.

Clearly global firms are becoming more aware of the need to develop communication skills as one enabling factor of successful collaboration. The range of practices available is growing, and we have dedicated our discussion to the more commonly applied practices. However, another critical element in supporting globally distributed work is the tools and technologies implemented and used by remote teams.

Tools and Technologies for Globally Distributed Teams

IT can play an important role in transferring information across distances and cultures. Dynamic dashboards – software that produces a dashboard of vital information at a glance – can facilitate the transfer of information about the project between teams. Financial information and reporting tools can work in the same way, and these tools and reporting structures can organise and enhance continuous improvement efforts. Furthermore, a reliable and high-bandwidth ICT infrastructure is required to ensure connectivity among remote sites. ICT facilitates the process of boundary crossing to overcome the challenges presented by geographically remote and culturally diverse team members. ICT can help to mitigate the negative impact of intercultural miscommunication and support decision-making in distributed environments.

Numerous tools and technologies have been introduced to overcome the challenges we have examined. Taking a broad perspective, Leonardi and Bailey (2008) distinguish between *communication, storage* and *transformational* technologies and discuss how they facilitate distribution of knowledge-intensive work. Communication technologies mediate the content of work between remote parties by transferring messages containing knowledge and information. Storage technologies such as knowledge management systems and version control systems enable and facilitate storage, retrieval and sharing of knowledge and information that is explicitly codified. These two types of technologies have been studied extensively in the context of globally distributed work. Leonardi and Bailey suggest a third type which they call transformational technologies referring to technologies that affords the creation, modification and manipulation of digital artifacts in the process of converting input into output (p. 412). They illustrate the role of transformational technologies with the following example: 'computer-aided engineering applications transform input like physical dimensions, location coordinates, and material properties into computational models that can be shared electronically among engineers around the world as they work together on analysis tasks.'

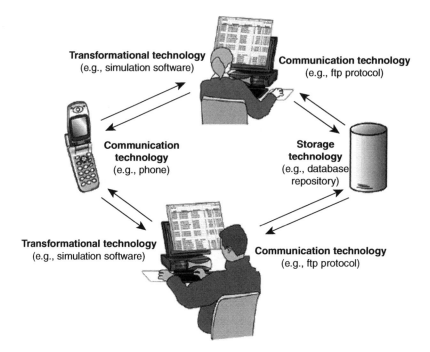

FIGURE 10.5 Technology supporting flow of knowledge and information in offshored or distributed teams
Source: Leonardi and Bailey, 2008.

Leonardi and Bailey also illustrate how all three types of technologies are used to accomplish work across time and space (see Figure 10.5).

Leonardi and Bailey (2008) argue that 'digital artifacts created via transformational technologies often embody implicit knowledge that must be correctly interpreted to successfully act upon the artifacts.' They study what problems might arise in interpreting this implicit knowledge across time and space and offer five practices and their constituent activities to facilitate transferring knowledge-intensive work offshore in scenarios that involve use of transformational technologies (summarised in Table 10.2).

Collaborative technologies

Among the many collaborative technologies for global teams are these:

- Teleconferencing, often combined with e-meetings
- Virtual whiteboards that allow document sharing

- Email
- Online chat (instant messaging)
- Voice over Internet protocol (VoIP)
- Video conferencing
- Internet and intranet
- Group calendars
- Discussion lists
- Electronic meeting systems.

TABLE 10.2   Practices to facilitate use of transformational technologies in transferring knowledge-intensive work offshore

Work practice	Constituent activity
Defining requirements	• Collect task information • Collect relevant information from Design Engineer • Define project • Prepare statement of requirements (SOR) (including type of analysis, type of model and issues to attend to) • Prepare PowerPoint file to complement SOR
Monitoring progress	• Place phone call to offshore/remote Performance Engineer (PE) to check on task status • Send e-mail to offshore PE to check on task status • Remind PE of deadline
Fixing returns	• Inspect completed work received from offshore team • Fix problems in received models and analysis
Routing tasks strategically	• Hold weekly status call with offshore managers • Monitor number of jobs currently with offshore team • Gauge number and timing of expected tasks to be sent • Reserve/confirm available resources • Send new jobs when resources clearly available
Filtering quality	• Compare returned work against defined requirements • Determine what aspects of returned work meet criteria • Ask offshore PE to redo aspects of returned work that fail to meet criteria or expectations

Source: Leonardi and Bailey, 2008.

Collaborative technologies recommended for global teams can be classified according to time and space dimensions. These collaborative technologies could be based on the following four categories: same place, same time, in which collaborative technologies are for co-located group decision support; same place, different time, in which work flow systems are used; same time, different place, in which telephone and chatting technologies are mainly applied; and different place, different time, of which bulletin boards are one example.

A more extensive classification of collaborative technologies is presented in Table 10.3. In this framework, there is a distinction among several types of collaborative technology that support the different needs of globally distributed teams in different time and place settings.

TABLE 10.3   Types of collaboration technologies

	Setting		
	Different place, different time (offline): support between encounters	**Different place, same time (online): support for electronic encounters**	**Same place, same time: support for F2F meetings**
Communication Systems: Aim to make communications among people who are not co-located easy, cheap and fast	• Email • Voice message • Text • Fax	• Phone/Voice-over-IP • Video • Multipoint video/audio-conferencing systems • Online chat	
Information-sharing Systems: Aim to make the storage and retrieval of large amounts of information quick, easy, reliable and inexpensive	• Document sharing systems • Portals and Web-based databases and repositories for searching remote information sources ·	• Screen sharing applications • Podcasting	• Presentation systems

(continued)

TABLE 10.3   Continued

	Setting		
	Different place, different time (offline): support between encounters	**Different place, same time (online): support for electronic encounters**	**Same place, same time: support for F2F meetings**
Collaboration Systems: Aim to improve teamwork by providing document sharing and co-authoring facilities	• Co-editing systems	• Shared whiteboard • Computer-assisted design	• Group decision support systems

Coordination Systems: Aim to coordinate distributed teamwork by coordinating work processes	• Synchronisers:
	  – Group calendar
	  – Shared project planning
	  – Shared work-flow system
	• Web-based scheduling /voting (e.g., Doodle poll)
		• Awareness or notification systems (e.g., active batch)	• Command-and-control centre support systems

Social Encounter Systems: Aim to facilitate unplanned interactions	Social media (e.g., Facebook, blogs, Twitter)	• Virtual spaces • Virtual worlds	

Source: Based on Huis, Andriessen and Soekijad, 2002 and modified by the authors to include modern technologies.

Socialisation and the Role of Face-to-Face Meetings in Global Teams

While the concept of globally distributed projects implies that team members work over distance, typically some of them do have an opportunity to meet in person. Studies that have focused on social aspects in globally distributed projects have suggested that firms should promote and hold F2F meetings to tighten interpersonal ties among remote counterparts in an attempt to improve collaborative work (Oshri et al., 2007b). Indeed, creating and renewing social ties between remote counterparts may open additional channels, supplementary to the technical solutions proposed, through which collaborative work can be improved. Using F2F meetings to advance social ties in globally distributed teams may also improve the formation of these teams as members get to know each other during meetings, learn about cultural differences among members of the team, discuss and agree on ways to resolve tensions, set up procedures to coordinate work activities and start working together towards a successful completion of a project.

We have observed that supporting interpersonal contacts between remote counterparts throughout the project life cycle is rather challenging to managers. So far, the emphasis in practice and research has been on F2F meetings that serve as a stage for bonding, socialising and creating social ties among remote counterparts. Nonetheless, F2F meetings alone may not create the conditions through which interpersonal ties such as trust and rapport can be created and renewed. F2F meetings tend to be short and often last only a couple of days. The agendas for these meetings often revolve around project and technical issues that need to be resolved, leaving little space for socialisation and one-on-one meetings. The emerging challenges in creating social ties among members of globally distributed teams are as follows:

- F2F meetings are short and tend to offer only limited social space that accommodates cultural differences.
- Most time spent in F2F meetings is dedicated to project procedures and technical issues, that is, they are formal to a great extent.
- F2F meetings are selective in the sense that not all counterparts are invited to these meetings.
- Short and infrequent F2F meetings offer sporadic interpersonal interactions between remote counterparts, which restrict the build up of interpersonal relationships.
- ICT offers limited opportunities for personal contact and social space as compared to F2F meetings.

While F2F meetings assist in acquainting counterparts of globally distributed teams with each other and addressing project and technical issues, these meetings, being sporadic, short, selective and formal to a great extent, do not support the long-term build up and renewal of interpersonal ties between dispersed counterparts very well. Therefore, managers of globally distributed teams need to pay attention not only to planning the actual F2F meetings but also to activities that can be carried out over distance before and after these meetings to help make the most of the meetings and help establish social ties in global teams. Table 10.4 summarises activities that we recommend to implement before, during and after F2F meetings on individual, team, and organisational levels.

F2F meetings activities provide insights into the way that managers of global teams can supplement collaborative tools and methodologies with human-related activities to ensure strong social ties among remote counterparts. We suggest that firms can move on from the traditional focus on F2F meetings as the main vehicle through which interpersonal ties are created and invest in before-and-after F2F meeting activities. In this respect, managers should consider the full life cycle of social ties when planning and executing collaborative work among remote sites.

The life cycle of social ties consists of three stages: introduction, build up and renewal (as shown in Figure 10.6). Each step represents an array of activities (presented in Table 10.4) that a globally distributed team may apply in order to move from the introduction stage to the building up of social ties, and finally to the renewal phase in which social ties are renewed through various activities during and after F2F meetings (Oshri et al., 2007b).

Managers should assess at which stage the dispersed team is prior to embarking on the introduction of specific activities. For example, dispersed teams that are in the introduction stage, such as the SAP team we investigated that included members located in Walldorf (Germany), Bangalore (India) and Palo Alto (USA) that had no prior experience of working together, require activities that foster social ties; these are different from activities for teams in the renewal stage, such as the LeCroy team, whose members from New York (USA) and Geneva (Switzerland) had a

TABLE 10.4   Individual, team and organisational activities supporting social ties

	Before F2F meeting (introduction stage)	During F2F meeting (build-up stage)	After F2F meeting (renewal stage)
Individual	• Increase awareness of communication styles • Offer language courses • Offer short visits of individuals to remote locations	• Create space for one-on-one interactions • Provide a sense of importance to each member to the team • Adjust communication styles	• Ensure real-time communication channels • Ensure mixed audio and visual cues • Offer short visits to remote locations • Offer temporary co-location
Team	• Introduce new team members • Increase awareness of team composition • Increase awareness of communication protocol • Appoint a contact person for each remote team • Set up mini-teams • Offer virtual F2F meetings	• Conduct kick-off meeting • Discuss differences between national and organisational cultures • Offer space for multiple interactions among counterparts • Offer team-building exercises • Organise social events • Discuss organisational structure	• Facilitate reflection sessions • Facilitate round-table discussions • Facilitate progress meetings • Conduct virtual F2F meetings • Offer F2F meetings
Organisational	• Distribute newsletters • Create and offer shared cyberspaces	• Support sharing of information from F2F meetings (e.g., photos)	• Encourage direct communication channels
Tools	Phone/teleconference, VoIP, email, collaborative technologies, shared knowledge repositories and shared databases, video conference, online chat, intranet, Internet		

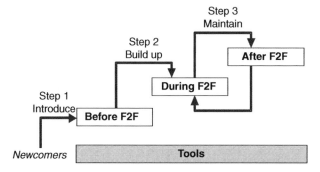

FIGURE 10.6 / The life cycle of social ties in globally distributed teams

long history of working together over distance on various projects (Oshri et al., 2007b).

As the project progresses and remote counterparts get to know each other, establish interpersonal ties and develop a collaborative mode of working together, renewing these social ties may require only a subset of the activities offered in Table 10.4. In this regard, the activities in Table 10.4 are not a recipe for building and renewing social ties but rather represent a set of possibilities available to managers who are seeking to strengthen social ties among team members. Each team and each team member differs in the way they bond with others. The manager's responsibility is to choose the most appropriate activity at the right time to ensure that social ties are renewed and the collaborative work strengthened.

From a social ties perspective, we have observed that globally distributed teams need to 'renorm' from time to time as newcomers join and change the dynamics of interpersonal ties within dispersed teams; in addition, disagreement and miscommunications can arise even in later stages of a project because of a lack of F2F interactions that resulted in fading interpersonal ties. For this reason, we recommend that managers consider renorming dispersed teams and renewing social ties through bonding activities, such as short visits or F2F meetings. These activities, we have learnt, should be offered not only in the early stages of team development but also later, because social ties may loosen over time and affect collaborative work.

Challenges in Multicultural Teams

Having multicultural teams in outsourcing and offshoring settings is often the norm. Without doubt, most multicultural teams will face certain challenges regardless of whether they are distributed or co-located. Smith and Blank (2002) distinguish four types of cultures, all of which are evident in global sourcing engagements.

- *Individual culture* refers to individual styles or personality differences (e.g., Myers-Briggs Type Indicator)
- *Functional culture* refers to differences associated with the nature of a profession (function) such as marketing, engineering and R&D
- *Organisational culture* refers to characteristic differences between companies
- *National culture* refers to differences associated with national culture (e.g., Hofstede characteristics).

A typical outsourcing/offshoring project is likely to accommodate multiple cultures such as functional (e.g., accounting and IT), organisational (e.g., client and supplier personnel) and national (e.g., home country and nearshore or offshore). Interestingly, different cultures may in fact have implications as to how individuals perform their work, coordinate activities, communicate with each other and interpret messages and cues. These challenges lead to communication barriers, misunderstanding and wrong assumptions as to how members of the team should react to cues and messages. A case study about a Dutch female manager, Mrs Lisette Breukink, who set up a captive development facility in St Petersburg, illustrates the cultural challenges she faced when she was professionally and socially interacting with her team in St Petersburg.

C A S E   S T U D Y

In a Russian Sauna with the Dutch Manager

In 1997 Lizatec, a small Dutch software house, faced a dilemma: where to get programmers? There were not enough good programmers in the Netherlands: Dutch programmers had a reputation for producing low-quality software and asking for high fees. The company started to look for opportunities to achieve better quality and reduce development costs. Lizatec started to think about offshoring, but to which country?

Lisette Breukink, one of three managers and co-owners of Lizatec, visited several companies in India to discuss the possibilities of outsourcing software work. However, this did not work out, mainly because of cultural differences. Lisette came back feeling that the men in Indian companies could not accept the idea of working under the supervision of a woman: that they just could not handle the fact that a woman would be their manager and give them instructions.

Lisette heard from some friends about Russian programmers and she convinced her Lizatec partners to try Russia. In late 1998, Lisette visited St Petersburg, interviewed some Russian programmers and a short time after that opened an offshore facility in St Petersburg. By early 1999, 12 software engineers were working at Lizatec's Russian facility (and by 2004 when this case was written there were 25).

Not everything went smoothly. There were many cultural adjustments that both sides had to make. Lisette related the three cultural vignettes described below.

Vignette 1

Dutch and Russian people have different perceptions of time. For example, the Dutch make appointments well in advance and work between 9am and 5pm, while the Russians are spontaneous and more flexible in working hours. If a deadline is approaching and there is still plenty of work to do, what do Dutch software developers tend to do? At 5pm they stop working and leave. What would Russian programmers do in this situation? When Russian developers from Lizatec were preparing the launch of a new product and a deadline was approaching, they said to Lisette, 'Why don't we go to your place, you cook dinner, and we work and eat: it is more cosy to work at home.' And this is what they did: Lisette went shopping for food and cooked dinner while the Russian programmers worked. Without knowing it, the

Russian programmers took a small risk when they asked Lisette to cook for them, because Dutch women are usually not good cooks, particularly compared to Russian women. The Russian programmers were lucky because Lisette is not a typical Dutch woman and can cook great meals.

Vignette 2

To motivate the Russian employees and keep them productive in the long run, you need to create a family-like environment at work. This is not typical for Dutch culture: Dutch people place strict boundaries between personal and organisational life, between home and work. The Dutch have formal relationships at work, while Russians need a home-like, friendly atmosphere in order to be motivated. Lisette explained: 'In the beginning the engineers made lunch by themselves – just dry sandwiches. They would come in early in the morning and by the end of the day they looked a little greyish and tired.'

Then, Lisette hired a cook. She later explained: 'I decided to hire a cook just to make a fresh salad and do some shopping; but she took her task very seriously and she started to cook three-course dinners in a corner of an office. So we ended up having a real dining room with a kitchen. And now every day we have a huge dinner at 2 o'clock.' This is another cultural difference: in Holland people have dinner in the evening, while in Russia dinner is in the afternoon (2–3pm), with a small supper in the evening.

Lisette explained that it then became possible for programmers to eat all their meals at work:

> If you are single, you don't need to do any shopping. Because you can come in and have breakfast (we have sandwiches for people who come in very early in the morning), then have dinner at 2 o'clock, and then leftovers are served for supper in the evening for people who want to work late. So there is always soup and salad. Now they can eat all day, and it is OK.

She continued: 'The cook is now like a mother for everybody. If you are on a diet, she will cook for your diet. It is just her life – cooking for these people, like a family. And after this cooking, everybody started to look healthier, because they ate real fresh vegetables and fresh meat. This is my investment in everybody working well: everybody started to be happier.'

Vignette 3

In Dutch and Russian cultures the human body is perceived and treated in different ways, in particular the naked body. What does this have to do with offshore software development? It is indeed related: when the Russian developers (most of whom are men) go together with their Dutch manager (a woman) to a sauna (*'banya'* in Russian).

Russian programmers do not place boundaries between work and home. So, it was natural for Lizette's engineers to organise various cultural and social events so that their Dutch manager would learn about Russian culture. During the first year, Lisette would go to Russia once a month for about a week. 'We went to the theatre, paint-ball shooting, bowling and to a music hall. Every visit somebody organised such an evening together,' she recalled.

One of the social events was to a summer house (*'dacha'*) on the outskirts of St Petersburg, to enjoy nature, have barbecues and drinks for dinner and, of course, use the *banya*. This is where cultural differences became apparent. The Dutch are very practical and treat their body as something functional: for them the sauna is associated with health and pleasure, and the sauna cannot be enjoyed if he or she has something on. So, Dutch people take their clothes off and walk in naked. The mixed sauna (men and women together) is very common in Holland (as in Germany and in Scandinavia). For tourists and foreigners who live in Holland, there are signs by the entrance to a sauna saying that entry in swimming suits is forbidden. However, this is not the case in Russia: Russians perceive the human body as essentially sexual. When Lisette asked her Russian employees how the Russian sauna worked – if they undressed and just walked in – the Russian programmers were shocked. They told Lisette that in Russian culture the naked body is a sexual object: 'If we see a naked body, we think about sex.' Therefore, in Russia, in a mixed sauna, people put a towel around themselves or wear a swimming suit.

Lisette was surprised: for her Dutch sensibility it sounded strange to be in a sauna and not be naked. 'Strange, I don't think about sex when I am in the sauna, it is too hot,' she said to the Russian developers. However, there was no choice but to respect Russian traditions and those of her employees. Lisette said to them: 'Tell me what to do and I will do the same.'

This was the first time that Lisette sat in the sauna wrapped in a towel.

The Role of the Client in Distributed Collaboration

So far, this discussion of distributed collaboration has mainly focused on the suppliers and client companies that adopted a global teams approach as part of the captive mode of working (e.g., by carrying out global projects with team members from different sites of the same company). We have noted that suppliers and other global companies should introduce and use cutting-edge methodologies, practices, tools and technologies to ensure that software solutions can be jointly developed by remote team members. In offshore outsourcing arrangements, the client is part of this distributed collaboration and can improve the degree of collaboration between the supplier's on-site and offshore teams. For example, the client can work with the supplier to ensure that there are no knowledge or expertise asymmetries between on-site and offshore teams. In such a case, the client can ask the supplier's offshore team to 'play back' the information the offshore team has acquired from the on-site team (Kotlarsky et al., 2014). However, such involvement is not always welcomed by clients, in particular if the client perceives the outsourcing contract as transactional in nature. Therefore, we highlight two propositions for the client that could improve collaboration among the client, on-site teams and offshore teams, and also improve the value delivered to the client from the outsourcing contract:

Proposition 1: Clients must understand the benefits they will receive from a supplier's collaborative system. In the pre-contract stage, clients need to obtain a detailed statement, in financial terms as far as possible, of the benefits to themselves of their supplier's collaboration practices. These benefits could include a speedier improvement in service performance, faster availability of expertise at lower rates and the supplier's commitment to a higher level of innovation in processes, services and technologies, resulting in observable performance improvements. Such benefits must be agreed on, documented and signed off on in the contract, with money or credits going to the client where they do not materialise.

Proposition 2: Clients must understand the costs of a provider's collaboration system. Generally these costs involve helping the supplier to coordinate service delivery by making the client's and supplier's staff available for knowledge transfer activities through methods such as seminars, interviews and offshore visits. Clients should agree to these costs contractually. They should also understand and agree contractually to the net benefits they will receive versus the net benefits the supplier will receive. As we have observed, when there is a large difference between the two, the disadvantaged party's commitment to delivering on the collaboration strategy falls off.

Summary

Offshore, nearshore and onshore teams have become part of globally distributed teams. For this reason, such teams should consider how they operate to ensure successful collaboration. Previous chapters have focused on key aspects of managing outsourcing relationships without analysing the specific context within which such collaborations take place. This chapter has considered the unique challenges that global teams face and strategies to improve their collaboration.

chapter 11

Captive and Shared Service Centres

Offshore captive centres are one of a broad range of sourcing models available to firms. While most of the literature on outsourcing and offshoring has focused on a third-party sourcing arrangement, this chapter will solely examine the option of in-house, however, from an offshore or nearshore location. The key aspects examined in this chapter are:

- The history of the captive centre industry
- The strategies captive centres have pursued
- The trends and changes in the captive centre industry
- Shared Service Centres and the captive model.

Background

Throughout the past few decades, large multinational companies such as General Electric, Texas Instruments and Motorola have established captive centres in various foreign countries, most notably India.[1] Captive centres are wholly owned subsidiaries that provide services, in the form of back-office activities, to the parent company from an offshore location. While traditionally they have kept most of their offshore tasks in-house, numerous information technology service providers that have emerged within the Indian marketplace have developed the capabilities to execute both simple and complex work projects – a few of the most recognisable companies being Tata Consultancy Services, Infosys and

Wipro. These companies can often provide services at a lower cost than their Western competitors.

This development has enabled Western multinationals to consider alternatives in the way they implement their offshoring strategies. As just one example, in 2006, SAP Hosting Services in Bangalore outsourced several of its services to Tata Consultancy Services, also based in Bangalore. Many other companies have pursued an approach in which certain specific, often noncore, activities have been outsourced to local service providers, while core activities remain in-house (i.e., in a captive centre). Other companies, such as Standard Chartered and Hewlett-Packard, have followed a different approach in which their captive centres provide services to both the parent company and external clients.

Other companies seem to have outgrown their offshore captive strategies. British Airways, for example, sold a majority stake of its captive centre to a private equity firm, Warburg Pincus, in 2002. Apple went even further and shut down its development centre in India in 2006.

The worldwide economic crisis beginning in 2008 has raised many questions about the continuing viability of captive centre models in sourcing. The worldwide drop in demand for goods and services has significantly affected companies in all industries. Questions of efficacy have surfaced as major Fortune 250 companies divested their captive endeavours throughout late 2008 and 2009. In October 2008, Citi divested its BPO centre in India to TCS and, in May 2009, it sold its Indian IT centre to Wipro. Similarly, AXA sold its 600-person centre to Capita Group in May 2009. Dell has also been a major contributor to the sell-off phenomenon. In October 2008, it sold its El Salvador support centre to Stream Global Services; in March 2009, it sold its Pasay consumer tech support centre to Teleperformance.

And this is just the tip of the iceberg. The year 2009 saw sales of captive centres in India by American Express, UBS and AIG as well. Indeed, some commentators predict that captive centres are no longer needed. David Rutchik of Pace Harmon, an outsourcing consultancy, believes that captive centres have become a drain on many companies: 'The larger issue is that these captive centres are difficult to manage and quite a distraction from a company's core business. They haven't been the panacea they were expected to be.'

Rutchik cites several reasons for this. First, captive centres represent a large, fixed cost for companies. In times of recession, getting these captive centres off the books and gaining some much-needed capital from the sales offers a short-term benefit. Second, as Indian and other outsourcing suppliers have improved their capabilities over the last few years, Rutchik thinks that captive centres may no longer seem worth the effort: 'It takes a lot of overhead and management attention to manage internal facilities ... You're exposing yourself to a lot of administrative burden just to do back-office type work in lower-cost locations.'

However, in spite of these and other divestitures, the captive centre model, according to numerous studies, has not collapsed. As of 2014, the number of new captive set-ups has been rising in particular in Central and Eastern Europe and China.

An examination of investments made by Fortune 250 global firms regarding their captive centres between 1985 and 2010 within the context that shaped their offshoring decision conducted by Oshri and van Uhm (2012) shows three key trends during this period: (i) multinationals have adopted captive models that allow the captive to operate lean as well grow quickly by taking external clients; (ii) while India is still by far the country with the highest number of captives, China and Eastern Europe has attracted the highest number of new captive set ups since 2006; (iii) certain functions are no longer attractive for captives such as IT support and some BPO, but R&D captive centres are on the rise.

These developments bring to the fore significant challenges. First, how should a parent company strategically perceive its captive centre in view of its allocation and use of resources? Second, what sets of capabilities should companies develop offshore to support the evolution of a captive centre?

C A S E   S T U D Y

GlobalSoftware

GlobalSoftware, a leading software developer, planned to set up a product development centre in India in the late 1990s. According to the co-director of the captive centre, 'India has excellent people and it provides many opportunities to grow fast.'[2] When the captive centre was established, the Internet boom was at its peak and IT companies were in need of talent and skills. Alain, the director of process improvement and performance management, recalls: 'There was an arbitrage of costs and to certain extent some pressure to recruit the people.'

In 1998, GlobalSoftware acquired IndiaTesting, a company that provided front-office software for marketing and business operations. The acquired company already had a team of 70 experienced software professionals, who immediately started to work on the parent company's new 'Sales Force Automation' project and were directly involved in testing and customisation. Within a few years, the captive centre was able to expand its activities. Testing was among the most important services because of its cost advantage and effectiveness. For cost reasons, the captive centre also hired many young people coming straight out of colleges in India. They were three to four times cheaper than engineers from the home country, claimed the captive centre manager of business research extension. In 2002, the captive centre employed 500 software developers and received investments of over US$125 million from its parent company. By 2006, it had increased the capacity to over 3,000 staff, many of them software developers.

Despite all the success, both the captive centre and the parent company had their worries. Top managers from the captive centre felt that the full potential of the captive centre had not materialised. In particular, managers thought that the software giant still considered its captive centre as a back office that should perform low-level tasks cheaply. One aspect of this was that all product development decisions regarding products that were partly or fully developed by the captive centre were still taken by the parent firm headquarters. This approach did not allow the captive centre to make recommendations about the firm's product portfolio and about the development of product features within the existing product line.

From the parent company's perspective, the captive centre's high staff attrition rate was a serious problem. This problem was not unique to GlobalSoftware – many Western companies in India as well as local IT suppliers faced the same challenge. 'If we have a high level of attrition,' said Alain, 'we do not get to build domain knowledge. And if we do not build domain knowledge, we do not get more responsibility from the parent firm, GlobalSoftware. If you have an attrition of 25%, every two years you virtually start from zero.'

Addressing the High Attrition Challenge

In order to cope with the high attrition levels, the captive centre sought to outsource some of the repetitive tasks performed in-house. These were some of the hosting services that provided technical support to both internal and external clients. The captive centre also perceived the outsourcing of these services as an opportunity to divert talent from low-value to high-value activities. To accomplish this, the company entered a due-diligence process with a service provider that was based nearby and which had long-term relationships with the parent firm. The outsourcing project was of small scale, about US$2 million per year and involved the transfer of knowledge and hosting services from the captive centre to the supplier over a period of three months, after which the supplier would assume full responsibility for these services. In order to successfully accomplish this outsourcing project, the captive centre and the supplier agreed on the governing structure, business processes and knowledge transfer mechanisms and procedures, and the timelines per each major milestone. As the supplier was one of the leading Indian suppliers in this area of services, Alain felt that he was in good hands. After all, the supplier had undertaken so many similar contracts that providing the captive centre with such services should not be a major challenge. Furthermore, there was also the perception that since the client and supplier were located nearby, any issue which might arise would be easy to handle over a face-to-face meeting. Having discussed these matters, GlobalSoftware and the supplier were ready to launch this outsourcing project.

By early 2006, not long after their collaboration had commenced, Alain was not satisfied with the supplier's performance. Things became even worse later that year. Alain complained:

> We are so busy managing the supplier that at times it feels that we could have kept this activity in-house and would be better off. They never catch up with our introduction of new services. We trained their staff and yet we see that knowledge is not retained within their teams. We assumed that their employees, who are Indians, have the same perception as we have regarding quality and service standards. We were wrong!

The project manager from the supplier's side, who was also frustrated with the situation, gave a different picture:

> True, we suffer from a high level of attrition that affects our ability to retain knowledge. However, the client does not help with their continuous introduction of new services. They want far more than what we can deliver for such a small project. Yes, we have excellent methodologies to capture and retain knowledge and we also have service standards. But how can we justify applying these methodologies, procedures and techniques when it comes to such a small project?

Alain had to rethink recent developments within the GlobalSoftware captive centre. Although the outsourcing project was not going so well, he had developed a good rapport with the supplier's relationship manager. He hoped that this personal connection with the supplier could be improved and that soon performance would also get better. But what should he do? He had been hoping to free up resources in order to focus on high-value activities and instead his workforce was now tied up in supplier management activities. Furthermore, he wondered whether this outsourcing contract was changing the original purpose of setting up the captive centre. If so, how did this strategy fit into GlobalSoftware's overall strategy?

Between 1990 and 2010, Global Fortune 250 companies established 408 captive centres worldwide (Oshri and van Uhm, 2012). Many of these firms owned more than one captive centre and a third of them changed their captive strategy over time, mainly from providing services to the parent firm to servicing external clients, outsourcing to local suppliers, or in some cases, being divested, moved or terminated.

Offshore captive centre strategies tend to evolve based on the strategic intent of the parent company and conditions in the destination country (Oshri, 2011). Therefore, offshore captive centres will gain momentum only as multinationals seek to reap the value of their initial investment in an offshore operation (and in some cases, minimise losses).

A Historical Perspective on Offshoring and Captive Centres

Offshoring has emerged as a major trend in international business. Over the past decade, the issue of whether to offshore business processes has become one of the most vigorously debated topics in management. Decisions concerning offshoring are rooted in much larger strategic business concerns. Generally companies consider offshoring when they face decreasing profit margins stemming from competitive pressures or are interested in accelerating their value-chain activities. Considering this choice is a strategic reaction for companies confronting rising costs and fiercer competition.

The roots of offshoring lie in the mercantilism and imperialism of the 17th century. The East India Company first established its own factories in India, recognising the cost-effectiveness, flexibility and viability of having a company foothold in the targeted trade country. The idea of establishing company-owned factories in host countries quickly swept commercial trade endeavours and expanded to such industries as sugar and rum-processing and trade. Thus, the concept of offshoring has been around for centuries. In the modern day, this has become more visible since US multinationals began to offshore labour-intensive manufacturing processes to low-cost developing countries such as Mexico and Panama.

One significant new development within the concept of offshoring began in the mid-1990s. Companies such as Citicorp and American Express set up offshore facilities to carry out enterprise-wide activities, such as converting data from one medium to another (e.g., converting paper documents to digital data in corporate databases). Since then, significant technological developments, such as telecom bandwidth, satellite technology and the Internet, have eliminated distance issues, enabling information to be sent around the world in seconds at marginal costs. Overall, a high degree of global collaboration has been evident since these developments in the 1990s.

In *The World Is Flat*, Thomas Friedman describes how a Web-enabled global playing field has been created as a result of the convergence of ten flattening factors, among them the introduction of search engines and work-flow applications and the growing tendency to outsource and offshore work. These factors offer a real-time platform for collaboration and knowledge sharing to almost anyone on the globe. Following these developments, information technology requirements such as software maintenance and development could be carried out at lower cost in countries such as Israel, Singapore, India, the Philippines and China.

In the late 1990s, numerous companies worldwide anticipated major IT problems at the turn of the millennium, dubbed the Y2K problems, for which significant numbers of programmers were required. Reliable, trained programmers were unavailable in local markets such as the USA in the numbers required to address the potential issues the new millennium presented. India had the resources available to adjust software to correct potential Y2K problems envisioned by the business community. One issue arose concerning the quality of the IT services provided in India: Would Indian companies compare to the expertise offered by programmers and software companies in the home country? The Centre for eBusiness at MIT found that projects developed in India only had 10% more bugs than comparable projects in the USA. Furthermore, Indian software development teams quickly began using quality assurance programmes such as Six Sigma and Capability Maturity Model Integration (CMMI) approaches to quality management issues, which made their processes more reliable and equivalent to those of Western software development teams. More and more companies witnessed the high quality of IT services that Indian companies offered, and soon other activities such as call centres, accounting services, payroll administration, debt collection and even clinical research were transferred offshore to India. Although most of the jobs transferred offshore were considered dead-end types of jobs in countries such as the USA, they offered relatively high pay to the offshore communities and were viewed with respect.

When companies consider the strategies available regarding offshore work, they basically look at two options. One is to offshore the desired activities and processes while still maintaining them in-house through the captive centre: wholly owned facilities with the purpose of processing activities that were previously done in a company's back office in the domestic country. Alternatively, they can outsource the activities and processes to an external supplier located offshore. Most companies initiate the process of offshoring by choosing one of these two options. Companies have steadily increased the volume of work outsourced to external suppliers located offshore, and a large number have also set up captive centres in offshore locations to maintain internal control of the business process.

Most captive centres are set up for one or more of the following three major reasons: to reduce costs, access skilled and qualified personnel, or expand and enter new markets. Indeed, captive centres have delivered value through cost savings, increased productivity and quality and innovation. One highly visible example of a successful captive centre offshoring activity is demonstrated by Dell's Indian captive centre, which developed process innovations that were later diffused worldwide to other Dell factories.

Some companies began their offshoring experience pursuing both options. For many large multinationals, offshoring some specific operations was seen as an ordinary development, as the CEO of Siemens explained: 'Offshoring is a funny thing for an international company. Where is your shore? My shore is as much in India and China as it is in Germany or the US.'

Multinationals have set up captive centres in various countries and regions, including India, China, Central Europe and Latin America. India has nevertheless become the dominant location for captive centres in the world. By late 2010, over 400 captive centres had been established by large multinationals in 34 countries representing an economic value of US$12.3 billion and employing over 440,000 professionals.

Among the most important factors affecting companies in their decision to set up captive centres in India are the country's vast human capital, the sophisticated level of education and the relatively low language barrier. Indeed, the Indian captive market employs over 200,000 employees and accounts for 30% of the Indian offshore services market.

The economies of offshoring are clear. A programmer in the USA, for example, earns about four times more a year in comparison to a programmer with the same qualifications and skills in India. Farrell found that US companies saved a significant amount of money when offshoring to India. She states that American companies save 58% on every dollar spent on jobs moved to India, with the main saving coming from the significant disparity in wages. Additional savings stem from bundling activities in one location, which results in a gain from economies of scale. Moreover, the shortage of qualified labour in the Western world is another main driver of the increasing number of companies that offshore business and other IT-related processes.

The technology boom in the 1990s, coupled with the Y2K effect on computer systems, resulted in a significant increase in programmer wages in Western countries. This strained budgets and forced companies to search for alternatives abroad in India, China and countries in Eastern Europe. Technological advancement and availability has been one of the main drivers of service offshoring worldwide. These technological developments made the dispersal of business activities across the globe over the last decade possible. The rapid development in telecommunications and related areas, such as the Internet, is another facilitating factor.

According to our research (Oshri and Kotlarsky, 2009), access to skills is the most important motivator affecting the decision to offshore IT and business processes, followed by cost saving as the second driver. The results of our survey represent the shift in executives' mindset regarding offshoring. It is about accessing skills and expertise not available in-house rather than only achieving reductions on the IT cost base. Offshoring is also about opportunities and not just exploitation. However, we acknowledge that in some business processes, cutting costs will continue to be the main driver, such as with call centre operations.

Research also suggests that a large percentage of businesses that are currently offshoring certain activities are also planning new projects abroad in the near future. Call centre activities are one of the projects frequently cited as an area for new implementation. This phenomenon is surprising because of growing evidence that some large firms, even those from the Fortune Global list, have closed their captive call centres because of customer dissatisfaction. Many of these companies have already moved their call centre operations back to their home country.

Setting up a captive unit in an offshore location is not free of challenges and involves more than simply hiring employees, renting a building and installing hardware. Considering the competitive nature of the offshoring market and high employee turnover, a significant investment is required to obtain high-quality HR professionals and processes, software development process optimisation, state-of-the-art training facilities, engagement management expertise and service management expertise.

Many other challenges arise through the adoption and implementation of captive centres. For example, some firms have struggled with ever increasing costs, employee attrition and the lack of integration and management support. Some experts suggest that the nature and purpose of captive centres must evolve for them to be successful. For example, WNS, previously owned by British Airways, has evolved from a basic captive providing services to a parent firm to a larger centre that now provides services to international customers as well. Small-sized captive centres are often hard to maintain because they offer little long-term career growth to employees, resulting in a high level of attrition. Such negative impacts on captive centres have led firms to explore a wider range of strategic options that are available offshore.

CASE STUDY

GlobalAirline

In 1996, Nicolas, the now former managing director of GlobalAirline, one of the biggest European airlines, received a warning alarm: if the company wanted to survive, it had to get in shape soon. Profits had declined and the cost-base of passenger processing activities had been rising. Nicolas put together a task-force that included the general manager of the engineering department. His task was to analyse cost savings. He noticed that passenger revenue accounting demanded high-volume, low-skilled work that could be moved to a cheaper offshore location. The passenger revenue accounting unit then had over 600 full-time staff. Though GlobalAirline was familiar with offshore outsourcing, it had not outsourced passenger revenue accounting because it 'was the blood of the organisation' and had to be kept under control, according to Nicolas.

In August 1996, GlobalAirline decided to establish a wholly-owned captive centre in India, to bring down costs while keeping control. The captive centre was to be run as an independent profit centre. India was chosen because the airline had direct flights from the headquarters location. GlobalAirline saw India's infrastructure as developed, which allowed for a relatively easy data-transfer process. Culture was not perceived as a problem: the company was already familiar with the local markets and many of the cultural aspects in India. Indian workers were fluent in English and, in addition, the Indian government provided significant tax breaks among many other benefits.

The captive centre was set up under an airline subdivision responsible for providing services and systems to external clients. A general manager who had experience of customer services, sales and marketing in foreign countries was sent to India to set up the captive centre. Shortly after its establishment, the captive centre started to offer additional services such as customer relations. 'Again, this was a high-volume activity, requiring a very quick turn-around,' said Nicolas. 'The prime reason for moving customer relations to the captive centre was that it was becoming very expensive as a department to run – it needed many extra staff.'

As a wholly owned subsidiary, the captive centre was not named after GlobalAirline. Its staff were employees of the captive centre, not of GlobalAirline, to prevent union problems. A wholly-owned subsidiary also had the flexibility to reach third-party clients. Nicolas said: 'It became easier for me to make deals. If the captive centre had had the parent company's name, there would have been major restrictions.'

The captive centre started off with 60 employees in a commercial space that could accommodate 300 people. But it grew quickly. Nicolas remembered:

> I had a number of companies coming to ask me what we were up to and wanted to know more about our services. Following this, GlobalAirline's top management quickly agreed that the captive centre should offer services to third parties because it could bring down costs.

However, 'there was a lot of scepticism among the middle managers back home about whether the Indian captive centre would work,' said Nicolas.

This scepticism was unjustified. The captive centre successfully acquired third-party clients within a short period of time, thanks to GlobalAirline's worldwide alliance programmes. When the captive centre was launched, the parent company had already formed an alliance with other airlines, which included a trading services programme. One key aspect to any success was information security. Being a wholly owned subsidiary that did not carry the parent company's name helped the captive centre to be less exposed to security breach attacks and made competitors less suspicious about confidentiality aspects when negotiating deals.

Consequently, in November 1996, the captive centre was already serving three external clients and was best known for supplying specialist computer skills such as ticketing and computer-based training. In 1998, the captive centre broke even as expected and started to offer services to other businesses outside the airline industry, such as insurance. Nicolas said: 'Again, the opportunity came partially through the parent company, because one of the management directors was also on the executive board of an insurance company.' By 2000, the captive centre was offering services to nine other airlines and had revenues of US$25 million a year.

Following the expansion of the GlobalAirline captive centre and its range of services to third-party clients, the captive centre management team sought ways to further develop the unit. At that point in time, the captive centre employed 1,500 staff, of whom 65% were serving the parent company and 35% were providing services to third-party clients. In fact, the 35% focusing on external clients generated 45% of the captive centre's total US$11 million revenue.

Dave, the former captive centre general manager, remembered that when he forwarded the five-year additional expansion plan to the management director of GlobalAirline, the director snapped: 'What have you smoked? You have put forward a plan for 12,000 staff, which is about 30% extra headcounts for GlobalAirline.'

The board of the parent company stressed that they were running an airline, not an investment house, and therefore rejected the plan. However, as an external commentator observed: 'The future strategy of the captive centre requires investments to fully exploit its growing third-party client base.'[3]

Capital was needed to develop skills relating to marketing and sales and building the scale of transactions within the captive centre. A clash arose between the parent company and its captive centre regarding the centre's strategic direction. Dave commented: 'It became obvious that the only way for the captive centre to advance was to be sold off.'

In 2001, GlobalAirline considered a takeover of its captive centre by an investment house. The basis for the negotiations was that any agreement should 'allow the future growth and development of the captive centre, with the airline company still retaining a significant stake in the business'.[4] The negotiations took over 18 months. According to representatives from the captive centre side, the airline did not want management overheads in India and was concerned with service quality and costs once the private equity firm assumed a majority stake of ownership. Losing key employees was another concern. The private equity firm wished to see the new captive centre managed without the parent company's influence. It was prepared, therefore, to sack old employees and let its people run operations.

Finally, in 2002, a deal was struck. GlobalAirline announced the sale of 70% of its captive centre equity stake.[5] GlobalAirline did not intend to be involved in management decisions relating to the captive centre, now that its major stake was held by the private equity firm. However, it hoped to still improve the financial performance from this transaction when the eventual value of its 30% stake in the captive centre would increase.

GlobalAirline chose the private equity firm for two reasons. 'Money-wise, they came with a good offer,' Dave remarked, 'and they had the right structure and culture to protect the interest of the airline, the captive centre's principal customer.' The takeover would also let the airline concentrate on its core business and let the captive centre develop new businesses outside the airline industry.

The private equity firm was interested in acquiring Global-Airline's captive centre because the captive had established a leading position in the BPO segment in India. Dave added: 'The basis of the captive centre, its infrastructure, set up, and management team, was very attractive.'

GlobalAirline's positive reputation, strengthened by its ISO 9000 certification and Six Sigma model, also helped the private equity firm make this acquisition decision. According to the private equity firm, during the divesture, the BPO sector worldwide was poised to witness tremendous growth, and the firm saw the buyout as a valuable investment in building a leading global organisation. The CEO of the private equity firm confirmed: 'With this captive centre, we now have deep domain knowledge of the sector. We will let the new company grow organically as well as through acquisitions in the Indian BPO market.' The new chairman of the captive centre also thought that the captive centre had a great potential to handle complex and varied business processes, as there was no other captive centre in India with such large-scale and advanced domain knowledge.

After the acquisition, the private equity firm allotted a considerable sum of money to further develop the services provided by the captive centre. The intention was that the captive centre staff would increase to 10,000 full-time employees in the next five years. 'We can grow organically at 50% a year to the foreseeable future,' predicted the new captive centre chairman.

Within its first year as an independent company, the captive centre revenue grew by 120%, and, by 2005, the BPO firm reported US$165 million in revenues. Supported by this rapid growth, the captive centre went public in July 2006. It then faced new challenges. The Indian government applied different regulations to public BPOs and captive centres. Tax breaks for captive centres shrank and in, June 2006, the captive centre was asked to repay service taxes to the government for the period 2003–2005. Meanwhile, however, the captive centre had to satisfy its shareholders, who wanted a higher return on their investment each year.

Despite the difficulties, the initial public offering still allowed both GlobalAirline and the private equity a return on their investments. In 2008, according to Dave, only 10–12% of the US$460 millions in revenues were being generated by the former parent company. The captive centre was able to increase its capacity to over 18,000 employees, who were considered as core staff and no longer as back-office workers. This attracted more talent to the captive centre and supported the knowledge-base developed offshore.

According to Dave, fast growth was possible because the private equity firm spent a great deal of money to 'rebuild the communication infrastructure and bring in some very senior management plus their contacts and networks.'

Fast growth, however, did not come easily. Dave added: 'The captive centre had to fight for contracts after larger multinational players like IBM had entered India – there are few contracts left in the market not taken by the big companies.'

> Accounting for 40%, travel was still the strongest segment of the captive centre's mainstream revenue. Banking, financial services and insurance, however, together generated 40% of the revenue. The emerging segments of manufacturing, retail and consumer products supplied the remaining 20% of the revenue. According to the director of investments and alliances at GlobalAirline:
>
> > The venture has turned out more successful than most of the airline leadership expected. There was no question that the airline made the right decision. The company has benefited from both its initial stake in what later became a successful commercial venture and also from the fact that its business processes are being done by a more efficient and viable entity.
>
> But have GlobalAirline done the right thing? Perhaps they should have maintained ownership of the captive centre, considering its success?

One area that requires more in-depth exploration is the question of why offshoring and outsourcing work for some firms but not others. The problem stems from the widely held view that offshoring is a universally applicable solution for reducing costs, creating flexibility and broadening access to the required talent pool that is not currently available in the home country at a reasonable cost. Contrary to popular belief, offshoring is not a single strategic model applicable to every business need, intention or process. Rather, it comprises a variety of models, each with its own risks and benefits to consider and address. Successful offshoring depends heavily on choosing the appropriate model to fit the specified business need as much as it does on a cost–benefit analysis of performing the same activities at home.

Captive Centre Strategies

Oshri (2011) identified six fundamental types of captive centres (see Figure 11.1). The basic captive centre focuses on providing services to the

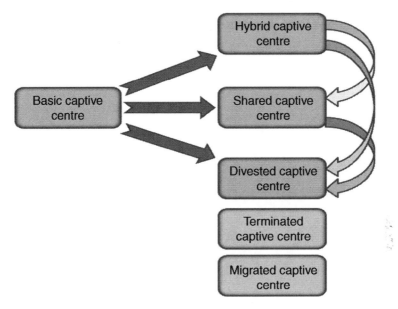

FIGURE 11.1 The six fundamental types of captive centres
Source: Oshri, 2011.

parent firm only, the shared captive centre services external clients as well, the hybrid option refers to the case when a captive centre outsources an offshored operation to a local supplier, the divested option encompasses the sale of part or all of the captive centre by the parent firm, the migrated captive centre suggests the relocation of the business unit to another location, and the terminated captive centre represents the case in which the captive centre was closed down.

Oshri's research shows that the basic captive centre has evolved into a hybrid, shared or divested model. In our data set, we identified three evolutionary paths: basic-shared-divested, basic-hybrid and basic-divested; however, it is possible to envisage nearly any evolutionary path depicted in Figure 11.1. In some cases, the captive centre will initiate its own evolutionary development (basic-hybrid); in other cases, especially those involving ownership changes, the parent firm will decide which path the captive unit will follow (basic-divested or basic-shared-divested). The terminated captive centre and the migrated captive centre do not offer an evolutionary path.

Future Trends in the Captive Industry

Today firms have allocated trillions to manage and process back-office operations. With an annual growth of about 5% in outsourcing and offshoring and the emergence of new offshoring locations (estimated at about 125 countries around the globe) that are offering IT and business processes services, captive centres will continue to play a role in sourcing arrangements. We have identified seven trends for the present and future of captive centres.

1. More captive centres will be built by large firms looking to reduce costs and access skills that are not available in-house.
2. Central and Eastern Europe will emerge as the most attractive location for European multinationals to set up captive centres in the next five years. Nearshoring, which is the sourcing of IT and business services to a relatively close country, will also be a strong trend in captive centres for North-American multinationals.
3. Captive centres will continue to be sold for two main reasons: many captive centres (at the moment about 60%) will struggle to become or remain successful and, therefore, will drive their parent firms to look for a buyer. Captive centres that have built large scale or developed an area of specialisation complementary to the commonly found expertise in the local supplier market will become attractive for an investment house or a local supplier and, therefore, will eventually be divested.
4. Large captive centres in maturing and mature outsourcing markets such as India will expand outsourcing offshore activities to local suppliers in an effort to transform the captive centre from a service and cost centre into a profit and innovation centre and free up talent to focus on value-adding activities.
5. Small- and medium-sized enterprises will explore ways to use existing captive centre facilities as pools of expertise in order to reduce costs as well as access skills at a global level. This will accelerate the evolution of captive centres into the shared captive centre model.
6. Many multinationals with captive centres will struggle to sell their offshore assets. These are mainly captive centres that failed to build up scale or develop a unique area of expertise that is complementary to the mainstream line of expertise commonly found in the local supplier market.

7. The captive centre concept will move from the experimentation stage to the maturity stage, significantly reducing the number of captive centre terminations.

CASE STUDY

WNS Buys Aviva's Captive Centres

On 10 July 2008, Aviva announced that it would sell its five captive centres (Aviva Global Services), located in India, to WNS. With the sale, it signed a contract, extending over eight years, in which WNS would provide offshore services to Aviva.

Since 2004, Aviva had offshored its finance and accounting division to captive centres in India and Sri Lanka. Aviva set up these centres using the build-operate-transfer (BOT) model and worked with three BPO suppliers: EXL, WNS and 24/7. The essence of this model is that the client contracts with an offshore or near-shore supplier to execute an outsourcing arrangement whereby the supplier builds and operates the service centre (a call centre or any other business process) for an extended period of time. The client retains the right to take over the operation under certain conditions and certain financial arrangements. On 3 July 2007, Aviva announced that it was bringing back over 300 accounting professionals from WNS to Aviva Global Services as part of the BOT agreement, signalling its intention to take over the virtual captive centre eventually.

A year later, however, Aviva announced that it was selling its offshore operations to WNS and signing a contract to receive BPO services worth US$1 billion. According to Aviva, it selected WNS because of its proven operational performance and the fit between the cultures and values of both firms. Aviva also believed that WNS truly understood the insurance industry and that the BPO supplier had demonstrated commitment and customer care.

The outsource services included life- and general-insurance processing services covering policy administration and settlement, finance and accounting, customer care and other support services. Aviva also indicated that by early 2009, 6,000 professionals would be transferred from Aviva Global Services to WNS, some of them transferred back only a year after they joined Aviva. It explained the reason for this strategic move as protection from rising inflation in India and fluctuating exchange rates.

WNS, which is facing increased competition in the BPO industry, benefited from its acquisition of Aviva Global Services. In 2009, the BPO provider's revenues increased by 17%, and it expanded its service offerings and market share.

Shared Service Centres: Introduction

Shared Services Centres (SSCs) are defined as service units that are 'consolidating and standardising common tasks associated with a business function across different parts of the organisation into a single service centre. These services are then provided by the service centre to other parts of the organisation' (McIvor et al., 2011, p. 448).

SSCs are increasingly used across public and private sectors and for a range of back office functions including HR, Accounting Finance, procurement and most recently, legal and IT. While there is considerable variation in the motivation to set up a SSC and their configuration, the overarching objective for most SSCs is to improve the service efficiency and quality.

Historically, SSCs are dated back to the 1980s with General Electric being among the first multinationals to set up service units around the globe. Reports suggest that GE's investment in SSCs resulted in significant savings.

The academic and professional literature has mentioned several reasons for setting up a SSC (Baldwin et al., 2001; Davis, 2005; Janssen and Joha, 2006). Among those are to: increase control, improve standardisation, access skills not available on-shore, improve information security, improve service levels and reduce overcapacity where there is duplication of services across multiple locations. While there are numerous drivers for setting up SSCs, the economic drive seems to have been the most dominant for large multinationals.

Shared Service Centres and Sourcing Models

To what degree are SSCs different than the insourcing or the captive model? In many ways, SSCs are just another form of insourcing or captive solution. The emphasis in the SSC professional and academic literature, however, has been on the corporate structuring phenomenon in which the decision to establish a SSC is driven by the search of consolidation and improved efficiencies through the centralisation of the service line. A good example is Diageo's initial move to shared services, a decision driven by the need to consolidate, increase efficiencies and standardise across multiple service lines.

While much of the literature perceives SSCs as a 'make' choice (between 'make' or 'buy' options), others have pointed out that SSCs should be also understood as the initiating move towards outsourcing, that is, the 'buy' option, by means of an evolutionary process (Gospel and Sako, 2010). In particular, Gospel and Sako describe the 'evolution' of shared services referring to the 'unbundling of corporate functions' as a dynamic process along a 'path chosen to create shared business services and to move to outsourcing' (2010, p. 1367). For example, Procter & Gamble created an SSC prior to outsourcing the entire centre to third-party suppliers and Unilever sought outsourcing as a means of creating an SSC in order to adopt global standardisation.

Indeed, SSCs tend to change organisational form and objectives. In their search for improved service levels, multi-nationals continue to seek new sources of efficiencies and lower cost locations by utilising various SSC models. Another example is Reuters, who embarked on organisational and business process centralisation by setting up SSCs. Driven by further pressure to reduce costs, transactional processes from some SSCs were migrated to a new centre in India which in turn outsourced processes to a local supplier.

SSCs are also quite similar to captive models (described by Oshri, 2011). Indeed, similarly to the evolution of captives, SSCs have evolved into different configurations over the years. Currently, the literature distinguishes between two primary SSC configurations:

- The intra-organisation where the SSC provides services for internal departments (basic and hybrid model by Oshri, 2011)

• The inter-organisation where the SSC provides services also to external organisations (shared captive model by Oshri, 2011).

The intra-organisation SSC may have numerous routes to provide services internally, for example, through a single SSC that is solely responsible for procuring and providing services to the organisational departments, or a network of SSCs that jointly provide services to the entire organisation based on their areas of speciality. SSCs also vary in the nature of the services they provide. For example, there are SSCs that are providing transaction-based services such as administrative tasks and data entry while other SSCs focus on transformation-based services in the form of planning, personnel development and performance management schemes.

Summary

In this chapter we examined the evolution of the captive and shared service centres and how this evolutionary path resulted in the diversification of the concept into new strategies. Of particular interest are the growth strategy, shared captive centre, which emphasise the potential in long-term investment in captive centres. At the same time, the hybrid model highlights the need to develop sourcing capabilities offshore, critical for the captive's ability to both focus on higher value activities and for the proper management of its supplier base.

chapter 12

Innovation Through Outsourcing

There are many reasons that companies of various sizes see the benefit of outsourcing particular aspects of innovation, here defined generally for a business context as deploying new and creative ways of achieving productivity or topline growth (Coulter and Fersht, 2010). Quinn (2000) lists reasons that include limited resources and capabilities within the organisation, a shortage of specialist talent, management of multiple risks, attracting talent in the company's non-specialised areas, and getting to market faster. So how can companies achieve innovation through all the various ways of sourcing available? Often they have an ad hoc approach to innovation, or what Linder et al. (2003) call a transactional approach. This approach, however, often fails to leverage organisational learning and develop innovation capabilities within the client firm as they work with suppliers. Clearly, an ad hoc approach cannot create a culture in which external contributions are accepted or welcomed. Moreover, it is difficult to measure innovative processes and outcomes when companies innovate on an ad hoc basis.

In this chapter, we look at how organisations go about achieving innovation through outsourcing in a systematic manner. This sets the context for our major, more restricted focus on whether, and, if so, how, IT and business process innovations can be achieved through using external ITO and BPO service providers. We want to stress that in this chapter we are not talking about sourcing innovation through offshore R&D centres which has been discussed in the context of offshore captive centres (Chapter 11), but about outsourcing engagement where the client is seeking to achieve innovation. The chapter starts by detailing the debate around whether innovation can be outsourced and, if so, under what conditions. We then look at the case for internal control and the research on how outsourcing innovation can become an organisational practice in outsourcing arrangements. Therefore, this chapter focuses on the following topics:

- The debate about innovation through outsourcing
- Tapping into the sources of innovation in the outsourcing context
- The case of innovation through outsourcing
- The Innovation Ladder: What should client firms do in order to achieve innovation through outsourcing.

The Innovation Through Outsourcing Debate

Over the past 20 years of ITO, BPO and offshoring, the record on innovation through suppliers has been one of many disappointments and false starts. In practice, clients and suppliers have found it difficult to draw up contracts that lead to innovation. Suppliers have created and tried to use innovation centres, and clients have created innovation funds or have set up multisourcing arrangements in which they hoped that greater collaboration and competition might lead to greater innovation. But time and again, such well-intended efforts have not yielded significant innovation. All too often, the promise of innovation has been too small a part of the overall contract and, moreover, has tended to be negotiated out of outsourcing contracts as both parties seek to reduce their risk and investment exposure (Willcocks and Lacity, 2006). More recently, Coulter and Fersht (2010) have suggested that an additional limitation for ITO and BPO alike lies with outsourcing suppliers that historically have been organised around the industry verticals of their clients. They argue that suppliers need to develop a new organisational model from their experiences of servicing multiple industries that bypasses an industry vertical's inherent resistance to collaborate and creates an environment of willing collaborators.

Certainly there is plenty of evidence that if an innovation agenda is to be productive, a lot needs to change from the way leaders perceive and are willing to invest in innovation through outsourcing. For example, a survey of client organisations taken in 2010 (Oshri and Kotlarsky, 2011) found that, while 53% of respondents indicated that innovative capabilities demonstrated by the supplier are either important or very important in their supplier-selection criteria, 66% expected the supplier to free up internal resources that could focus on higher value activities. Only 35% of the respondents indicated that they expected their suppliers to help them innovate.

A 2009 Forrester Research survey found that 38% of IT outsourcing customers cited a lack of innovation or continuous improvement as their biggest challenge with suppliers. But even before the downturn, IT analysts were registering considerable scepticism among clients about suppliers' innovation pitches (Overby, 2007; Savvas, 2007). More recently, looking at BPO, Fersht (2010) surveyed 588 senior decision-makers in client, supplier and advisory organisations. While 43% of clients viewed innovation as a critical element in BPO, more than half of all BPO buyers were disappointed with their current state of innovation. Customer care, recruitment, payroll and management reporting were noticeably failing to meet clients' expectations. Buyers saw their major impediments as ineffective change management and un-empowered internal governance teams. The report concluded that the BPO innovation gap represented a huge opportunity for clients and suppliers alike, if only they could act on it.

There has been a long-standing debate around whether innovation through outsourcing can in fact be achieved. At the heart of this debate is the dichotomy between the service and innovation mentalities. The service outsourcing mentality is based on the ability to clearly define the scope and nature of the service and capture these dimensions in a Service Level Agreement. On the other hand, innovation requires an open-ended mentality in which it is not always possible to define the outcome of the innovation effort, let alone develop a clear commercial model that will ensure compensation for the supplier for their innovation effort. Overby (2010) rightly argues that in fact the problem lies more with clients' critical mistakes in attempting to procure innovation from external suppliers. She cites three such errors: clients do not know what they want (a failure to define innovation in the context of corporate objectives), clients choose the wrong suppliers (they do not adequately examine the supplier's culture, history, suite of services and innovation track record), and clients do not set up effective innovation metrics (therefore avoiding traditional

IT metrics; in addition, most service-level agreement regimes and pricing models deter innovation).

The Role of Strategy and Internal Capability to Innovate When Pursuing Innovation Through Outsourcing

All this would suggest that, before looking to the market for innovations, companies should first consider whether innovating through outsourcing is a strategy. As Chesbrough and Teece (1996) and Chesbrough et al. (2006) point out, the virtues have sometimes been oversold. Companies that place a great deal of emphasis on external sourcing while neglecting to nurture and guard their own capabilities may be taking many risks. One approach, therefore, is to build internal capability to innovate. This is particularly important in firms that are highly dependent on innovation for market leadership. Westerman and Curley (2008) provide a useful example here of building IT-enabled innovation capabilities at Intel. Their study charts how from 2003, Intel adopted a staged approach and built a global network of IT innovation centres, together with a virtual innovation centre that acted as a focal point for making new innovation tools and activities available throughout the company. They suggest seven lessons:

1. Take the lead in innovation. Do not wait to be asked
2. Build momentum early, and use it to expand scope
3. Measure and publicise progress
4. Culture is not a prerequisite; it can be changed to be more innovative
5. Build an enabling environment and infrastructure for innovation
6. Do not innovate alone: obtain external people and funding
7. Gain and maintain executive support.

Chesbrough and Teece (1996) distinguish two types of innovation: autonomous and systemic. *Autonomous* innovation can be pursued independently from other innovations, whereas the benefit of *systemic* innovation can be realised only in conjunction with related, complementary innovations. The two types of innovations call for different organisational strategies. Autonomous innovation can be very well managed in decentralised virtual networks, while systemic innovation requires a high level of information sharing and the capabilities to coordinate adjustments throughout an entire product system. Such capabilities of coordination and integration are usually available within a well-managed organisation rather than a loosely connected network.

IBM is a good example. In the early 1980s, IBM had an open architecture based on standards and components that were widely available. This architecture enabled IBM to take advantage of a third-party development of software applications and hardware accessory products. It also relied on the market to distribute the product. As a result, IBM greatly reduced its costs to bring a PC to market and outperformed Apple, the market pioneer at that time. However, IBM has since lost its advantage as other competitors have tapped into the same sources in the market, over which IBM has little control. Moreover, most of the profits from the PC architecture have migrated upstream to the supplier of the microprocessor (Intel) and the operating system (Microsoft). IBM's experience shows that key development activities that depend on one another must be conducted in-house to capture the rewards from long-term R&D investments.

A company that cultivates and strengthens its unique competencies and capabilities is also able to maintain the position of a dominant player in a network, and thus to drive and coordinate systemic innovation. As Chesbrough and Teece (1996) observe, the most successful companies withhold dominant control in a network. For example, Toyota was much larger than its suppliers and was the largest customer of most of them. As a result, it could compel those suppliers to make radical changes in their business practices.

Tapping into External Innovation Sources

A plethora of studies and commentators have supported the notion of increasingly working and innovating with external parties in order to compete effectively in the global economy. Hagel and Seely Brown (2008) point to the importance of new forms of connection and coordination and the value of offshoring. Pralahad and Ramaswamy (2004) see co-creating value with customers as among the best future competitive plays. Davenport et al. (2006) argue that globalisation, aided by rapid technological innovation, has changed the basis of competition. It is no longer a company's ownership of capabilities that matters, but rather its ability to control and make the most of critical capabilities, whether or not they reside on the firm's balance sheet. A new strategic mindset is required that supports co-shaping value innovation and open innovation processes.

To put flesh on this rationale, Stanko et al. (2009) researched the sourcing habits and innovative performance (patents produced) of 359 companies. The most successful companies used outsourcing in four circumstances:

- When a company needed to add lots of new knowledge to innovate – for example, finding out how to work with an unfamiliar chemical compound to develop a new line of pharmaceuticals
- In the early stages of a project, when there are many technical hurdles to overcome and the outcome is far from certain
- When intellectual property is not well protected in the industry. In this situation, since new ideas spread quickly, it may not be possible to differentiate products with innovations. Therefore, businesses turn to outsourcing to limit spending
- When a company has a great deal of experience with outsourcing. The costs and benefits of outsourcing are more certain for experienced firms, and they can better manage the situation to produce effective results.

Where companies make the decision to leverage externally sourced innovation, they should establish deliberate, consistently available channels to match their strategic requirements. Once established, these channels can be used as needs arise. Linder et al. (2003) identify five types of external innovation channels:

1. *Building innovation on the market*. One source of innovation that companies can turn to are universities and private research labs. Another way to tap into innovation on the market is through strategic procurement, that is, by seeking differentiated products or innovative processes from suppliers.
2. *Investing in innovators*. Companies can take equity positions in organisations focused on small or emerging markets. This often helps to resolve the innovator's dilemma that arises when established firms resist innovation that might undermine their existing offerings. By investing in an equity partnership, a company can participate in and nurture an emerging market.
3. *Co-sourcing*. Companies sometimes band together to share the costs of innovation, for example, to address regulatory requirements that

affect them all. Some high-tech firms sponsor professors in universities who work in promising areas and share any intellectual property that is produced. Joint venture is another way to co-source innovation.

4. *Community sourcing.* This refers to innovation produced by loosely connected communities of sophisticated users. One successful example is the open source software industry. Another is eBay, which uses community-based innovation extensively to identify new sales categories and expand its capabilities.

5. *Resourcing.* Companies can support their research staff by contracting with external suppliers for on-demand talent and innovative new tools. For example, DuPont Crop Protection hires high-quality researchers in India, Russia and China who are paid much less than their counterparts in the USA. Aventis S.A. identifies cutting-edge technologies in the market and brings them in-house to support product development.

How to Achieve Innovation Through Outsourcing: The Innovation Ladder

Oshri and Kotlarsky (2011) have developed a framework that they called the Innovation Ladder (Figure 12.1) to help client companies to incorporate innovation in their outsourcing strategy. The emphasis in our approach, as opposed to some other studies we have seen, is that we believe that the innovation strategy should be integrated into the outsourcing strategy of the client firm. The Innovation Ladder is a full cycle approach from the beginning of the outsourcing relationship until the delivery of innovation. Yet, client firms can pick and choose some steps depending on the breath of innovation sought and on the nature of the relationship they establish with their suppliers.

Step 1: Strategise innovation

A journey into innovation through outsourcing should start at the early stages of strategising the outsourcing project. These early stages of the outsourcing life cycle often involve the identification of objectives and the potential areas for improvement derived from the outsourcing engagement. At this point in time, it is imperative that executives consider the impact expected on the firm, from operational or strategic

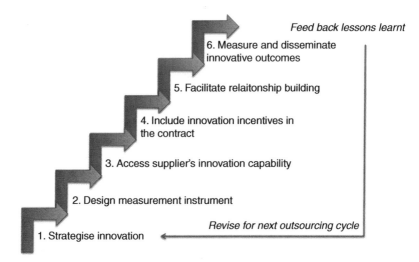

FIGURE **12.1** The innovation ladder in outsourcing
Source: Oshri and Kotlarsky, 2011.

perspectives, and the two levels of innovations: incremental and radical (see Figure 12.2).

In principle, executives should consider the four areas of improvements when strategising innovation in outsourcing. To start with, executives should discuss the *incremental improvements expected at the operational level* in business processes that are considered to be noncore to the firm's competitive position. Such business processes can be, for example, finance and accounting, human-resource management and procurement, which are becoming prominent candidates for outsourcing; however, with little attention to the improvements sought to be achieved from the suppliers.

Client firms should also seek *incremental improvements in critical operations* outsourced to a third-party service provider. One example of such business process is business analytics. Our study (by Oshri and Kotlarsky, 2010) reports that 26% of the respondents outsourced business intelligence to a third-party service provider. In this regard, executives should consider incremental innovations in a critical business function that benchmark with best practices in the industry. For example, executives can ask: What gaps exist between our level of critical operations and the industry best performer's level of these critical operations?

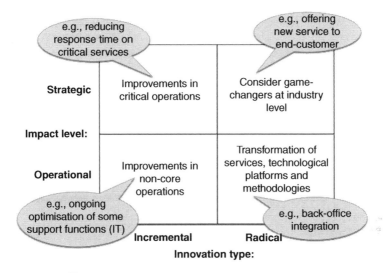

FIGURE 12.2 / Impact of incremental and radical innovation on the operational and strategic levels of the client firm
Source: Oshri and Kotlarsky, 2011.

Combining the areas of improvements in noncore and critical business operations will allow executives to form their 'wish list' of incremental improvements, which can be captured in the contract.

Executives should also consider radical innovation that can be achieved in their outsourcing engagements. This would require executives to consider the transformation of existing services and technological platforms but also scenarios in which the solution or the process through which the desired outcome will be achieved is not yet defined. In terms of the *impact at the operational level through radical innovation*, executives should discuss what services and technological platforms are candidates for major transformations. Such decisions can be made by considering specific service performance, cost/value ratios, and benchmarking against cross-industry service performance.

The fourth, and most challenging, strategise stage should be about problems or strategic moves that are still unknown and, therefore, the solutions for them are still to emerge. Here we are considering the *impact at the strategic level of radical innovation*. Executives should discuss scenarios of major shifts in the industry landscape and competitor strategies as a threat and an opportunity to shape their competitive environment. In this regard, executives should ask the following questions: What business models may emerge in the industry? What business models may become obsolete? What new services and service delivery methods may emerge and how prepared is the organisation to either shape the environment or benefit from such changes? Decision-markers at this stage may also consider entry to new markets and/or new industries as a strategic move of the firm, or as a result of mergers and acquisitions that create a need for executives to re-consider how to maximise benefits from new markets/industries. The purpose of such discussions is two-fold: first, to shift executives' attention from focusing on the operational/transformative level in outsourcing to consider strategic issues that are still to emerge, as a response to the dynamic and highly competitive environment; and second, to discuss and formulate a framework within which such challenges will be shared with trustworthy suppliers.

By bringing together these four aspects of innovation in outsourcing during the early stages of the planning, the client firm will be able to devise an approach to realising the innovation potential from each setting.

Step 2: Design measurement instrument

As a second step, client firms need to develop the measurement instruments for the incremental innovation expected to be delivered by the suppliers and design a framework for which radical innovation will be pursued with selected suppliers. The measurements for incremental innovation should be developed against the benchmark in the industry. With this, the objectives captured in Step 1 will be translated into specific expectations regarding incremental improvements expected from their prospective suppliers. While designing measurements for incremental innovation (e.g., a percentage of cost reduction, a percentage of improvement in time-to-marker or a percentage reduction in process duration), it is important to relate these targets to Key Performance Indicators (KPI) of the client's firm and to Key Success Factors (KSF) at the industry level. In this stage executives should ask the following questions: Which services/technological platforms/methodologies are lagging behind the standard performance in the industry? Which business function candidates for outsourcing are key for operational excellence? The answers to these questions will assist executives in identifying the services and technologies that are candidates for incremental innovation and also to realise the expected improvement measurement as benchmarked against industry performance. This analysis will address the design requirements of incremental innovation in the early stages of the outsourcing engagement. The contract should also have a clear reference to how the supplier will be rewarded if it improves the measurements further (e.g., bonus as a percentage of additional cost savings that result from process improvement).

The design of a collaborative framework for radical innovation should take a different approach. As the challenge is not clearly defined at the operational and strategic levels, client firms should devise a radical innovation framework to create conditions within which preferred suppliers will be introduced to significant and game-changing challenges that require radical innovation. The radical innovation framework includes procedures and processes within the client firm that scout threats from competition and markets, and translate those into descriptive scenarios that can be shared with external partners. The radical innovation framework should also outline the knowledge-sharing platforms, their participants, structure and frequency of interactions between the participants, to ensure that suppliers bidding for the outsourcing project are aware of the commitment required from them in exploring radical innovation opportunities, which would allow them to budget for additional resources required for such activities. Last but not least, the radical innovation framework will include a proposed contractual approach once the client firm and supplier(s) have agreed on the best way to tackle transformative and game-changing challenges. Our recommendation is that a *joint venture* arrangement, separate from the ongoing outsourcing engagement, will be the main vehicle through which radical innovation is carried out.

Step 3: Assess supplier's innovation capability

How would you know whether your supplier could innovate for you? Well, you won't. The common perception is that most suppliers are capable of innovating in an incremental fashion with an impact on their client operations. Fewer suppliers are capable of offering incremental innovation at the strategic level, usually as a reaction to client requests and by setting up a separate contract for such projects. Can you then identify the supplier that is capable of delivering both incremental and radical innovation for you on an ongoing basis?

Oshri and Kotlarsky (2014) developed a set of questions to consider when assessing the bidding supplier's ability to innovate and, therefore, may help client firms to select those supplier(s) that meet the client's expectations in terms of both service and innovation.

Question Number 1: How do you understand and define innovation in the context of outsourcing?

Most suppliers define innovation as 'anything that the client firm considers to be innovation for them'. This is clearly a very broad definition – is this definition helpful in achieving innovation in outsourcing? Yes and no. It is helpful in the case of radical innovation where the client and the supplier will be facing major challenges to clearly define what the solution would look like and its impact on business performance. However, this definition is not so helpful in the case of incremental innovation, in particular where the impact is at the operational level, simply because such advancements could and should have been captured in the outsourcing contract. Treating such improvements as an innovation project suggests that the client did not develop a complete roadmap for the service when outsourcing it and, therefore, did not scope development efforts to be included in the contract. The supplier, on the other hand, is treating requests for changes from the client as innovation projects, though these developments could have been handled as an extension of the contract. In an ideal world, the supplier should have gone the extra mile and helped the client firm realise and scope these requests as part of the contract; however, considering the limited exposure the supplier has to the client's service roadmap, such expectation is, in fact, unrealistic. Yet, both the client and the supplier should avoid treating incremental/operational changes as innovation projects; these are simply specifications the client has missed while scoping the project.

Question Number 2: What is your strategic approach to achieve innovation through outsourcing?

We have learnt that most suppliers have a clear operational approach in how opportunities to improve services can be taken forward, but only a few suppliers can clearly articulate their strategic roadmap to instilling innovation within the outsourcing setting. Developing a strategic innovation capability requires two fundamental elements in the supplier's service philosophy: First, that any innovation engagement must deliver value. The key aspect here is that the innovation engagement is not necessarily delivering a monetary value but the value can be in the form of learning, collaborating, experimenting and even failing (but learning from the failure). Second, that innovation through outsourcing is perceived to be systematic, which means that both the supplier and the client will be looking to create opportunities to innovate throughout the outsourcing engagement.

Question Number 3: Do you have a proven methodology to deliver innovation through outsourcing?

Without doubt, most suppliers will be able to walk you through what they can do but only if you ask them for innovative solutions. They will be able to point out resources available within the firm that can carry out an innovation project. So it is true, most suppliers will be able to innovate for their clients; however, it will not be a systematic capability and very likely it will be one that lacks organisational assets to constantly search and leverage opportunities to innovate.

An alternative approach is to develop an innovation methodology which requires an investment from the supplier but at the same time signals the supplier's readiness and its potential to deliver innovation in a regular and systematic manner.

The *innovation methodology* at IBM, for example, is made of five steps. It includes the following: (i) agreeing on the *definition of innovation*, (ii) defining a *scope of the innovation* project (the contractual setting of the innovation project), (iii) *deciding on key areas* (themes) to focus on, (iv) *developing an action plan* for each innovation project and (v) *deciding on the governance process* of the innovation programme (a joint governance structure where both the client and IBM are committed to deliver value).

Question Number 4: What organisational assets bring together your innovation methodology and strategy to ensure a systematic delivery of innovation through outsourcing?

There can be numerous organisational assets that suppliers could develop to support the systematic delivery of innovation in outsourcing settings.

First and foremost the organisational structure needs to include leadership and operational roles that make the link between the service outsourcing and the innovation organisational structure. For example, IBM set up an innovation leadership structure within the outsourcing organisation in 2008. This network of roles was instituted into the regional and account level of the outsourcing organisation. In addition, there was a network of innovation managers at the account level that completed this highly structured and formulated organisational structure for innovation within IBM.

Second is the provision of research and development laboratories and the links between innovation leaders and this asset. Many suppliers have established R&D laboratories; however, technological inventions produced by these R&D centres do not always find their way to the outsourcing account level. Demonstrating links between the innovation network and the R&D assets is key in signalling the supplier's ability to both innovate and deliver innovation at the outsourcing account level.

Third is a change management and awareness programme for innovation within the service outsourcing organisation and also with the client. This programme should be designed to achieve a shift in the mindset of the players involved in service outsourcing so that they develop innovative mentality and pursue opportunities to innovate.

Last but not least is the entrepreneurship approach that innovation leaders need to pursue in seeking solutions for business problems. While formal structures and a systematic approach are key here, there is an informal and entrepreneurial component that needs to be nurtured and encouraged. Entrepreneurship in the outsourcing context can manifest itself in various forms and shapes. For example, where appropriate, entrepreneurship can be the ability of innovation leaders to divert from the formal innovation methodology and apply agile structures that bring together speed, creativity and 'out of the box' solutions.

Question Number 5: What KPIs would you use to measure the returns on the innovation project?

This is probably one of the most challenging aspects of innovation in outsourcing for both the supplier and the client. This is simply because value is a dynamic, ever-changing concept that is often difficult to capture in basic service outsourcing projects (do not confuse value with cost saving!). Figure 12.3 depicts the different mentalities observed in service outsourcing versus innovation settings.

Concept	Outsourcing	Innovation
Value specification	Easy to specify and scope	Difficult to specify and scope
Ways to monitor and measure value	SLAs met, service on par or better, operations orientated (function KPI)	Realised impact on business performance and firm's competitiveness (industry KPI)
Time dimension	Immediate	Long term
Fee schemes	Fees for service, time and materials, outcome-based	Good will, JV schemes, outcome-based (?)
Stakeholders	Mainly technical champions with some business knowledge	Combination of business and technical champions

FIGURE 12.3 / **Comparing service outsourcing and innovation mentalities**
Source: Oshri, 2014.

In the context of innovation through outsourcing, value is particularly challenging for both the supplier and client. In service outsourcing value is fairly defined, measurable and determined at the delivery point. However, in innovation in outsourcing, value can manifest itself in various ways. Sometimes the value in engaging in innovation can be monetised; however, in many cases the value will be abstract, though noticeable. For example, IBM and its clients gained extensive media coverage for some of their joint innovation projects, though it was not always clear what the exact return on these investments was.

In conclusion, we propose that client firms start such a journey by asking: *Can this supplier innovate for me?* Part of this answer is still the responsibility of the client firm: to demand innovation, collaborate, participate in knowledge-exchange sessions and be proactive about innovation opportunities. But a substantial element in the innovation premise still lies with the supplier, simply because without an innovation strategy, systematic innovation methodology and a clear understanding of the expected returns, innovation in outsourcing will still remain the 'holy grail' of the outsourcing industry instead of a common and successful practice.

Step 4: Design a contract for innovation

Once the supplier-selection phase has been concluded, the attention of the parties involved shifts to the contract and its content. One very clear result from this study is that most outsourcing contracts are not designed to accommodate innovation. Many of these contracts focus on defining service levels, pricing and penalties, tilting the attention of the supplier to a 'service' mentality as well as the client's mindset to monitor outsourcing performance based on well-defined SLAs. Accommodating innovation through outsourcing contracts requires a different attitude. Contracts that accommodate incremental innovations should elaborate on both improvement targets and innovation processes that will commit both the client and the supplier to follow and monitor, including desired targets and rewards if these targets are met or outperformed. In this regard, and often beyond the regular SLA clauses, the incremental innovation clauses should be specific regarding the relationship mechanisms put in place by both the client and supplier that will support the supplier's effort to deliver incremental innovation according to the improvement measurements.

The clauses in the contract that refer to radical innovation should provide an elaborative description of the methodology through which suppliers will become partners. In this regard, the contract should describe the process put in place to share transformative and game-changing challenges with the suppliers, the expected participation from the suppliers in such forums and the preferred legal agreement to pursue solutions in the form of radical innovation by one or more suppliers. Our recommendation is that this kind of partnership is established where a clear specification of resources and capital is defined, as well as the approach to appropriate value and manage intellectual property is outlined.

Step 5: Facilitate relationships building

It is without doubt that building relationships between the client firm and the supplier is imperative for the success of either incremental or radical innovation. However, the relationship plays a different role in incremental and radical innovation. We have already discussed the various ways client firms can represent the potential leverage for innovation through relationship management. At this point in time, we wish to discuss how relationship management should be executed in incremental and radical innovation.

When incremental innovation is sought, relationship building between the client and the supplier comes second to the contract regardless of the contract type (all but joint venture). Client firms, therefore, should focus on developing relationships with their suppliers as a complementary element to monitoring the contract. Relationships in incremental innovations should in fact be facilitated through the formal channels, which are already captured in the contract. Some examples of such mechanisms include the regular meetings, shared portals and communication procedures which are elementary in each outsourcing project; however, becoming imperative for incremental innovation.

Radical innovation, however, begs for a different approach according to which client firms need to invest in the interpersonal side of the relationship with the supplier, as a complementary step to the contractual approach. It is imperative that trust and rapport between senior managers (e.g., relationship manager) will be developed and renewed to encourage a collaborative atmosphere between the client and supplier staff (Oshri et al., 2007b). While personality clashes and cultural differences might play a negative role in developing rapport and trust between individuals from the client and supplier teams, there are always opportunities to enhance the relationship dimension by organising informal social events, the use of social media tools and through open and preferably face-to-face communication channels. Clearly, it takes a major commitment from senior managers to develop a collaborative atmosphere, which in our view is only one enabler among many to set up and launch a radical innovation project.

We also see opportunities in harnessing social media and open source platforms to support relationship building between the client and supplier. Social media platforms that serve as collaborative tools will enhance the collaborative experience of the client firm in particular when the supplier and client teams are remote. Similarly, Web 2.0 platforms will enable stakeholders to co-innovate and co-create services regardless of their physical location.

Step 6: Measure innovation performance

Most client firms fail to measure the return on innovation delivered by their suppliers. In the academic literature there is general agreement that innovation improves business performance. It flows from this that client firms should invest more in understanding the nature of innovation delivery, its impact on the operational functions within the value chain, as well as on the firm's strategic positioning within the market. Such an exercise will allow decision-makers to realise the value delivered by partners and will inform executives regarding the opportunities that emerge in outsourcing relationships. Most firms can, in fact, measure the return on the outsourcing investment, in a quantifiable form, should they follow steps 1 and 2 of the Innovation Ladder. For incremental innovation at the operational and strategic level, client firms should have developed clear measurement instruments as part of step 1 and 2. These measurement instruments may have to be revisited during the project life cycle. Using the measurement instruments as reference points, the client firm should seek to evaluate whether its incremental innovation targets have been met.

Radical innovation is more challenging to measure; however, the client firm should seek both qualitative and quantitative inputs regarding performance. In terms of qualitative feedback, the client firm should seek input regarding the quality of the network created to arrive in radical innovation. Periodical surveys among members of the joint venture consortium regarding the quality of collaboration, motivation to contribute, assessment of each partner's contribution and intention for future collaboration can provide an indication regarding the 'health' of the joint venture consortium and the potential to tap into this pool of expertise in future projects targeting radical innovations. Quantifiable measurement tools to assess the impact of the radical innovation on business performance should be in the form of benchmarks against industry performance. In particular, as radical innovation was sought to improve the competitiveness of the firm either through operational excellence or strategic positioning, the client firm should judge the impact of the radical innovation through industry-wide performance indicators. For example, the quality of service provided, represented through various measurable indicators such as customer satisfaction, is one performance indicator that can be used by service firms.

Step 6 is not the last step in the Innovation Ladder. If anything, it is a step that calls for reflection and a stage that offers an opportunity to redesign the innovation framework. Feedback collected during these six steps should serve the client firm in its journey to achieve innovation in outsourcing.

C A S E   S T U D Y

KPN: Challenging Suppliers for Innovation

KPN provides high-quality telephone, Internet and television services and products and is an all-around supplier of ICT services. Consumers in the Netherlands use fixed and mobile telephony, Internet and TV from KPN. Business customers use an entire array of innovative and reliable services that include everything from telephony, Internet and data traffic and management all the way through to the management of ICT services. In Germany, Belgium and elsewhere in Western Europe, the services of the KPN group consist mainly of mobile telephony. KPN made a profit of €2.5 billion in 2007 on annual sales of €12.6 billion.

Between 2009 and 2010, the Netherlands business underwent a radical transformation. The All-IP network announced in March 2005 moved into its final phase with the implementation of a new access network. In addition, KPN pursued a radical simplification of its business at the front end in retail segments and at the back end in network operations. The significant cost reductions that would be generated by this simplification would be used for reinvestment in revenue growth and would lead to improving margins.

Hans Wijins was the senior vice-president for innovation at KPN. For Wijins, the maturing of the global outsourcing services market had made it possible to do very large jobs and make large steps in innovation:

> You can't outsource innovation. Our responsibility is for time to market, for business development for innovation; we must have the architects. We don't outsource our vision. But we really do believe that innovation can only be done if we use a lot of capacity outside of the company. I really believe that we have to use the knowledge and the power from places like India.

Wijins saw the client as responsible for making the innovation plan for the next few years. He felt that a lot of sector-based innovation no longer succeeded and that KPN would have needed to find trans-sector innovation in the future. Requirements had to be very clear, and this started at board level. The first step was the strategy to market, and the next was the architecture:

> As an example, we put the designing teams from the several suppliers together in one building and in five months together they built the new IT solution. Designing, building, and testing their own part are the responsibilities of each supplier; we have the integration function and the architecture.

KPN used a lot of innovation power from its network of suppliers, and not just IT: 'We are only the facilitator. We bring together those technologies in IT and in our network and take the products to the customers. We are not the most innovative party. We have to challenge the suppliers for innovation.'

Wijins stressed that KPN wanted to collaborate and not just manage contracts. A client that only manages the contract has much more difficulty working with several suppliers:

> If they are competitive, then we have a special meeting and say this behaviour is unacceptable; you have to work together. Collaboration only happens if there is a higher-level goal for everyone. We put in the necessary incentives for them to put their best people on it and they can't succeed without the help of the other suppliers.

The sourcing strategy, therefore, was long-term relationships with several partners that are focused on quality and delivery. KPN did not want to outsource everything to one party and essentially say, 'Okay, we are not involved any more.' The board wanted to be involved in its own destiny. 'I think that we have to co-create.'

For KPN, innovation is related to what it brings in for the business. In outsourcing the network, cost-cutting is not the main goal. Wijins summed up: 'We are looking to suppliers that can help us in transformation and not only in the existing network. It has to be a combination of cutting costs and innovation together.'

This case study highlights the following learning points for innovation:

• Do not outsource innovation, but make an innovation plan
• Trans-sector innovation will be the way forward
• Use the innovation power from your network of suppliers
• Suppliers need to collaborate with each other
• Collaboration happens only if there is a higher level goal for everyone
• There is a need to co-create.

Summary

This chapter shows that achieving innovation through outsourcing is increasingly realistic as both clients and suppliers are maturing in their ability to go beyond traditional outsourcing relationships and build the governance arrangements and organisational structures necessary for innovating. But innovation with large-scale, long-term impact requires collaboration within clients, and with and across their external suppliers. Without this, innovation, and the consequent high performance, cannot be delivered. Thus, collaborating to innovate requires a change in objectives pursued, relationships with suppliers and how work and innovation are conducted. As part of such change in both the client and supplier's mindset, the parties will need to consider new forms of contracting where risk and gains are shared to incentivise innovation, collaboration and high performance.

Appendix A

/ More information about the comparative analysis of attractive European destinations

Costs		UK	France	Germany	Netherlands	Czech	Ireland	Spain	Poland
	Average wage per skilled employee and managers (US$) (2011)[1]	33,513	27,452	24,174	29,269	15,115	41,170	26,856	14,390
	Average rental office space per square metre (€/sq.m/yr)[2] (2013)	717 (London) 234 (Outside London)	915	533	500	339	437	439	415
	Cost of telecom, Internet access (US$ per month)[3] (2012)	27.25	12.43	27.4	12.37	18.76	31.06	31.72	11.27
	Cost of power (Kw/H) (2011)[4]	0.158	0.142	0.253	0.298	0.147	0.209	0.209	0.135
	Corporate taxes[5,6] (2011)	20–24%	33.33%	29.8%	25%[7]	19%	12.5%	25–30%	19%

(continued)

(Continued)

		UK	France	Germany	Netherlands	Czech	Ireland	Spain	Poland
Availability of skills	Size of the labour market (2011)[8]	31.72 million	27.99 million	43.51 million	8.33 million	5.4 million	2.3 million	22.97 million	5.58 million
	Size of the local supplier market indicator (0.1–1.0)	0.92	0.41	0.53	0.73	0.34	0.83	0.62	0.28
	Quality of delivery skills indicator (0.1–1.0)	0.9	0.65	0.65	0.66	0.71	0.9	0.68	0.74
	Quality of sourcing management skills indicator (0.1–1.0)	0.93	0.65	0.74	0.91	0.55	0.83	0.87	0.5
Environment	Level of corruption (2013)[9]	74	71	79	84	49	69	65	58
	Quality of life (index) (2013)[10]	148.12	151.36	204.84	160.54	122.18	149.64	141.05	90.47
	Serious crime per capita (per 1 million people) (2006)[11]	<0.7	8.0	2.5	8.7	<0.8	5.5	0.8	9.8
	Accessibility to the country indicator (1–100)	90	85	80	70	60	65	75	55

(continued)

(Continued)

		UK	France	Germany	Netherlands	Czech	Ireland	Spain	Poland
Quality of infrastructure	Average downtime per year Recovery time per year (2011)[12]	25 hrs 13 hrs	24 hrs 16 hrs	14 hrs 9 hrs	12 hrs 13 hrs	16 hrs 15 hrs	19 hrs 21 hrs	11 hrs 8 hrs	31 hrs 20 hrs
	Availability and quality of real estate[13] (2012)	93.7	89.0	84.7	86.4	54	65.9	79.9	65.9
	Quality of overall infrastructure (2012)[14]	5.6	6.4	6.2	6.2	5.5	5.2	5.8	4.0
	Quality of electrical supply (2012)[15]	6.7	6.7	6.7	6.7	6.4	6.4	6.0	5.3
	Scale and quality of roads[16] Rail (2012)	5.5 4.9	6.6 6.4	6.2 5.7	5.6 5.7	3.6 4.5	4.8 4.0	5.9 5.6	2.3 2.5
Risk profile	Risk to personal security (fraud, crime and terrorism)	80.222	80.9	84.98	86.67	74.77	62.33	66.71	70.99
	Risk of labour strikes indicator (0.1–1.0)	Moderate– low	High	Moderate– high	High	Moderate– low	Moderate– low	Moderate– High	Moderate– low
	Political unrest (Political Instability Index)[17] (2010)	4.6	5.3	3.8	4.0	3.7	4.6	5.5	4.5

(continued)

(Continued)

	UK	France	Germany	Netherlands	Czech	Ireland	Spain	Poland
Natural disasters[18] (economic damage per year US$ X 1,000): (2009)[19] Disaster reported (2009)[20]	960,215 Flood, Storm	1,256,829 Storm	1,171,036 Flood	145,829 Flood	161,470 Flood	11,389 Flood Epidemic	846,784 Drought Flood Wildfire	266,650 Flood
Cost inflation (2012)[21]	2.8	2.3	2.2	2.4	3.3	1.3	2.5	3.6
Intellectual property risks (2013)[22]	Not listed	Not listed	Not listed	Not listed	Not listed	Not listed	On a watch list	Not listed
Market potential — Attractiveness of local market (GDP growth rate and GDP$) (2012)[23]	0.2 35,657	0.1 35,246	0.9 39,491	–0.5 42,772	–1.0 26,208	0.7 41,682	–1.5 32,045	2.4 21,261
Access to nearby markets Indicator (0.1–1.0)	0.95	0.74	0.72	0.84	0.52	0.86	0.68	0.45

Notes

2 Sourcing Models: What and When to Outsource or Offshore

1. The cloud infrastructure combines physical and abstraction layers. The physical layer consists of the hardware resources (e.g., server, storage and network components) that are necessary to support the cloud services. The abstraction layer consists of the software deployed across the physical layer (NICT, 2011).
2. Situation described in this case took place in 2011.
3. Numbers are based on information provided on the InnoCentive website www.innocentive.com/ (Accessed 3 July 2014).
4. Spence R. Cambrian House: The wisdom of crowdsourcing. *Canadian Business Online.* http://www.canadianbusiness.com/entrepreneur/managing/article.jsp?content=20070212_140822_6416 (Accessed 15 December 2010).
5. Numbers are based on information included on the Cambrian House website: www.cambrianhouse.com (Accessed 14 July 2014).
6. http://www.cambrianhouse.com/how-it-works/crowds-test-it/ (Accessed 15 December 2010).
7. http://www.chaordix.com/what-we-do/ (Accessed 9 July 2014).
8. The URL for its international page is http://international.ohmynews.com/ (Accessed 10 July 2014). A brief history of OhMyNews can be found at http://en.wikipedia.org/wiki/OhmyNews (Accessed 10 July 2014).
9. Min J.K. (January 2005). Journalism as a Conversation. *Nieman Reports* 59:4. pp. 17–19.
10. This section on online crowdsourcing environments and marketplaces was written by Evgeny Kaganer, Erran Carmel, Rudy Hirschheim and Sandra Sieber for the second edition of the handbook. It was revised and extended by the authors for this third edition.
11. These marketplaces are examples of Online Sourcing Environments (OSEs) we introduce later in this section.
12. http://www.lionbridge.com/microsoft-crowdsourcing-case-study/.
13. http://researcher.ibm.com/researcher/view_project.php?id=3832.

14. http://www.gequest.com/.
15. http://www.engadget.com/2013/02/07/google-mapathon-2013-india/.

3 Country Attractiveness for Sourcing

1. Link to conference site: http://www.cnoutsourcing.com/English/index.asp.

4 The Attractiveness of Western Countries for Outsourcing Services and Backsourcing

1. http://world.bymap.org/Airports.html.
2. http://smartinnovation.forumpa.it/story/70050/uk-preparing-move-4g-and-starts-planning-5g-mobile.
3. This section is written on the basis of master dissertation of Lars Bognar under supervision of Julia Kotlarsky.

5 Supplier Configurations and Capabilities

1. Though configuration C also presents an opportunity to reduce the burden of day-to-day management of multiple suppliers, it is less popular because it requires a client to engage in additional efforts of selecting a new supplier (service integrator).

6 Supplier Selection, Retained Management Capabilities and Legal Issues

1. Fixed fee is a core principle of *fixed price* contract and *fee-for-service* types of contract. The main difference between these two contract types is the volume of work for which fees are fixed.

8 The Outsourcing Life Cycle and the Transition Phase

1. Specific techniques and frameworks to use at this stage are discussed in Chapter 2.
2. Supplier-selection process is discussed in detail in Chapter 6.
3. The term 'wave' is an industry term to refer to a chunk of work (here, group of applications).

11 Captive and Shared Service Centres

1. For more about captive centre strategies, see Oshri (2011).
2. Singapore Press Holdings Limited (13 August 1999). Bangalore tech par signs on more investors. *Straits Times*, p. 1.
3. *Dow Jones International News* (23 November 2001). GlobalAirline starts W. GlobalAirline stake sale talk. *Dow Jones International News*, p. 1.

4. *Reuters News* (23 October 2001). GlobalAirline in talks for unit sell-off in India. *Reuters News*, p. 1.

5. *Financial Times* (4 April 2002). Companies & Finance UK – GlobalAirline sells business outsourcing arm to W. *Financial Times*, p. 1.

Appendix A

1. OECD, 'OECD Statistics', Organisation for Economic Co-Operation and Development, 2011 [Online]. Available: http://stats.oecd.org/ (Accessed 13 May 2013).

2. Cushman and Wakefield, 'Office Space Around the World', A Cushman & Wakefield Research Publication, pp. 1–35, 2013.

3. World Economic Forum, 'The Global Competitive Report', 2012 [Online]. Available: http://www3.weforum.org/docs/WEF_GCR_Report_2011-12.pdf.

4. EuroStats, 'Energy Price Statistics', European Commission, August 2012 [Online]. Available: http://epp.eurostat.ec.europa.eu/statistics_explained/index.php/Energy_price_statistics#Further_Eurostat_information [Accessed 13 May 2013].

5. HMRC, 'Corporation Tax rates', HM Revenue & Customs, April 2012 [Online]. Available: http://www.hmrc.gov.uk/rates/corp.htm [Accessed 13 May 2013].

6. VAT. Live, '2013 European Union VAT Rates', 11 May 2013 [Online]. Available: http://www.vatlive.com/vat-rates/european-vat-rates/eu-vat-rates/ [Accessed 13 May 2013].

7. KPMG, 'Services', KPMG [Online]. Available: http://www.kpmg.com/DK/da/in-english/setting-up-business-in-denmark/Sider/services.aspx [Accessed 13 May 2013].

8. OECD, 'OECD Statistics', Organization for Economic Co-Operation and Development, 2011 [Online]. Available: http://stats.oecd.org/ [Accessed 13 May 2013].

9. Transparency International, 'Corruption Perceptions Index 2012', Transparency International, 2012 [Online]. Available: http://www.transparency.org/cpi2012/results [Accessed 13 May 2013].

10. Numebo [Online]. Available: http://www.numbeo.com/quality-of-life/rankings_by_country.jsp.

11. N. Master [Online]. Available: http://www.nationmaster.com/graph/cri_mur_percap-crime-murders-per-capita.

12. CATechnologies, 'The impact of IT downtime on employee productivity', CATechnologies, 2011.

13. K. Lieser and A. P. Groh, 'The attractiveness of 66 countries for institutional real estate investments', IESE Business School, 2010.

14. WorldEconomicForum, 'Quality of overall infrastructure, The Global Competitive Report, 2012' [Online]. http://www3.weforum.org/docs/CSI/2012-13/GCR_Pillar2_2012-13.pdf.

15. WorldEconomicForum, 'Quality of overall infrastructure, The Global Competitive Report, 2012' [Online]. http://www3.weforum.org/docs/CSI/2012-13/ GCR_Pillar2_2012-13.pdf.

16. WorldEconomicForum, 'Quality of overall infrastructure, The Global Competitive Report, 2012' [Online]. http://www3.weforum.org/docs/CSI/2012-13/ GCR_Pillar2_2012-13.pdf.

17. The Economist, 'Views Wire', The Economist Intelligence Unit, 2010 [Online]. Available: http://viewswire.eiu.com/site_info.asp?info_name=social_unrest _table&page=noads [Accessed 13 May 2013].

18. Prevention Web. 'United Nations Office for Disaster Risk Reduction' [Online]. Available: http://www.preventionweb.net/english/.

19. revention Web. 'United Nations Office for Disaster Risk Reduction' [Online]. Available: http://www.preventionweb.net/english/.

20. Prevention Web. 'United Nations Office for Disaster Risk Reduction' [Online]. Available: http://www.preventionweb.net/english/.

21. World Economic Forum, 'The Global Competitive Report' 2012 [Online]. Available: http://www3.weforum.org/docs/WEF_GCR_Report_2011-12.pdf.

22. USTR, '2011 Special 301 Report', Executive Office Of The President of The United States, 2011.

23. OECD, 'OECD Statistics', Organization for Economic Co-Operation and Development, 2011 [Online]. Available: http://stats.oecd.org/ [Accessed 13 May 2013].

References

A.T. Kearney (2011), *Offshoring Opportunities Amid Economic Turbulence. The 2011 A.T. Kearney Global Services Location Index*™, A.T. Kearney, New York.

Agarwal, M.K., Frambach, R.T. and Stremersch, S. (2000), "Does size matter? Disentangling consumers' bundling preferences", Vrije Universiteit, Amsterdam, Faculty of Economics, Business Administration and Econometrics.

Armbrust, M., Fox, A., Griffth, R., Joseph, A.D., Katz, R., Konwinski, A., Lee, G., Patterson, Rabkin, A., Stoica, I. and Zaharia, M. (2009), "Above the clouds: A Berkeley view of cloud computing", Technical Report EECS-2009-28, EECS Department, University of California, Berkeley.

Aron, R. and Clemons, E.K. (2004), "Process complexity & productivity in off-shore outsourcing of services: Evidence from cross country, longitudinal survey data", Wharton Working Paper, http://opim.wharton.upenn.edu/wise2004/sun311 .pdf, *Proceedings of the Workshop on Information Systems and Economics*, http://opim.wharton.upenn.edu/wise2004.

Aron, R. and Singh, J.V. (2005), "Getting offshoring right", *Harvard Business Review*, 83(12): 135–143.

Baldia, S. (2007), "Intellectual property and knowledge process outsourcing in India", *Business & Technology Sourcing Review*, Q4(10): 7–10; Mayer Brown Web site, http://www.mayerbrown.com/publications/article.asp?id =3975&nid=6.

Baldwin, L., Irani, Z. and Love, P. (2001), "Outsourcing information systems: Drawing lessons from a banking study", *European Journal of Information Systems*, 10: 15–24.

Bhagwatwar, A., Hackney, R. and Desouza, K.C. (2011), "Considerations for information systems 'Backsourcing': A framework for knowledge re-integration", *Information Systems Management*, 28(2): 165–173.

Bhimani, A. and Willcocks, L. (2014), "Digitisation, 'Big Data' and the transformation of accounting information", *Accounting and Business Research*, 44(4): 469–490.

Bonabeau, E. (2009), "Decisions 2.0: The power of collective intelligence", *MIT Sloan management review* 50(2): 45–52.

Bruno, G., Esposito, G., Iandoli, L. and Raffa, M. (2004), "The ICT service industry in North Africa and the role of partnerships in Morocco", *Journal of Global Information Technology Management*, 7(3), 5–26.

Carmel, E. (1999), *Global Software Teams: Collaborating Across Borders and Time Zones*, 1st ed. Prentice-Hall P T R, Upper Saddle River, NJ.

Carmel, E. (2003), "The new software exporting nations: Success factors", *The Electronic Journal on Information Systems in Developing Countries*, 13(4): 1–12.

Carmel, E. and Abbott, P. (2007), "Why nearshore means that distance matters", *Communications of the ACM*, 50(10): 40–46.

Carmel, E., and Tjia, P. (2005), *Offshoring Information Technology. Sourcing and Outsourcing to a Global Workforce*. Cambridge University Press, New York.

Chesbrough, H. and Teece, D.J. (1996), "Organizing for innovation: When is virtual virtuous?", *Harvard Business Review*, January–February: 65–73.

Chesbrough, H., Vanhaverbeke, W. and West, J. (eds.). (2006), *Open Innovation: Researching a New Paradigm*. Oxford University Press, Oxford.

Chua, A.L. and Pan, S.L. (2008), "Knowledge transfer and organizational learning in IS offshore sourcing", *Omega*, 36: 267–281.

Coulter, L. and Fersht, P. (2010), *Service Providers Siloed by Vertical Industry Are Stifling Innovation with Clients*. HfS Research, London.

Cramton, C.D. and Webber, S.S. (2005), "Relationships among geographic dispersion, team processes, and effectiveness in software development work teams", *Journal of Business Research,* 58(6): 758–765.

Crowston, K., Li, Q., Wei, K.N., Eseryel, U.Y. and Howison, J. (2007), "Self-organization of teams for free/libre open source software development", *Information and Software Technology*, 49(6): 564–575.

Cullen, S., Seddon, P. and Willcocks, L.P. (2005), "Managing outsourcing: The lifecycle imperative", *MIS Quarterly Executive* 4(1): 229–246.

Cullen, S. and Willcocks, L.P. (2003), *Intelligent IT Outsourcing: Eight Building Blocks to Success*. Elsevier, Chichester.

Davenport, T., Leibold, M. and Voelpel, S. (2006), *Strategic Management in the Innovation Economy*. Wiley, New York.

Davis, T. (2005), "Integrating shared services with the strategy and operation of MNEs", *Journal of General Management*, 31(2): 1–17.

Dibbern, J., Winkler, J., and Heinzl, A. (2008), "Explaining variations in client extra costs between software projects offshored to India", *MIS Quarterly,* 32(2): 333–366.

Doan, A., Ramakrishnan, R., and Halevy, A. Y. (2011), "Crowdsourcing systems on the world-wide web", *Communications of the ACM,* 54(4): 86–96.

Ejodame, K. and Oshri, I. (2014), "Understanding the backsourcing process: A knowledge perspective", *Eights Global Sourcing Workshop*, 23–26 March 2014, Val d'Isere, France.

Espinosa, J.A., Slaughter, S.A., Kraut, R.E. and Herbsleb, J.D. (2007), "Team knowledge and coordination in geographically distributed software development", *Journal of Management Information Systems*, 24(1): 135–169.

Ethiraj, S.K., Kale, P., Krishnan, M.S. and Singh, J.V. (2006), "Where do capabilities come from and how do they matter? A study in the software services industry", *Strategic Management Journal*, 26: 25–45.

Farrell, D. (2006), "Smarter offshoring", *Harvard Business Review*, 84(6): 85–92.

Feeny, D., Lacity, M. and Willcocks, L.P. (2005), "Taking the measure of outsourcing providers", *MIT Sloan Management Review*, 46(3): 41–48.

Feeny, D.F. and Willcocks, L.P. (1998), "Core IS capabilities for exploiting information technology", *Sloan Management Review*: 9–21.

Fersht, P. (2010), *Desperately Seeking Innovation in Business Process Outsourcing: Enterprises Speak Out.* HfS Research report, HfS Research, London.

Frey C.B. and Osborne, M.A. (2013), "The Future of employment: How susceptible are jobs to computerisation", Working Paper, available on http://www.futuretech.ox.ac.uk/sites/futuretech.ox.ac.uk/files/The_Future_of_Employment_OMS_Working_Paper_1.pdf.

Gino, F. and Staats, B.R. (2012), "The microwork solution", *Harvard Business Review*: 92–96.

Gospel, H. and Sako, M. (2010), "The unbundling of corporate functions: The evolution of shared services and outsourcing in human resource management", *Industrial and Corporate Change*, 19(5): 1367–1396.

Government Accounting Office Report (2001), "Leading commercial practices for outsourcing of services", Available online: http://www.gao.gov/new.items/d02214.pdf.

Hagel, J. and Seely Brown, J. (2008), *The Only Sustainable Edge.* Harvard Business School Press, Boston.

Harris, J. and Blair, E.A. (2006), "Functional compatibility risk and consumer preference for product bundles", *Journal of the Academy of Marketing Science*, 34(1): 19–26.

Hendry, J. (1995), "Culture, community and networks: The hidden cost of outsourcing", *European Management Journal*, 13(2): 193–200.

Hennart, J. (1988), "A transaction cost theory of equity joint ventures", *Strategic Management Journal*, 9(4): 361–374.

Hirscheim, R. and Lacity, M. (2000), "The myths and relaities of Information technology Insourcing", *Communications of the ACM,* 43(2): 99–107.

Howe, J. (2008), *Crowdsourcing: How the Power of the Crowd Is Driving the Future of Business.* London.

Huis, M.A.A., Andriessen, J.H.E. and Soekijad, M. (2002), "ICT facilitation of distributed groups and communities", in *Building Blocks for Effective Telematics*

Application Development and Evaluation, Verbraeck, A. and Dahanayake, A. (eds.) Delft University of Technology, Delft, The Netherlands, pp. 39–46.

Iivari, J., Hirschheim, R. and Klein, H. (2004), "Towards a distinctive body of knowledge for information systems experts: Coding ISD process knowledge in two IS journals", *Information Systems Journal*, 14: 313–342.

Janssen, M. and Joha, A. (2006), "Motives for establishing shared service centers in public administrations", *International Journal of Information Management*, 26(2): 102–115.

Jarvenpaa, S.L. and Mao, J.Y. (2008), "Operational capabilities development in mediated offshore software services models", *Journal of Information Technology*, 23(1): 3–17.

Kaganer, E., Carmel, E., Hirschheim, R. and T. Olsen (2013), "Managing the human cloud", *MIT Sloan Management Review*, 54: 23–32.

Kakabadse, N. and Kakabadse, A. (2000), "Outsourcing: A paradigm shift", *Journal of Management Development*, 19(8): 670–728.

Koh, J. and Venkatraman, N. (1991), "Joint venture formations and stock market reaction: An assessment in the infomration technology sector", *Academy of Management Journal*, 34: 869–892.

Kotlarsky, J., Levina, N. and Kuraksina, E. (2013), "Evaluation of Russia's attractiveness as IT offshoring destination", in *The Oxford Handbook of Offshoring and Global Employment*, Bardhan, A., Dwight, J. and Kroll, C. (eds.) Oxford University Press, New York. pp. 435–464.

Kotlarsky, J. and Oshri, I. (2005), "Social ties, knowledge sharing and successful collaboration in globally distributed system development projects", *European Journal of Information Systems*, 14(1): 37–48.

Kotlarsky, J., Oshri, I., Kumar, K. and van Hillegersberg, J. (2007), "Globally distributed component-based software development: An exploratory study of knowledge management and work division", *Journal of Information Technology*, 22(2): 161–173.

Kotlarsky, J., Oshri, I. and van Fenema, P.C. (2008a), *Knowledge Processes in Globally Distributed Contexts*. Palgrave, London.

Kotlarsky, J., Scarbrough, H. and Oshri, I. (2014), "Coordinating expertise across knowledge boundaries in offshore-outsourcing projects: The role of codification", *MIS Quarterly*, 38(2): 607–627.

Kotlarsky, J., van Fenema, P.C. and Willcocks, L. (2008b), "Developing a knowledge-based perspective on coordination: The case of global software projects", *Information and Management*, 45(2): 96–108.

Lacity, M. and Willcocks, L. (2009), *Information Systems and Outsourcing: Studies in Theory and Practice*. Palgrave, London.

Lacity, M. and Willcocks, P. (2012), *Advanced Outsourcing Practice: Rethinking ITO, BPO, and Cloud Services*. Palgrave, London.

Lacity, M.C., Willcocks, L.P. and Zheng, Y. (2010), *China's Emerging Outsourcing Capabilities: The Services Challenge*. MacMillan, London.

Lee-Kelley, L. and Sankey, T. (2008), "Global virtual teams for value creation and project success: A case study", *International Journal of Project Management,* 26(1): 51–62.

Leonardi, P.M. and Bailey, D.E. (2008), "Transformational technologies and the creation of new work practices: Making implicit knowledge explicit in task-based offshoring", *MIS Quarterly,* 32(2): 411–436.

Levina, N. and Ross, J.W. (2003), "From the vendor's perspective: Exploring the value proposition in information technology outsourcing", *MIS Quarterly,* 27(3): 331–364.

Levina, N. and Su, N. (2008), "Global multisourcing strategy: The emergence of a supplier portfolio in services offshoring", *Decision Sciences,* 39(3): 541–570.

Levina, N., and Vaast, E. (2008), "Innovating or doing as told? Status differences and overlapping boundaries in offshore collaboration", *MIS Quarterly* 32(2): 307–332.

Lewis, A. (2006), *Outsourcing Contracts – A Practical Guide.* City & Financial Publishing: London.

Liker, J. and Choi, T. (2004), "Building deep supplier relationships", *Harvard Business Review,* 82(12): 104–113.

Linder, J.C., Jarvenpaa, S. and Davenport, T.H. (2003), "Toward an innovation sourcing strategy", *Sloan Management Review,* 44(4): 43–49.

Mahnke, V., Wareham, J. and Bjorn-Andersen, N. (2008), "Offshore middlemen: Offshore intermediation in technology sourcing", *Journal of Information Technology,* 23(1): 18–30.

Malhotra, A. and Majchrzak, A. (2005), "Virtual workspace technologies", *Sloan Management Review,* 46(2): 11–14.

Mani, D., Barua, A. and Whinston, A.B. (2006), "Successfully governing business process outsourcing relationships", *MIS Quarterly Executive,* 5(1): 15–29.

McCarthy, I. and Anagnostou, A. (2003), "The impact of outsourcing on the transaction costs and boundaries of manufacturing", *International Journal of Production Economics,* 88: 61–71.

McIvor, R., McCracken, M. and McHugh, M. (2011), "Creating outsourced shared services arrangements: Lessons from the public sector", *European Management Journal,* 29(6): 448–461.

Mell, P. and T. Grance (2011), *The NIST Definition of Cloud Computing.* U. S. Department of Commerce, National Institute of Standards and Technology, USA.

Metters, R. (2008), "A typology of offshoring and outsourcing in electronically transmitted services", *Journal of Operations Management,* 26(2): 198–211.

Mockus, A. and Weiss, D.M. (2001), "Globalization by chunking: A quantitative approach", *IEEE Software,* 18(2): 30–37.

NASSCOM (2012), *The IT/BPO Sector in India – Strategic Review 2012.* NASSCOM, New Delhi.

Nelson, P. (2008), *Capital Markets, Law and Compliance: The Implications of MIFID*. Cambridge University Press, Cambridge.

Neo Group (April, 2005), "Best practices in communicating global outsourcing initiatives", Internal Report by Neo Group, Available on http://www.neogroup.com/PDFs/Whitepapers/OIv3i04_0405_Best-Practices-Communication.pdf.

Nevo, D. and Kotlarsky, J. (2014), "Primary vendor capabilities in a mediated outsourcing model: Can IT service providers leverage crowdsourcing?", *Decision Support Systems*, 65: 17–27.

Oshri, I. (2011), *Offshoring Strategies: Evolving Captive Center Models*. MIT Press, MA.

Oshri, I. (2013), "Choosing an evolutionary path for offshore captive centers", *MIS Quarterly Executive*, 12(3): 151–165.

Oshri, I. (2014), "Innovation through outsourcing: Have you got the goods", *National Outsourcing Association Year Book 2014*.

Oshri, I. and Kavari, K. (December 2013), "Enterprise cloud: The state of the nation", *Professional Outsourcing Magazine*, 15: 34–38.

Oshri, I. and Kotlarsky, J. (July 2014), "Four ways to multisource", *Professional Outsourcing Magazine*, 17: 50–54.

Oshri, I. and Kotlarsky, J. (2009), "The real benefits of outsourcing", A WBS White Paper for Cognizant.

Oshri, I. and Kotlarsky, J. (2010), "Innovation in outsourcing", a Warwick Business School report for Cognizant.

Oshri, I. and Kotlarsky, J. (2011), "Innovation in Outsourcing", a WBS White Paper for Cognizant.

Oshri, I., Kotlarsky, J. and Liew, C.M. (2008), "Four strategies for offshore 'Captive' Centers", *Wall Street Journal*, 12 May.

Oshri, I., Kotlarsky, J. and Willcocks, L.P. (2007a), "Managing dispersed expertise in IT offshore outsourcing: Lessons from TATA Consultancy Services", *MIS Quarterly Executive*, 6(2): 53–65.

Oshri, I., Kotlarsky, J. and Willcocks, L.P. (2007b), "Global software development: Exploring socialization in distributed strategic projects", *Journal of Strategic Information Systems*, 16(1): 25–49.

Oshri, I., Kotlarsky, J. and Willcocks, L.P. (2008), "Missing links: Building critical social ties for global collaborative teamwork", *Communications of the ACM*, 51(4): 76–81.

Oshri, I. and Ravishankar, M.N. (2014), "On the attractiveness of the UK for outsourcing services", *Strategic Outsourcing: an International Journal*, 7(1): 18–46.

Oshri, I. and van Uhm, R. (2012), "A historical review of the information technology and business process captive centre sector", *Journal of Information Technology*, 27(4): 270–284.

Oshri, I., van Fenema, P.C. and Kotlarsky, J. (2008), "Knowledge transfer in globally distributed teams: The role of transactive memory", *Information Systems Journal*, 18(4): 593–616.

Overby, S. (2007), "What does it take to get IT outsourcers to innovate?", *CIO Magazine*, 8 October.

Overby, S. (2010), "IT Outsourcing: Three reasons why your vendor won't innovate", *CIO Magazine*, 5 May.

Power, M.J., Desouza, K.C. and Bonifazi, C. (2006), *The Outsourcing Handbook: How to Implement a Successful Outsourcing Process*. Kogan Page Limited.

Pralahad, C. and Ramaswamy, V. (2004), *The Future of Competition: Co-creating Unique Value with Customers*. Harvard Business School Press, Boston.

Punongbayan and Araullo (2012), *Doing Business in The Philippines for Business Process Outsourcing Companies*. Report by Punongbayan & Araullo, Philippines. Available online from http://www.punongbayan-araullo.com/pnawebsite/pnahome.nsf/section_docs/VM010C_21-6-12.

Puryear, R. and Derrick, C. (2006), "Are you sending your problems offshore?", *Harvard Business Online*, January.

Quinn, J.B. (1999), "Strategic outsourcing: Leveraging knowledge capabilities", *Sloan Management Review*, 40(4): 9–21.

Quinn, J.B. (2000), "Outsourcing innovation: The new engine of growth", *Sloan Management Review*, 41(4): 13–28.

Quinn, J.B. and Hilmer, F.G. (1994), "Strategic outsourcing", *Sloan Management Review*, 35(4): 43–55.

Reinhardt, A., Kripalani, M., Smith, G., Bush, J., Balfour, F. and Ante, S.E. (2006), "Angling to be the next Bangalore", *Business Week*, 30 January.

Ross, J. and Beath, C. (2005), "Sustainable value from outsourcing: Finding the sweet spot", *MIT Research Brief*, 5, 1A.

Rottman, J.W. (2008), "Successful knowledge transfer within offshore supplier networks: A case study exploring social capital in strategic alliances", *Journal of Information Technology*, 23: 31–43.

Rottman, J.W. and Lacity, M.C. (2006), "Proven practices for effectively offshoring IT work", *Sloan Management Review*, 47(3): 56–63.

Sarker, S. and Sahay, S. (2004), "Implications of space and time for distributed work: an interpretive study of US–Norwegian systems development teams", *European Journal of Information Systems*, 13(1): 3–20.

Savvas, A. (2007), "Firms sceptical about outsourcing innovation", *Computer Weekly*, 8 February.

Smith, P.G and Blanck, E.L. (2002), "From experience: leading dispersed teams", *The Journal of Product Innovation Management*, 19: 294–304.

Srikanth, K., and Puranam, P. (2008), "Integrating Distributed Work: Comparing Task Design, Communication, and Tacit Coordination Mechanisms", *Strategic Management Journal*, 32(8): 849–875.

Stanko, M., Bohlmann, J. and Calentone, R. (2009), "Outsourcing innovation", *MITSloan Management Review*, November.

Stewart, T. (2001), *The Wealth of Knowledge: Intellectual Capital and the Twenty-first Century Organization*. Nicholas Brealey, London.

Su, N. and Levina, N. (2011), "Global multisourcing strategy: Integrating learning from manufacturing into IT service outsourcing", *IEEE Transactions on Engineering Management*.

Szulanski, G. (1996), "Exploring internal stickiness: Impediments to the transfer of best practice within the firm", *Strategic Management Journal*, 17: 27–43.

Taxén, L. (2006), "An integration centric approach for the coordination of distributed software development projects", *Information and Software Technology*, 48(9): 767–780.

Tisnovsky R. (2006), "IT Outsourcing in the Small and Medium Businesses – There is a Light at the End of the Tunnel", *Everest Research Institute Report*.

Vlaar, P. W. L., van Fenema, P. C., and Tiwari, V. (2008), "Cocreating understanding and value in distributed work: How members of onsite and offshore vendor teams give, make, demand, and break sense", *MIS Quarterly*, 32(2): 227–255.

Vashistha, A. and Khan, I. (2008), "Top 50 emerging global outsourcing cities", Available online: http://www.epam.com/company/news-events/press-about-epam/2008/Top-50-Emerging-Global-Outsourcing-Cities.html.

von Hippel, E. (1994), " 'Sticky information' and the locus of problem solving: Implications for innovation", *Management Science*, 40(4): 429–439.

Warner, A. and Brown, N. (2005), *Increase the Success of Your Knowledge Transfer Effort*, Available on: http://www.cio.com/article/2448571/it-strategy/increase-the-success-of-your-knowledge-transfer-effort.html.

Wegner, D.M. (1986), "Transactive memory: A contemporary analysis of the group mind", in *Theories of Group Behavior*, Mullen, G. and Goethals, G. (eds.) Springer Verlag, New York, 185–205.

Wegner, D.M. (1995), "A computer network model of human transactive memory", *Social Cognition*, 13: 319–339.

Westerman, G. and Curley, M. (2008), "Building IT-enabled capabilities at Intel", *MIS Quarterly Executive*, 7(1): 33–48.

Whitla, P. (2009), "Crowdsourcing and its application in marketing activities", *Contemporary Management Research* 5(1).

Willcocks, L.P., Griffiths, C. and Kotlarsky, J. (2009), *Beyond BRIC. Offshoring in Non-BRIC Countries: Egypt – A New Growth Market*. The LSE Outsourcing Unit report. LSE, London.

Willcocks, L. P., Hindle, J., Feeny, D. and Lacity, M. (2004), "IT and business process outsourcing: The knowledge potential", *Information Systems Management*, 21(3): 7–15.

Willcocks, L.P. and Feeny, D. (2006), "The core capabilities framework for achieving high performance back offices", in *Global Sourcing of Business and IT Services*, Willcocks, L.P. and Lacity, M. (eds.) Palgrave, London, pp. 67–96.

Willcocks, L.P. and Lacity, M. (2006), *Global Sourcing of Business and IT Services*. Palgrave, London.

Willcocks, L.P. and Lacity, M. (2009), *The Practice of Outsourcing: From IT to BPO and Offshoring*. Palgrave, London.

Willcocks, L., Lacity, M. and Craig, A. (2015), *South Africa's BPO Service Advantage: Becoming Strategic in the Global Marketplace*. Palgrave, London.

Willcocks, L., Lacity, M. and Cullen, S. (2006), "Information technology sourcing: Fifteen years of learning", Working Paper, Source: http://is2.lse.ac.uk/ WP/PDF/wp144.pdf#search=%22Information%20Technology%20Sourcing %3A%20Fifteen%20Years%20of%20Learning%22.

Willcocks, L.P., Oshri, I. and Hindle, J. (2009), "Client's propensity to buy bundled IT outsourcing services", White Paper for Accenture.

Willcocks, L. Petherbridge, P. and Olson, N. (2002), *Making IT Count: Strategy, Delivery and Infrastructure*. Butterworth, Oxford.

Willcocks, L., Venters, W. and Whitley, E. (2013), "Cloud sourcing and innovation: Slow train coming? A composite research study", *Strategic Outsourcing – An International Journal*, 6(2): 184–202.

Wong, S.F. (2008), "Drivers of IT backsourcing decision", *Communication of the IBIMA*, 2(14): 102–107.

Index

Note: The letter 'n' 't' 'f' following locators refers to notes, tables and figures respectively.

Printed and bound in the United States of America